AGAINST THE TIDE

I want nothing for
myself; I want
everything for the Lord

Watchman Nee

倪柝聲

THE STORY OF WATCHMAN NEE

AGAINST
THE TIDE

ANGUS I. KINNEAR

CHRISTIAN LITERATURE CRUSADE
Fort Washington, Pennsylvania 19034

CHRISTIAN LITERATURE CRUSADE
Fort Washington, Pennsylvania 19034

Printed in Great Britain
by Richard Clay (The Chaucer Press) Ltd
Bungay, Suffolk.

Contents

To Jean

Foreword

IN EVERY age of human history men and women have emerged with qualities of character and intellect which have been recognized by their contemporaries as qualifying them for leadership. In the history of Europe the names of Garibaldi, Napoleon, Cromwell, and Churchill at once come to mind. North America has produced an Abraham Lincoln, a George Washington, and an Ike Eisenhower. All these men have impressed their personalities on their contemporaries and their convictions have altered the course of history. They were men of destiny.

So too in sacred history. Abraham was the founder of Israel, Moses moulded a community of Hebrew slaves into a potentially great nation. David despite his humble origin became king of Israel and Judah. But what is so refreshing and so encouraging to us who know ourselves to be far from perfect is to see the honesty of the sacred historians in depicting the lives and the work of their heroes. Moses was not always the meekest of men and even after he had learned meekness he impetuously forfeited the hoped-for privilege of leading his people into the Promised Land. David, the man after God's own heart, at the height of his power sank to the lowest moral depths and set in motion a sequence of tragic events affecting his family and the nation.

The history of the Christian church is studded with the names of 'men of destiny'; Paul, Augustine, Francis of Assisi, Luther, Calvin, Xavier, Knox, Wesley, Zinzendorf, Livingstone, Carey, Hudson Taylor, C. T. Studd, etc. But no one who has read the intimate biographies of these men can be unaware that they were all very human and that their sanctity did not deliver them from errors of judgement nor even serious mistakes which affected their followers, the Christian church as a whole and the missionary movement in every continent.

China, like the other great fields of missionary endeavour, has produced her national heroes—men of spiritual stature to serve their own generation in the will of God. Pastor Hsi, the converted scholar and drug addict, pioneered the church in Shansi in the last century and composed hymns of beauty and spiritual understanding. Heroic Chinese Christians chose death rather than deny their faith in the Boxer massacres of 1900. Men like Wang Chi-t'ai called the church to revival in 1910. Ting Li-mei also exercised his gifts as an evangelist in the early years of the Nationalist revolution. Dr. James Yen pioneered mass education in China in the name of Christ. Dr. Ch'eng Ching-yi, in the early days of the Chinese Communist Party, when the Chinese church was being seriously threatened, summoned the church to revival and dependence on God alone. Dr. John Sung and Dr. Andrew Gih profoundly stirred the Christian church and led many to faith in Christ during the '30s. Marcus Cheng was a gifted Bible teacher and writer, while Dr. Chia Yü-ming was an outstanding Biblical scholar and convention speaker right up to his death at the age of over 90. And in an era when association with foreign missionaries was embarrassing and unpopular men like Chang Lin-shen (True Jesus Church), Ching Tien-yin (Jesus Family), and Watchman Nee (Little Flock) headed movements independent of foreign missions and the traditional denominations. Wang Ming-tao maintained an individual independence without starting a separate movement and exercised a nation-wide influence on the churches.

The list of outstanding Chinese Christians is long but the records of most of them have never been written and so everyone will welcome the life story of a man whose name has become a household word among Christians all over the world. Watchman Nee personally wrote and published only one book but he left an almost complete record of his sermons, lectures, and conference addresses which were published in the several magazines he edited. Some of these Angus Kinnear has collected and skilfully edited under such titles as *The Normal Christian Life*, *Changed into His Likeness*, and *Love Not the World*. Over the years Dr. Kinnear has also collected much historical information about the life and work of Watchman Nee, whom he came to know personally in England in 1938.

Calvin Chao, a first generation Christian who became an outstanding evangelist and student worker, once said that it takes a third generation Christian to produce the maturity and depth of insight needed to expound the mysteries of the Gospel with the pen of an Andrew Murray or a Bishop Handley Moule. Watchman Nee, unlike Calvin Chao and other contemporary leaders, was a third generation Christian and to him was certainly given an insight into Biblical truth which is unique. Few modern Chinese preachers have so glorified Christ and from the depth of his experience and the breadth of his reading so edified their hearers as did Watchman Nee.

But, like David and Paul, Wesley and Studd, Watchman Nee was not free from human error and human frailty. His insistence on the 'one locality one church' principle led him into separatism and a denunciation of all churches other than his own and this inevitably caused deep division in the Body of Christ. His well-intended but misconceived venture into industry and commerce alienated him from his own church people, hindered his usefulness to God for at least five years, and provided a weapon for the Communists to use against him. His belated attempt to emulate the early Church and to impose on his churches the practice of having all things in common again divided his followers and presented his enemies with ample grounds for criticism and condemnation. These were the kinds of aberration which almost inevitably occur when a single individual both starts and then controls a movement, lacking the credal checks and doctrinal safeguards of the more established churches. Church history, ancient and modern, contains plenty of examples of this principle. So lessons are to be learned from Angus Kinnear's biography.

But when the history of the Chinese church comes to be written it will be impossible to ignore the life and work of an oustanding leader whose influence will last and whose legacy may well be a Christian fellowship which will survive the fires of persecution and the attempts being made to destroy the Christian church in China. Watchman Nee was surely another 'man of destiny' who endured to the end as seeing Him who is invisible. In twenty years of imprisonment he never betrayed his Lord. Among his converts, colleagues, and followers, as in other branches of the church, there are many of like courage and faith in God who live on to continue the testimony.

LESLIE T. LYALL

Preface

THIS account of the life and ministry of Watchman Nee is presented from the standpoint of an observer at a distance who has at no time been involved in the China scene. When in 1938, as a young missionary about to leave Britain for India, I was privileged to spend some valuable weeks with him, I found my whole outlook on Christian life and service greatly enriched and given a fresh direction and purpose; and now that there has fallen to my lot the task of setting his remarkable story in writing he has once again profoundly affected my thinking. For, as one might expect, his message proves to be inextricably woven into his life. By setting the one in the context of the other and making full use of his own many interpretive anecdotes we are able to trace God's hand in the course of his pilgrimage through a scene of world-shaking events.

Over years I have been privileged to meet and converse with many who knew Nee intimately and it is largely to these that I owe the vivid picture it has been possible to reconstruct in these pages. Some earlier encounters were, alas, all too brief and it is to my sorrow that prevailing circumstances have not allowed me to pursue some of them further. Of these personal accounts many have helpfully dovetailed to reinforce one another, but for some details I have had to rely – and have felt it right to do so – upon the evidence of single witnesses quoting from memory. Furthermore I have occasionally, where the evidence was slender, had to make my own prayerful deductions as to precise timings and sequences and, for the sake of brevity, to take a few short cuts. For any errors and inconsistencies I must assume personal responsibility, as also for my assessments of Nee and his colleagues. I wish to apologize in particular for any pain or inconvenience that might possibly arise from my misunderstanding of the meanings, causes, or motives behind events.

I have been given a great deal of assistance by many people, and in the first place I must record the immense debt I owe, in all my work for Watchman Nee, to the gifted versions and transcriptions by the late Miss Elizabeth Fischbacher of the best of his preaching and writing. She has skilfully captured and preserved the spirit of the man and her contributions have appeared, hitherto unacknowledged, in the series of books by Nee I have been privileged to edit. They are drawn upon again in the present volume. In the interpretation of events the view I have taken owes much at several critical points to the mature spiritual wisdom of another servant of God. I refer to Watchman's friend from boyhood days, the late Mr. Faithful Luke.

At different periods I have received much help in the form of reminiscences and impressions, private documents, translations, etc., from the following: T. Austin-Sparks, Hubert L. Barlow, David Bentley-Taylor, Joy Betteridge, Dorothy Beugler, Lena Clarke, Elizabeth Fischbacher, Theodore Fischbacher, Mrs. Nancy Gaussen, Doris E. Hinckley, Herald Hsu, Hilda Holms, Victoria Holms, Mary Jones, Sophia Jorgensen, Stephen Kaung, Witness Lee, Gaylord Leung, Serene Loland, Faithful Luke, Leslie T. Lyall, James Ma, Shepherd Ma, George McHaffie, Kristeen Macnair, Simon Meek, Joy Meggach, D. Vaughan Rees, Mrs. Carol T. Stearns, Newman Sze, A. G. Taylor, Mary Wang, K. H. Weigh, Mary Weller, Mrs Betty Williams, Lucas Wu, Alan C. L. Yin. Printed sources are acknowledged in the Notes.

I should like also to express my gratitude to Miss Jean Wood and Miss Rosemary Keen of the Church Missionary Society and to Dr. Jim Broomhall and Miss Irene King of the Overseas Missionary Fellowship for their willing help, and to Hugh Fuller of Victory Press for his encouragement and long patience while I have been writing this book. And I wish to thank most warmly the four who have read through the manuscript and helped so constructively with advice, Gaylord Leung, Janet Killeen, Leslie T. Lyall, and my wife Jean who also did all the typing.

A word about the transliteration of Chinese names. Except where older spellings have been universally used I have tried to follow the Wade-Giles system, but without the 'frills'. That is to say, as in newspapers and reference books I have omitted the accents and apostrophes as being meaningless to the great majority of English readers. Inconsistencies and misspellings are due to my own ignorance of Chinese. To reduce the number of difficult personal names in the text I have supplied a Who's Who of the Nee family and other main characters in the story.

The *Notes on the Text* (at the end of the volume) besides acknowledging valuable sources and supplying hints for further reading are designed to embody a fairly full bibliography of Watchman Nee's writings and edited addresses available in English up to the date of this publication, linked where possible with their date of origin and historic setting.

The task of preparing this book has been a rewarding one in which I have been aware of the constant help of God. To His hands, for His use, I now entrust it.

ANGUS I. KINNEAR
London, 1973.

Who's Who

THE NEE (NI) FAMILY (in the Foochow dialect: Nga)

WATCHMAN'S GRANDFATHER:

The Rev. Nga U-cheng (U. C. Nga) of Foochow, born c. 1840; Congregational pastor with the American Mission Board, Foochow. Died 1890.

WATCHMAN'S PARENTS:

Ni Weng-hsiu (W. H. Ni) or Nga Ung-siu of Foochow, born 1877, the fourth of nine boys. Officer in the Imperial Customs Service. Died in Hong Kong 1941.

Lin Huo-ping (Peace Lin) of Foochow, born 1880. Died in Swatow 1950.

THEIR NINE CHILDREN:

1. Ni Kuei-chen, born 1900 (Mrs. H. C. Chan).
2. Ni Kuei-cheng, born 1902 (Mrs. P. C. Lin).
3. Ni Shu-tsu or Henry Nee (or in the Foochow dialect Nga Shu-jeo) born in Swatow 4 November 1903; re-named (i) Ni Ching-fu, (ii) Ni To-sheng or WATCHMAN NEE. Married Charity Chang. Died in Anhwei Province 1 June 1972. They had no children.
4. Ni Huai-tsu or George Nee, research chemist.
5. Ni Sheng-tsu, died in school years.
6. Ni Tek-ting (Mrs. L. H. Wong).
7. Ni Teh-ching (Mrs. Chang).
8. Ni Hong-tsu or Paul Nee.
9. Ni Hsing-tsu or John Nee.

THE CHANG FAMILY

CHARITY'S FATHER:

The Rev. Chang Chuen-kuan (C. K. Chang) of Foochow, pastor in Tientsin with the Christian and Missionary Alliance.

HIS CHILDREN:

1. Chang Pin-tseng or Beulah Chang (Mrs. G. S. Ling).
2. Chang Pin-fang or Faith Chang (Mrs. K. L. Bao).
3. Chang Pin-huei or CHARITY CHANG (Mrs. Watchman Nee). Died in Shanghai October 1971.
4. Chang Yi-lun or Samuel Chang.

SOME CHRISTIAN LEADERS AND WORKERS

*An asterisk denotes those directly associated with the Church Assembly Hall ('Little Flock' Movement).

*John Chang (Chang Kwang-yung) early Shanghai worker.
*James Chen (Chen Tseh-hsin) of Amoy, worker in Hong Kong.
*Stephen Kaung (Chiang Sheo-tao) worker in Chungking.
*Miss Ruth Lee (Li Yuen-ju) worker in charge of Shanghai Book Room.
*Witness Lee (Li Shang-chou) of Chefoo; later senior worker in Shanghai and the Philippines.
*Philip Luan (Luan Fei-li) of Shantung, worker in Hangchow.
*Faithful Luke (Liok Tiong-sin) of Kutien, worker in Singapore.
*Shepherd Ma (Ma Muh) Christian merchant in Shanghai.
*Simon Meek (Miao Shou-hsun) of Lieng Chieng, worker in Manila.
 Mary Stone, M.D. (Shih Ma-yu) first Chinese woman doctor and founder of Bethel hospital, Shanghai.
 John Sung, Ph.D. (Sung Ju-un) revivalist preacher associated with the Bethel Evangelistic Band.
*Daniel Tan (Chen Chu-yen) of Amoy, worker in Singapore.
*John Wang (Wang Lien-chun) elder in Foochow.
 Leland Wang (Wang Tsai) of Foochow, founder of China Overseas Missionary Union.
 Wang Ming-tao, fundamentalist pastor of the Tabernacle, Peking.
*Miss Peace Wang (Wang Pei-chen) worker in Shanghai.
 Wilson Wang (Wang Tse) of Foochow, brother and colleague of Leland Wang.
*K. H. Weigh (Wei Kwang-hsi) of Kutien, worker in Hong Kong.
*K. S. Wong (Wong Kai-seng) Christian merchant in Singapore.
*Lukas Wu (Wu Jen-chieh) of Tsinkiang, worker in Manila.
*Dr. C. H. Yu (Yu Cheng-hua) ophthalmologist, elder in Shanghai.
 Miss Dora Yu (Yu Tsi-tu) evangelist and Bible teacher used in the conversion of Watchman Nee. She died in 1931.
*Alan C. L. Yin, Christian manager of Sheng Hua Pharmaceutical Company.

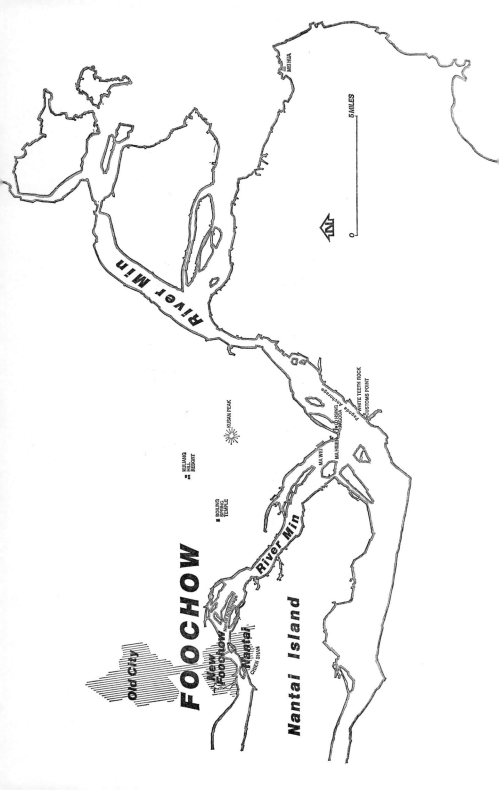

1

THE GIFT

Spring was well advanced in the Middle Kingdom and the season of Pure Brightness had given way to the season of Corn Rain. The night air was clear, with fleecy clouds drifting across a silvery moon. Foochow-fu had closed its seven gates beneath their fantastic storeyed towers. From the crumbling, crenellated walls obsolete cannon looked out over broad rice-fields and spreading suburbs. Foot-traffic had ceased on the eight-century-old Bridge of Ten Thousand Ages that linked the town on the north bank with Chung-Chou and Nantai Islands. Tonight no mist shrouded the huddled sampans of the boat-dwellers on the River Min.

Among the close-packed streets and houses the day's cacophony had long since died. Gone were the rhythmic noises of the streetside craftsmen, the song of bamboo coolies hefting giant loads, the grind-ing of huge pestles hulling rice, the unending slip-slip of straw sandals, the squeal of trussed pigs borne to market, the cries of hawkers and the whining pleas of beggars. All these had fallen silent and so too, very gradually, had the last home-bound footsteps through the narrow lane: a sedan chair with toiling bearers bring-ing home a late-working scholar official; a chattering band of long-shoremen returned from loading a junk to catch the tide; a shuffling addict drawn along by his ceaseless craving for the deadly 'foreign smoke'. Now at last all was still. In the rambling Nga home the large household slept.

Po-po! po-po! Beside her sleeping husband Lin Huo-ping stirred uneasily on her mat, aware tonight of the third child secretly within her. She listened. From Kuei-chen and from the little one there was only quiet breathing. *Po-po! po-po!* Again that staccato sound, and louder. It must be the night watchman on his circuit, alert while most men slept, to give the alarm of fire or thief or any danger. *Po-po! po-po!* The assuring clapper-note (*to-sheng*) of his bamboo rattle was receding now as the voice came reed-like, calling: 'Past mid-night, neighbours. All is well!'

An oil lamp with floating wick bathed the little room in its faint glow. The flame guttered and flared as Huo-ping lay back, assured that all was well. She closed her eyes once more, but not to sleep.

Again, perhaps for the hundredth time, she whispered *Let it be a boy!'* She recalled with burning resentment today's household gossip, the barbed, mocking words that had made this visit to her in-laws' home so painful. Chinese society placed a premium on male offspring, and to her gentle Nga Ung-siu she had already borne two girls. Her Cantonese mother-in-law had been furious. The unfortunate wife of her eldest son could conceive only females—six of them—and Ung-siu's woman, she affirmed, was another just like her. 'Avenge me, O God,' Huo-ping cried now in bitterness, 'and take away this reproach!' Then somehow there came back to her mind the half-hearted promise she had made and as quickly forgotten when a year back her second child was on the way. 'God,' she had prayed then, in words that echoed Hannah's, 'If you will give me a little boy, I will give him back to You to be Your servant all his days.'[1] They were good familiar words. She had known the Samuel story from childhood. But now, all at once they aroused in her heart an impulse she had not felt before. She would not only say them : she would mean what she said. She did not hesitate. 'I'll keep my word, Lord!' she exclaimed. Quiet then came to her at last. Smiling she drifted back again to sleep.

Long weeks were to pass, and a return journey by sea to their home in Swatow. But her pangs came at length, and oh, the inexpressible relief when she heard her husband cry, 'It's a boy!' Tension was released in tears as joy overwhelmed her. This time therefore, when the red-tinted duck-eggs went out to the neighbours and friends, it was to announce the longed-for son and heir.

Thus on 4 November 1903 Henry Nga came into the world to be the delight of his quiet father and his strong-willed mother. Chinese names are significant, a child being given or assuming a new one at some fresh turning-point in his career. At first, in the family tradition, he was Nga Shu-jeo in the Foochow dialect, or in Mandarin, Ni Shu-tsu, 'He who proclaims his ancestor's merits.' Years later however, conscious of a new mission in life, he sought a fresh name expressing his sense of duty to his people as God's seer and spokesman. For a while he called himself Ching-fu, 'one who gives warning or admonishes'; but this concept seemed harsh and he was not wholly satisfied. It was his mother who then proposed To-sheng, a gong-note or tocsin,[2] reminding him of her promise in the waking night while the watchman beat through the streets his bamboo gong or rattle (*to*) to emit its far-reaching note (*sheng*). So he became Ni To-sheng, or in English, Watchman Nee, and thus we shall generally know him. He disciplined himself through life to be like Samuel, alert while others slept, God's priestly bell-ringer who should warn His people of peril or arouse them to a new day's dawning.[3]

HONOUR YOUR ANCESTORS

FOOCHOW is the Fukien provincial capital and one of China's gateways to the southern ocean. For generations it had been home to the Nga (or Nee) family, whose members went each spring to a nearby hillside to tend the graves of their ancestors. In 1839, around the time when Watchman's grandfather Nga U-cheng was born, hostilities had broken out between China and Britain over the galling imperial restrictions on foreign trade. The three-year Opium War that followed ended in China's humiliation and the forcible opening of diplomatic relations with the West. The Treaty of Nanking, by which in 1842 Hong Kong was ceded to Britain outright, also opened Foochow and four other seaports to foreign commercial intercourse with all its scandals and abuses. While the native coastal trade went on, in timber, paper, fruits, and textiles, there now arose alongside it a new and unwelcome business settlement of foreign factories and residences on the mid-river islet of Chung-Chou and the farther hill-slopes of Nantai island.

Fifty years earlier the learned Emperor Chien Lung, knowing perhaps something of British encroachment in India under Clive and Warren Hastings, had patiently explained in a letter to George III of England that his Empire's self-contained economy had no room for the curious products of people living far away in the depths of the sea. 'As your envoy can see for himself, we possess all things. I set no value on objects strange and ingenious, and have no use for your country's wares.' In official circles that view still prevailed. Yet Europe increasingly demanded Chinese porcelain, silk, and lacquer, and since by imperial edict barter was denied them, the English merchants must pay in silver. This serious problem was only resolved when they found that the Chinese could be induced to buy Indian opium. The principle of exchange could then be made to work to the foreigner's advantage, and by 1851 the resistance of the Son of Heaven had been so eroded that opium was legalized.

The thing that above all else caused trade to soar was Europe's demand for tea. By 1853, when Nga U-cheng was around fourteen, the first cargoes of Foochow tea, brought down-river from the Wu Yi Shan highlands, were already being shipped from the Min River anchorage to markets in Europe and America. Soon the tall China clippers with great names like *Taeping* and *Thermopylae, Ariel* and *Flying Spur*, were to make this port second only to Shanghai in the prosperous tea trade.

The entry to China of Protestant Christianity as an accompaniment of the foreign trade was another consequence of the Opium War and the Nanking Treaty. Of the events of 1842 a contemporary Western writer could say with astonishing complacency: 'The ways of God's dealings with this people began to open, and He entered into judgement with them that He might show them His mercy.'[1] The vermilion pencil of the emperor had decreed that the Christian faith be tolerated throughout the Middle Kingdom, but the decree had been extracted under military pressure. Nevertheless it threw wide the door for Western missionaries with their social concern and evangelistic zeal to move in and stake out new claims for righteousness in Chinese hearts.

This they quickly did. At Foochow the first missionaries to arrive in 1847 were Congregationals of the American Board, to be followed the same year by American Episcopal Methodists and in 1850 by Anglicans of the English Church Missionary Society. The missionaries were not slow to protest against the iniquitous opium traffic; yet as red-haired aliens claiming extra-territorial privileges they could scarcely be distinguished in native minds from the traders and their trade.

The first school offering Western-style education was opened by the American Board in a suburb of the old city in 1853 and it was here that as a boy Watchman Nee's grandfather Nga U-cheng heard of the love of God in Jesus Christ and was won to him. Four years later in 1857, the year in which the first Christian church in Foochow came into being, he was one of a group of four pupils baptized in the Min River. He progressed so well that the missionaries trained him as an evangelist, and soon with other young men he was proclaiming the gospel of the Lord Jesus in this city of half a million souls. Eventually he was ordained a pastor, the first Chinese to be so honoured in the three north Fukien missions.[2] He had a gift for expounding the Scriptures for which, after his death in 1890, he was long to be remembered.

It was when as a maturing young man his time came to marry that his big test came, for very few women in Fukien as yet believed in Christ and for him no local Christian girl could be found. Foochow folk of those days were extremely conservative and would on no account transgress custom to intermarry with those of another province; yet he must either look farther afield or compromise his testimony. It says much for him that his faith prevailed over tradition. From Canton, 450 miles away by coastal boat, he accepted a Kwangtung girl who proved to be God's choice for him and made him a true, if somewhat sharp-tongued, life-partner.

They were blessed (in Chinese eyes) with nine boys. Of these Watchman's father Nga Ung-siu was the fourth, being born in 1877. As a pastor's son he was given Christian elementary schooling, and then went on to study the Confucian classics for the competitive examinations. Foochow was a literary centre where twice in every three years several thousand students from the prefecture gathered for the first degree examinations, and again twice in five years from the whole province for those of the second degree. With age-old ceremony at the appointed time Ung-siu and a throng of others entered the vast examination area north-east of the city, by a gateway that bore the characters: 'For the Empire: Pray for Good Men.' Confined there for three days in his own individual cell he adorned his scroll of ruled paper with columns of beautiful characters, pouring out his classical knowledge in a poem and two essays on the theme now set. The papers were judged with strict impartiality, and his success in the second degree gained him, shortly before his marriage, the post of a junior State Customs officer.

His young wife Lin Huo-ping had been born in 1880 of peasant stock, the last of a big family. Very poor and darkened by superstition they lived in fear of demons and dragons and fox-fairies. It was a famine year in Fukien, and with so many hungry mouths to feed she stood little chance of survival. Even in normal conditions an infant girl, just because she was one too many, might be exposed or drowned or buried alive by her father. Indeed a child still living, if sickly or pining from hunger, might be cast, along with the dead, into the high aperture of Foochow's capacious baby-tower, an urn-shaped granite receptacle at the town's edge designed to save the expense of child-burials. For just a few girls the Roman Catholic orphanage outside the southern gate offered a home. The inscription over its entry ran: 'When thy father and thy mother forsake thee, the Lord will take thee up.'

But Huo-ping's father did not forsake her utterly. For the three or four dollars he so desperately needed he sold her, through a go-between, to a better-off family in the city who thought of bringing her up as a slave girl. But she was a lively child, and soon this family was approached, again through an emissary, by a merchant named Lin in a foreign firm in Nantai. His concubine was barren and desired to adopt her as a daughter, so again Huo-ping changed hands. In the providence of God the merchant too loved children, and here she found a home. Though there were already two boys and a girl in the family the couple took the spirited little newcomer to their hearts and brought her up as their own child.

When she was six, according to the almost universal custom, her adoptive mother began binding her feet. By this procedure, the toes were balled under the sole and the as yet unossified heel and tarsus forced together, the bindings being tightened daily to withstand growth and hobble her for life. As a peasant girl Huo-ping would have escaped this treatment, for the Foochow field-women had long resisted the custom. They strode about fiercely adorned with daggers in their hair, and took their place alongside boys and grown men in the rice cultivation. But though she wept copiously each morning from the cruel pain, she never once thought of resisting. She was a merchant's child now, destined for better things, Lily feet were a part of the price she must pay.

But that year Mr. Lin became ill with a mysterious disease that defied the skills of all the doctors. Now it happened that a business superior of Lin's named Chang had become a Christian Methodist, and this man suggested that they ask the Methodist pastor to come and pray for him. They could scarcely refuse, and prayer was answered, and so impressed were the Lins with his dramatic recovery that they sought Christian instruction. Believing at length in the Lord Jesus they threw out the ugly little idols from their place of honour in the home and Mr. Lin and his wife were baptized into the Methodist church near his place of employment. Because it was closer at hand for them however, the concubine and her child attended the Church of England. To Huo-ping's great joy the painful foot-binding now ceased and she could run again freely. As she learned the hymns and Bible stories she found her heart warming to divine things. Her new happiness soon proved infectious. Asked by her primary teacher why she was always singing she told him the family's story, with the eventual result that he too with his wife and children joined the church.

A foreign business man had opened a primary school in their neighbourhood with Christian teachers, and here Huo-ping was sent to study, going on in 1891 at the age of eleven to the American-staffed Methodist Mission School for Girls. She did consistently well in class, and through spiritual failure and repentance she tasted too something of the mercy and forgiveness of God. Yet her religion still remained, she says, one largely of merit attained through good works.

It was when she was nearing the top of the school that there returned to Foochow from training in Philadelphia a young Chinese woman doctor, Hu King-en, at that time only the second woman in all China to have graduated in Medicine. Her arrival in 1895 to work in a mission hospital in the town aroused ambitions in some local girls, and next year, at the age of sixteen, Huo-ping asked her teacher to begin negotiations for her too to enter a medical school in the U.S.A. Her secondary school progress was such that to her joy the provisional answer was favourable. She therefore prevailed on her father to send her, in company with a school friend, to the Chinese Western Girls' School in Shanghai to improve her English. It was her first venture forth from Foochow and the sea voyage was exhilarating. The city, when she reached it, had wheeled vehicles in the streets and turbaned Sikh police in the International Settlement, and still at that date the park-gates along the Bund bore notices 'No dogs: no Chinamen.'

Among Chinese of a strange staccato speech she was soon home-sick, but ambition held her there. She began to excel in her studies, and to be captivated too by the higher living standards of this semi-foreign city. Soon she was expropriating the fees sent for her music lessons and using other devices to raise the dollars with which to dress herself more fashionably. 'I learned there,' she writes, 'much of the pride of life and some of the sins of the flesh.'

One particular encounter was to prove significant in the plan of God. A certain Miss Dora Yu, a girl not many years older than herself, visited the school one day to address the pupils. Yu Tzi-tu was from a cultured background and like many others had encount-ered Christianity while at a western-style school. Successful in her studies she had set out for England to train in Medicine. Passing the Suez Canal her ship anchored in the Mediterranean. There God met her, calling her to abandon her career and return to China to preach Christ to her people. She went to the ship's captain into whose care she had been entrusted, and told him what had transpired. Thinking her out of her mind he became angry; but she stuck so firmly to her request that at last he agreed to tranship her to a liner returning from Marseilles. Back in Shanghai her reception by her incredulous family was no less cool, but her quiet testimony was so convincing that they had to recognize the hand of God upon her. From that day she steadfastly set herself to witness to her Lord through preaching and Bible teaching, and all the more effectively because she received no foreign salary but trusted God alone for her needs.

Hearing Dora's story from her own lips Huo-ping was much moved. She called on her in her room to offer her a treasured gold ring, the gift of her own mother, and her obvious reluctance to accept such a present from a young girl went even further to con-vince Huo-ping of her genuineness. 'Then,' she says, 'I knew she loved God and not money.'

But to Huo-ping herself at the age of eighteen it was no call of

God that came, but sheer catastrophe that struck. Her mother had been pining for her and had all along opposed her going to America, and when in Foochow the Cantonese widow of Pastor Nga U-Cheng sent a man seeking a match for their son she leaped at the offer. Unknown to Huo-ping a marriage with Ung-siu was arranged, and now a letter backed with full parental authority broke to her the news. It put paid to her dreams of doing Medicine, for no Fukien girl had as yet so violated custom as to break such a parental arrangement. *Huo-ping* means Peace, but Turmoil would better have described her now. For days she was in agonies of near-despair. The lovely sea voyage home, with the vessel threading its way among the rocky coastal islands, was passed under a dark cloud of depression. In her heart she nursed a growing hatred for the mother to whom she owed her life, for now the residue of that life seemed in ruins.

On her arrival home she was called in and formally given Nga Ung-siu's photograph and the betrothal gift that clinched the contract. By it she was irrevocably tied to this man she had never seen. As the summer of 1899 dragged by and the marriage arrangements moved forward her heartache was unabated. Only unwanted girls were given as brides, she told herself. Others could be independent and rise to professional fame. Life, for her, was at an end. 'Marriage: how I *hated* that word!'

October arrived and the season of Cold Dew. On the nineteenth day they celebrated in Nantai the union of the late Congregational pastor's son Nga Ung-siu (who as a government officer in the Maritime Customs with a new posting to Swatow must henceforth be, in Mandarin, Ni Weng-hsiu) and Lin Huo-ping the adoptive daughter of the wealthy and generous convert businessman. It was a day of joy and hopefulness. The young couple went for two weeks to reside in the Nga home where Mrs. Nga senior ruled over seven sons and five daughters-in-law. The brief time there in the uneasy role of junior wife was, she discovered, more than enough to restore her affection for her own sweet mother. She determined that if she had children her girls should never suffer as she suffered, then and later, at the hands of the women of that house! It was thus a relief when the time came to set out, bag and baggage, for Swatow and the new appointment.

Amid the farewells of both families Ni Weng-hsiu took his young bride the eleven miles down river by sampan to the ocean anchorage at Pagoda Island to board the coastal boat. It was crowded with deck passengers, their bedding and bundles and little pig-skin trunks, and with livestock of every kind, but the congestion and discomforts of the sea voyage were offset by the rugged coastal beauty as the silt-laden river waters gave way abruptly to a clear green sea. A cruise of two hundred and fifty miles brought them at length to Swatow, the little treaty port at the rock-bound mouth of the Han River. Though tiny compared to Foochow it had a rich hinterland and its brisk trade would fully engage Mr. Nee in his taxation work. Here in the official quarter the young couple now set up home.

That year of 1900 was one of uneasy peace. Away in the northern provinces the *I Huo Chuan* or Righteous Harmony Fists, whom the foreigners knew as the 'Boxers', were murdering Chinese Christians and spreading anti-foreign madness. The astute and unprincipled Empress Dowager had gone further, and seeking to harness the dangerous movement to her own ends had issued an order to destroy all aliens China-wide. Happily the southern viceroys elected at great personal cost to stand by the 'unequal treaties' and ignore her edict. In Foochow city at the critical time floods providentially broke the Min River bridge, cutting off the murderers from their intended victims. At Swatow too a precarious quiet reigned. Into this quiet was born Kuei-chen, to be greeted with spontaneous rejoicing as God's undoubted gift. When however a year later Kuei-cheng arrived their joy was more qualified. Such was the strength of tradition that a sense of guilt weighed upon the parents. Why should God have to trust them with a second mere girl? Simple Christians as they were, their confidence in God was severely tested. Happily their anguish brought them back to their knees to put their problem to Him.

And then, back once more in Swatow, the third pregnancy reached term, and at length there came the delighted father's cry, 'It's a boy!' In young Shu-tsu God had given to Huo-ping the desire of her heart. Weak Christian though she was she kept her pact. Like Hannah she brought her treasure back to Him. 'It was this boy that I prayed for, and the Lord has given me what I asked. Now I lend him to the Lord; for his whole life he is His.'[3] God had found for Himself a watchman.

3

REVOLUTION

During the years that followed the Nee children increased to nine in all, five boys and four girls. After Kuei-chen, Kuei-cheng and Henry (Shu-tsu, who is Watchman) came George (Huai-tsu) and a third son, Sheng-tsu, who was to survive only to school days. After an interval two more girls followed, Tek-ting and Teh-ching, and finally two boys, Paul (Hong-tsu) and John (Hsing-tsu).

As a junior official in the Maritime Customs Ni Weng-hsiu's salary of 35 taels a month was not large. Moreover nearly half of this went back to his widowed mother. So the growing family must at first be content with the necessities of life, food, and clothing, and a house to dwell in, though with fresh vegetables and sea-foods at hand to garnish their rice they grew up fit and healthy. Childhood toys were simple and locally made of pottery and bamboo and paper, and there were kites to fly at Christmas time when the monsoon winds blew strongest.

But Lin Huo-ping was full of drive. To help their finances she enlisted her father's aid to build up in Swatow an export business in piece goods of drawn-thread work and figured cloth. This soon proved very profitable with a steady flow to markets in Malaya, Great Britain, and the United States. Her husband too came to be valued by his superiors as a careful and exact man and through conscientious work in the Service he attained steady promotion. Some years of prosperity passed, and then a transfer to Suchow, a city fifty miles west of Shanghai, put an abrupt end to the cloth business and threw the family's affairs into disorder. After twelve months there he was urged by his mother to apply for a fresh posting to Foochow on compassionate grounds and to his joy obtained it.

While in Swatow the parents themselves had taken care of the children's education, drilling them in propriety and good manners and teaching them their first brush-written characters. Once back in Foochow however Ni Weng-hsiu engaged as tutor a *hsiu tsai* or graduate of the first degree. From this man in due course they learned calligraphy and the literary and moral principles contained in the Four Books and the Five Classics which had formed the basis of Chinese moral culture for two millennia. For though in 1905 the old civil examination system had been abolished and the road to official advancement lay henceforth through new schools modelled on those of the West, yet no child might escape these Confucian studies and still claim to be educated. Young Watchman proved quick to learn, and usually outdid his elder sisters to win the dollar prize that the tutor sometimes offered for good work. The Nees were musical, and their tutor instructed them too in the ancient Chinese system called The Melodies, while Huo-ping herself taught them Christian hymns with their Bible lessons. Later when her husband could afford one he bought them a piano, and himself copied out sheet music for the children to play.

Traditionally a Chinese father would rule with a heavy hand, but this was not in Ni Weng-hsiu's nature. Grave like his own father, he was disinclined to scold. Though always approachable he kept in the background, occupying himself as a Chinese man should with his official duties and his men friends. In the home it was Huo-ping who wielded the rod. To her, discipline was the family's glory and she ruled her high-spirited children by fear. It was a family principle that domestic tidiness was a duty shared equally by all. Her pleasure was to have the home clean and orderly with everything where it belonged. If something were found out of place, none might shrug off responsibility : the one nearest at hand was responsible to put it back. Watchman was no angel and tended to leave behind him a trail of litter and breakages for which he was regularly punished. His elder sisters recall how sometimes this punishment was overdone and then they would conspire to shield him by confessing themselves to some of the mess he had made.

They were fortunate in having another Foochow family, the Changs, living close to them on the Nantai shore overlooking the bridge. Chang Chuen-kuan was a dear Christian friend and remote connection of their father. His children's ages approximated to their own and the two families were always on relaxed, easy terms together. The two eldest Chang daughters were special friends of the Nee girls, while little Charity always tagged along behind Watchman. In their childhood ploys he was the one who had the ideas and took the lead and thus he became 'eldest brother' to them all.

From their home it was but a short walk to the busy fish-market whence an ancient granite-piered bridge with worn flagstones led out to the tight-packed islet of Chung Chou, and from this the much longer Bridge of Ten Thousand Ages completed the crossing to the north shore and the thronged road to the city gate of old Foochow. That was too far for the children to venture alone, but on the bridge close at hand they could spend long and fascinating hours. Here they might find traders' stalls and picture shows, a geomancer fore-casting auspicious days for funerals or a dentist extracting teeth before the amused onlookers, or maybe even some victim of Man-chu justice, restrained round the neck by the heavy cangue bearing his offence inscribed on its planking. Above the island lay the close-packed sampans of the river dwellers, ever busy with life, while in the stream below the shallow arches the cormorant-fishers on tiny rafts worked their patient birds, rewarding each with a dose of mix-ture from a bottle for the fish it caught but, because of the tight ring round its neck, could never swallow.

From the quay near their father's office on the south bank the children would watch the coastal junks come up the sweep of river to the Nantai anchorage, their flaring bows painted with great direction-seeking eyes, their stiffened sails brown against the blue of the Kushan hills. They were of as many designs as their ports of origin and the cargoes the children saw unloaded were even more varied. There was too a brisk out-going trade in agricultural pro-ducts and in tea and timber from the hills, but the export industries were minor, being limited to silk and lacquer and such domestic articles as oil-paper umbrellas and red wooden 'pillows'. In this Foochow was behind the times, for elsewhere China had entered upon great industrial changes with textile factories springing up in the coastal towns, railways probing into the interior and foreign engineers diligently exploiting her mineral resources.

It was perhaps in Watchman's sixth year that the family returned to Foochow and he would be nine when revolution broke upon the country to sweep away the dynasty. We must pause for a moment to view the world in which he grew up. For the present the Viceroy of Chekiang and Fukien in his yamen in the old city was but a subject of Manchu overlords represented by the Tartar general and his indolent Bannermen who occupied, with their heavily painted women-folk, a special quarter within the walls. But the régime had outlived its value and, since the Boxer episode, was totally dis-credited, so that among educated Chinese these were years of mounting unrest directed against both alien rule and grasping West-ern exploitation. Increasing numbers of students had gone abroad to benefit from the new learning and to return with minds in a turmoil of revolutionary ideas.

Their hero was one who for twenty years had laboured for China's renewal. Dr. Sun Yat-sen, of humble Cantonese origin and Protestant Christian faith, was the prime ideologist of Chinese revo-lution. Though his lack of administrative flair was to be his undoing, his Three Principles of nationalism, democracy, and socialism (*san-min-chu-i*) were destined to capture and hold the popular imagination. He had long been compelled to work from exile, for the Manchu régime was still being bolstered up by the foreign powers for their own ends. Then in November 1908 the Emperor Kuang Hsu died. Intelligent but weak, he had been wholly dominated by the superstitious old Empress Dowager who had proved herself China's evil genius, self-seeking and reactionary to the last, and whose own death followed next day. Few mourned her going, but the heir to the throne was Kuang Hsu's three-year-old nephew, now proclaimed Emperor under the name Hsuan Tung.

There followed three years of uncertainty marked by a growing conviction that the dynasty had forfeited the mandate of Heaven. Then on 10 October 1911 ('the Double Tenth') the accidental discharge of a conspirator's bomb set off revolt in Wuchang, capital of Hupei province, and the train of events began which was to result in the imperial abdication, the rise and decay of the Republic, the Nationalist dictatorship and the eventual triumph of the Communist Party.

In December Sun Yat-sen returned from overseas and at the 'southern capital' of Nanking was elected first Provisional President of the Republic of China. There he declared a government based on the will of the people. To symbolize their rejection of Manchu rule his followers began to cut off their queues, the form of wearing the hair imposed upon the Han men as a mark of their subjection. No longer now would the school-boys in Foochow stand in file on the hostel verandah plaiting each others' pigtails. Was not the Tartar general suing for mercy while his soldiers ran in terror for the hills? After two millennia the king-pin of Chinese civilization, the Dragon Throne itself, had been torn from its vital place in the fabric of government to be hopefully superseded by a democratic republic.

But Sun and the southerners prominent in revolution with him were mostly exiles out of touch with the mood of their country, nursing vague dreams of a China reshaped on the Western pattern but unaware that for effective democracy she lacked the essential foundations. Inevitably a northerner arose to challenge him. Yuan Shih-kai, a general of the Empire with personal designs on the throne, contrived quickly to displace him as President. Before being forced back into exile in August 1913, Dr. Sun was constrained therefore to organize a 'Second Revolution' in the seaport cities of the south.

On a local scale the Nee family became closely involved in these affairs. Sun's 'Love One's Country' movement captured their hearts, and whereas Ni Weng-hsiu was a retiring man who could not utter a word in public, his wife was the reverse, eloquent and forceful and ready to assert her new-found release from feminine subservience.

Careless of the fighting and bloodshed around she set out on a tour of lectures, having first publicly donated to the cause her own gold bangles and jewellery in a gesture that many men and women were moved to follow. By energetic correspondence she formed a Women's Patriotic Society backed by prominent local leaders, serving it herself as General Secretary. When in July 1913 Sun Yat-sen arrived in person in Foochow,[1] Huo-ping was given an official role in the Presidential reception. It turned out that Dr. Sun's private secretary Miss Song was a Shanghai class-mate of hers, and with her she attended every feast and function throughout the four-day tour.

Watchman was now ten years old, able to listen with a boy's inquisitive ears to the political talk. The Revolution had surely brought new hope to his country. At first too an up-surge of pro-foreign feeling had promised the rapid expansion of Christian missionary enterprise, so who could tell what doors might open to him one day for study overseas? But a year later war broke out in Europe to create disillusion with the West. At home too the Revolution seemed stillborn, with the land dismembered by rival war-lords and by Japanese encroachments under the guise of aid in war participation. On 18 January 1915 Japan presented her Twenty-One Demands which, starting with claims upon Shantung Province, would have gone on to make of all China a puppet state.[2] That year President Yuan announced his own delighted reversal of all their hopes by proclaiming his ascent of the Dragon Throne, but he was destined only to end his days in shame.

In 1916 at the age of thirteen, impressionable and buoyed with hope, Watchman entered the C.M.S. vernacular Middle School in Foochow to begin his Western style education. In due course he would go on to the English-medium High School of St. Mark's. This was part of an Anglican complex in Nantai comprising primary, middle, normal, high, and divinity schools, having nearly four hundred on the roll and known together as Trinity College, Foochow. The missionary staff were mainly Irish from Trinity College, Dublin.[3]

As he passed up through the school Watchman did well enough in his class work, overcoming occasional setbacks through illness for which friends blamed Huo-ping's mother who constantly spoiled him. Often indeed he came out top in his class. He tells us how, like any school boy, he enjoyed as a youngster stamping 'Ni Shu-tsu' in opaque red ink on books and papers and whatever lay to hand, using a home-made version of the personal seal or die that would one day take on a more treasured significance. In manner he was generally straightforward, if perhaps a shade priggish with a keen sense of justice, for once when a street hawker visiting the school complained that one of his wares was missing Watchman aroused popular resentment by indicating the boy who had taken it. He showed little enthusiasm for the team games—basket-ball, volley-ball, football—in which the other boys joined, seeming to lack the stamina for them, but he was growing fast now into a lean, lanky lad, a head taller than most of his fellows.

He had soon acquired facility in the unfamiliar northern dialect, known to westerners as 'Mandarin', which was now coming to the fore as the national tongue or *pai-hua*, the 'plain language' of the people. All his early reading had been in books in the classical style beloved of literary men and still demanded by the fossilized State schooling system; but now China was passing through a gigantic cultural renaissance. In response to popular demand pioneer writers and poets were turning for a medium of expression to the vernacular that had hitherto been left to the gutter-press novelists, and as a consequence Watchman and his schoolmates read cheap novels surreptitiously under their desk-tops. By 1922 the Ministry of Education itself would give sanction to this development, ordering all school textbooks to be rewritten in the national language. It was a change destined to have tremendous effect on the spread of ideas through literature in the years ahead, and not least in the freer dissemination of Christian thought in popular circles.

But religion generally was just now in disfavour among students. Indeed in 1918 an Anti-Religious movement had been promoted through the magazine *New Youth* by Chen Tu-hsiu, Dean of the Peking School of Letters and a most influential leader of educated thought. His movement was to blossom in the Great Federation of Anti-Religionists of 1922 and the emotional outbursts against Christianity that followed,[4] and Chen himself was later to become Secretary General of the Chinese Communist Party. And an event of even greater influence that must claim our attention here is the May Fourth Movement. With the victory of World War I and the Versailles Treaty of 1919 China expected the return of the German concessions in Shantung, instead of which they were awarded by Britain and France to their other ally, Japan. Indignation among young Chinese on the discovery of what they felt was a sell-out by their own incompetent government led on 4 May 1919 to a massive spontaneous protest by Peking students,[5] prominent among whom was a young man of twenty-three named Chou En-lai. There followed student-led strikes in Shanghai and Foochow and a proliferation of new Marxist ideas, helped forward by the Soviet government's offer in 1920 to renounce Russian extra-territorial rights. The May Fourth Movement was to prove highly significant in paving the way for Chinese Communism.

Watchman was now in his sixteenth year and susceptible enough to the explosion of student feeling aroused by these events. But he had also just completed Middle School, and the stimulus of his approaching move to St. Mark's may have done something to counter in him the all-pervading disillusion affecting those around him. There were so many grounds for this. Sporadic fighting dragged on in the Province between northern warlords and a divided and weakened Kuomintang, their armies readily turning from soldiering to banditry (if the distinction matters) whenever pay was short. Some of his school friends returning from rural areas brought back tragic stories of civil chaos and mounting peasant distress.

In his home too there was much to disenchant a growing boy. His mother's involvement with the Party had begun to lose its glamour for them all. Earlier, in recognition of her political zeal the Fukien governor Suen Tao-ren had nominated her for an award, and Peking had responded by promoting her to the Order of the Second Class for Patriotism. Once this honour was hers however her zeal lapsed. Love of country gave way, she tells us, to enjoyment of praise and position for its own sake. Social and cultural entertainment took the place of her former church going, and 'from contact with unbelieving revolutionaries I became almost an unbeliever myself'. Daily the society ladies came to her home in Nantai to play cards and *mahjong*, and when one day the pastor called on her to ask for a subscription to some work for God, she said to him mockingly, 'Sit down here and let us see what my winnings amount to. If I win a lot I'll give Him some!' Even the outward mask of a Christian, she says, had gone.

Moreover Huo-ping's discipline of the children, generally fair and impartial, seemed now to be marked by impatience and injustice. One day in January 1920 at the end of the winter holidays a valuable ornament in the house was found smashed. Settling in her mind where the fault lay, Huo-ping decided that Watchman, as the certain culprit, should confess. When he declined to do so she subjected him once more to the indignity of a thrashing. She was not without remorse on later discovering that after all he was innocent, but she left him nevertheless to nurse his grievance. He went back to his second term at High School sore and embittered.

The same month some unexpected news reached her. Dora Yu, the woman who years earlier had so impressed her in Shanghai, was coming to Foochow at the Chinese New Year to conduct a fortnight's revival meetings in the Methodist Tien An Chapel. Miss Yu had become known as a gifted evangelist and had travelled widely among missions in northern China and Korea, as well as establishing her own Bible seminary in Shanghai. Huo-ping had not seen her since that day in 1898 when she had been moved to make her a gift. Now at the start of the Foochow meetings she invited her to an evening meal with a group of her gambling friends. She spoke warmly to them of the visitor, and at the end announced, 'Tomorrow Miss Yu will preach at the Heavenly Peace Hall. Please all be there.' Someone asked, 'And you?' 'Of course I shall go,' she answered.

February 15 came and the first meeting. Huo-ping was on time with the others and sat well forward as the preacher, her bound feet encased in tiny brocaded shoes, stood stiffly up to announce as her text God's words to Eve: 'Neither shall you touch it, lest you die.'[6] From these words she preached that day and the next with great power on spiritual death as separation from God. But the subject bored Huo-ping. She had known all this from a child and she decided two meetings were enough. Her friends were fretting at the loss of gambling time.

So on the third day, and again on the fourth, out once more on the hard-topped table clattered the white *mah-jong* bricks amid cries of rejoicing, but not without a pang of conscience in Huo-ping's heart. 'I sat there playing,' she recalls, 'as one already dead. I knew God's Holy Spirit was dealing with me.' After two uneasy days she could stand it no longer. 'I am a Christian,' she exclaimed suddenly to the others. 'Miss Yu has come a long distance to preach here. Not to attend is a breach of propriety. Say what you like, I shall not play tomorrow!'

Next day Dora Yu saw her arrive and came at once to greet her. 'Where have you been?' she asked innocently. 'I was not well,' Huo-ping lied. Miss Yu looked at her kindly. 'May God Himself shine on you and heal you,' she replied. The words struck home. How far removed was sickness from *mah-jong*! In stark reality she saw her deceitfulness for what it was. All through the address she shifted guiltily in her seat as the preacher's telling phrases found her out. Forty years old and a public figure, she could not conceive that anyone should so expose her. This was certainly going to be her last meeting. Yet when Miss Yu asked 'Will you be here tomorrow?' how could she excuse herself? And when tomorrow came, though God accused her still, His servant now recounted afresh the sufferings of Jesus on the Cross for sinners. 'Her every utterance was just for me,' she says. 'Thank God, each day a strength beyond mine brought me back for more.' The climax came when she confessed to Him her need and thanked Him for His mercy. His grace had triumphed.

Her husband, who had attended some of the meetings, was mystified. 'You neither sleep nor eat,' he protested. 'Instead you do nothing but shed tears. Others are happy when they are converted! If this is the effect it has on you, give it up and stay away!' 'But you don't know my inward state,' she exclaimed. 'I have lied to you; I have diverted so much of our family money to games of chance,' and she went on to recount the ways in which she had defrauded him. Then came his turn to confess his faults to her and soon they were both in tears. The 'Peace' that her name implies had come to her at last. The playing-cards and the *mah-jong* bricks she never touched again.

The high-school boys were free to attend Miss Yu's meetings and a number were doing so. With her new-found joy Huo-ping had assumed the role of interpreter, and was putting Miss Yu's *pai-hua* into the Foochow dialect for their sake. Watchman had till now absented himself. Susceptible as he already was to the agnostic mood of his friends he had been more than ever disillusioned by Christianity's failure as a vital force in his own home. Though his mother had invited him to attend he could be as stubborn as she was, and had declined. How could she expect otherwise? So now came the crunch. She knew she should confess her injustice to her eldest son, but her pride rebelled against such humiliation. It would be without precedent. Did not Confucius himself teach that parents were never in the wrong?

Something else however she could put right and she was determined to do so. With three dollars in her hand she set out to buy a Bible and hymnbook with which to recommence family worship. Next day she began to play and sing the first hymn—but the Spirit of God arrested her. If she was to worship God publicly she must first, she knew, confess to Him her faults. 'But,' she protested, 'how can *I*, a mother, confess to *my son*?' Quite distinctly God said, 'You must do precisely that. It is the only way.'

While her husband and the children looked on mystified she turned suddenly to Watchman and threw her arms about him. 'For the Lord Jesus' sake,' she cried, 'I confess to beating you unjustly and in anger.' 'You did, honourable Mother,' was his matter-of-fact reply, 'and I hated you for it.' 'Please forgive me!' she pleaded, looking him in the eyes; but he turned away without answering her appeal. Family prayers went on.

That night God took hold of Watchman. He had been deeply moved by Huo-ping's confession. Never had he heard of a Chinese parent accepting such loss of face. If his own mother could be thus transformed, then surely there must be something powerful in this visitor's preaching. Christianity must be more than a mere creed. He would go and see for himself. Next morning he arose early. 'I am ready now,' he told his mother, 'to come and hear Yu Tzi-tu.' He went, and before the meetings were over, her preaching had brought him also to repentance for his sins, and he had found in Jesus Christ a living Saviour and Friend. In an act of youthful committal he pledged himself to serve God wholly and utterly, and never went back on his word. God in turn responded with a new birth in his spirit that would wholly revolutionize his life. He had heard the mother's prayer in the night those years ago and was keeping His side of the compact.

Can we recognize God's hand too in the timing of these events? As we have already seen, powerful ideologies were competing for the allegiance of all thinking Chinese, and radical conversions were in the air. In these very months a man ten years Watchman's senior was devouring Marxist writings that were only now becoming available in the Chinese language, and through them arriving at profound inward convictions. Born in 1893 to a Hunan peasant family, Mao Tse-tung, sometime assistant librarian at Peking University and latterly a political agitator in Changsha, had arrived in Shanghai in the Spring of 1920 on a visit to Chen Tu-hsiu. They discussed Marx's works together, and it was through Chen's confession of political faith that Mao now became a convinced and life-long Communist.[7]

From such feeble trickles as this a nearly overwhelming flood was to break forth. Yet somehow against this tide Watchman Nee's course had already been straightly set.

4

DEDICATION

WHEN in his eighteenth year Watchman Nee turned to Jesus Christ, the committal he made was an outright one. He told a close friend later that during those few days of Dora Yu's meetings he weighed the matter carefully knowing it must be all or nothing. Did it not say of the disciples of Jesus that 'they left all and followed him'?[1] To be saved, he saw, was to yield lifelong obedience to One who makes total demands.

And why not? In one of the shops of the old city's lacquer street an anonymous craftsman had already spent six years on three hard-wood leaves of a four-leaf screen, carving reliefs of flowers in the natural wood, white against the black lacquered surface. For this he was paid eighty cents a day, 'rain, shine, holidays, or revolution', as the shop-owner put it, plus his rice and vegetables and a plank to sleep on. Having once acquired skill for this work he might make only two such screens before eyes and nerves failed and he was flung out with the beggars.[2] If human creative gift could be thus expended for an avaricious employer, was anything too good to give back to a God who had not withheld His own Son?

Soon Watchman came upon Paul's words: 'Present yourselves to God as men who have been brought from death to life, and your members to God as instruments of righteousness.'[3] 'God required of me therefore,' he said afterwards, 'that I now regard all my faculties as belonging to Another. I dared not squander a few cash of my money or an hour of my time or any of my mental or physical powers, for they were not mine but His. It was a great thing when I made that discovery. Real Christian life began for me that day.'

At once there was a wrong to be righted. In one school subject, the laboriously taught Scripture Knowledge, Watchman had till now preserved an apathy that ensured him consistently low marks. He had been not a little affected by the anti-religious mood of his seniors. Yet as the scion of a Christian family he disliked the loss of face this entailed in a Mission high school. He had therefore resolved to help himself in examinations by writing selected facts on his palms and concealing them in his flowing sleeves. This was enough to win him 70 per cent marks, which, since it more nearly approached his standard in other subjects, aroused no suspicion in his teachers.

Born anew however he at once abandoned the practice, and now, try as he would, he could not get pass marks. God, he realized, could not help him while his sin remained unconfessed. But he had reason to hesitate. The school Principal had warned that any boy found cheating would be summarily expelled, and expulsion would destroy any hope of a University scholarship and eventual study abroad. (The final two years at Trinity were at that time equivalent to the first University year at St. John's C.M.S. College, Shanghai.) So it was for him a real struggle to decide that Jesus Christ was more precious to him than a career. He went to the Principal and told him frankly what he had done and why he must confess it—and to his relief he was not dismissed.

Three months after Watchman's conversion Dora Yu paid a return visit to Foochow, stopping on her way northwards from Amoy to address the girls at the C.M.S. high school, and again 'many lives were transformed'.[4] At this period the district was militarily disturbed, with sporadic fighting in the countryside and the city swinging pendulum-like between Northern and Southern spheres of influence. Around 9 May the high-school boys were involved in anti-Japanese demonstrations for on this National Day of Shame China remembered each year Japan's Twenty-One Demands of 1915. The unrest continued and for a second year running the school curriculum was much disorganized.

Seeing this, and feeling the need to adjust himself to a whole new direction in life, Watchman quietly disappeared. His classmates had no idea where he had gone, and his family kept the secret until his return many months later. He had in fact taken ship to Shanghai, a city where the New Tide movement in education, fostered by the recent visits of John Dewey, Bertrand Russell, and Tagore, was making a big impression on student minds. Not, however, any longer on his. He had gone there to join Miss Yu's Bible School for a year's training in the Scriptures that till now he had found so difficult. He put his heart into the work and he could not have had a better teacher. From her he learned above all the secret of trusting God alone for his needs, as she had done through life. She taught him too to let God's Word speak to his own heart and not merely—essential though that was—to store his mind with its text.

When he returned his mother said to him firmly: 'Go back now to Trinity and finish your college course.' He did so, and since the entire class's curriculum had suffered he had little difficulty in catching up. But he was a changed student, and now he did not waste a moment. He plunged into his studies with a will, but he also made a list of the boys in his year and began systematically to pray for each one and to witness to them at every opportunity. At first, because he carried a Bible with him everywhere, they laughed and scornfully dubbed him 'Bible Depot'. But he was constantly reading it and knew what it contained. (He had set himself, we are told, to go through the New Testament several times a month.) He was ready to talk earnestly with any of them about its message for them, and by his changed life and evident sincerity, together with his winning smile, slowly he won their interest.

A young Foochow student of the Canton naval school, Wilson Wang, had transferred from nautical training to enroll in Watchman's class in the 6th year at Trinity, and he was one of the first to join him in informal student prayer-meetings in the college chapel. It was more than a year before solid fruits began to be seen, but slowly, as a result of talks in Watchman's room, several boys came under conviction and one by one discovered in Christ the new joy they had been seeking. Chief among these were Simon Meek from Lieng Chieng district near the coast, and Faithful Luke and K. H. Weigh who were both from Ku-tien farther up the river.

Not content with witnessing in the school, a handful of these high-school boys began to carry the gospel out into the town, making use of Sundays and festivals and the frequent student strikes as occasions for this. They procured a loud and resonant gong, and with it went singing through the streets, proclaiming to all who would pause and listen the good news of a living Saviour. There was incessant noise anyway in the town, of drums and firecrackers and squealing pigs, the cries of traders and vociferating coolies, and the cacophonous bands that attended funerals. No one minded a little more. They handed out leaflets and carried placards, and they wrote big-character posters plainly stating the way of salvation. These they pasted up on public walls to compete with the gaudy red cockerels advertising cigarettes, the chromos depicting the merits of kerosene lamps, and the lurid wall-paintings of the man-eating blue tiger, terror of hill dwellers in the Fu-tsing jungles to the south. The Chinese language, being written vertically, lends itself to sandwich-board publicity, and soon a fresh idea inspired them. They made themselves white cotton singlets which they adorned with red appliqué characters bearing the message: 'God loved the world of sinners', 'Jesus Christ is a living Saviour'. The suburbs on both sides of the river became aware of a spiritual awakening among the Christians.

At Ma Wei (Pagoda Anchorage) Watchman early discovered a kindred spirit who was to become a valued friend. When disembarking there on his return from Shanghai he had, at Dora Yu's suggestion, called on Miss M. E. Barber, a former Anglican missionary now working independently. Born at Peasenhall in Suffolk, Margaret Barber had sailed for Foochow with the C.M.S. in 1899 and for seven years had taught in the girls' middle school. The Mission records reveal her as a zealous and devoted worker and 'a very radiant personality'. When on furlough in England in 1909 however, she had felt God challenge her about baptism as a believer, and had gone for this to D. M. Panton, minister of Surrey Chapel, Norwich. Understandably her bishop wrote advising her not to come back to Fukien, notwithstanding which she returned at the age of forty-two, trusting God for her supplies and backed by the prayers of the Surrey Chapel congregation.

She was joined by an independent Chinese preacher, Li Ai-ming, and to avoid embarrassing her former colleagues at Nantai she found at low rental the bungalow of a retiring missionary of the American Board at White Teeth Rock (Pei Ya Tam) across the anchorage from the Lo-hsing pagoda at Ma Wei. Here, joined from home by Miss M. L. S. Ballord, twenty years her junior, she based her future operations.

For ten years the two of them laboured patiently among local women and, where possible, men. Periodically they paid visits to Foochow to distribute tracts in the city's markets, feeling, as single women missionaries do, the limitations placed upon their sex and the anomaly of their situation on the mere doorstep of a vast and spiritually dark province. Back in her first year in Foochow Margaret Barber had witnessed the baptism as a Christian of the second priest from the nearby Boiling Spring hill temple, once famous for its Buddha's tooth. Such things did not happen now. The winning of rural China for Christ seemed a far-off dream—unless, they told themselves, God Himself should choose and call for the task young men and women from all over the land. Yet why should He not do so? They began to make this their constant prayer.

One day early in 1921 a warship of the Republic dropped anchor off White Teeth Rock and a young Naval officer came ashore. Walking past the Customs station he was arrested by the sound of hymn-singing coming from a mission building and went in and introduced himself. This was Wang Tsai (Leland Wang) a native of Foochow and the elder brother of Watchman's classmate Wilson Wang. After passing out from Chefoo Naval College he had been posted to a ship stationed at Nanking, and while there he had been wonderfully converted to Jesus Christ. He was now twenty-three and had already determined to relinquish his commission and become a full-time preacher of the gospel. Here on their doorstep was a token that God was answering the two women missionaries' prayers.

The Wangs' home was in the Chien Shan suburb on the Nantai side of the river, on the hill slope a little above that of the Nees, so Wang Tsai was soon brought into touch with Watchman and his friends. Once his discharge from the Service was through he returned there to make it his headquarters as an evangelist, a ministry in which he proved to have a real gift. Being slightly older and more experienced than them all he was warmly welcomed and looked up to by the student group.

The Nee home too, with the transformation God had wrought in Huo-ping's life, became now a centre of action and movement of a fresh kind. It took people a little while to adjust to the idea of the worldly political speaker turned Christian witness, but soon, with her forthright testimony and her sensitive use of Scripture, Mrs. Nee came into demand as a Methodist preacher in meetings for women and girls throughout north Fukien. As, with a friend's help, she attained more facility in the *pai-hua* these engagements would take her even farther afield. She walked very close to God and sought His will in everything, keeping short accounts and making swift amends for her mistakes, and it seems that God signally honoured her witness.

Though again often away from home, she was sensible nevertheless of the needs of her large family. One hot season, after speaking at a fortnight's meetings for the Foochow Y.W.C.A., she declined the invitation to stay on for a much needed rest, feeling God had warned her of something impending at home. Back there that evening, as she strolled with her husband at the waterside before the house and watched the ceaseless coming and going of the river craft, she was moved to remark, 'It is so dry tonight, I fear there may be a fire.' In the early hours cries in fact awakened them to the fierce crackle of flames from bamboo and thatch house-roofs along the street. They prayed, and she received from God a strong assurance that their own home would not be touched and that she need not even wake the smaller children. Sure enough, the wind changed quarter and blew from the south, and the fire that had destroyed a dozen houses stopped short just three doors from their own.

Ni Weng-hsiu was much moved by this evidence of God's care, but he was not pleased when only seven days later, as again they walked to and fro in the hot evening, his wife spoke apprehensively of another fire. The uproar that this time aroused them at 4 a.m. was even more terrifying than the previous one. A strong rain-laden wind was helping the flames which were leaping northwards from the market area near the bridge. 'As you see it,' her husband asked, 'will our house be burned this time?' She lifted her heart to the Lord, and could only reply, 'It may be.' So they roused the older children first, and then the stampede began of packing and evacuating essentials. In the midst of this, suddenly Genesis 18 came to mind, and Abraham's (as she felt) premature conclusion of his prayer for Sodom.[5] God seemed to rebuke her with the question, 'Why don't you pray?'

So she abandoned her activities and knelt once more. 'O God,' she prayed, 'in this quarter of Foochow my family is the only one that believes in You. Give me some answer to these unbelievers so that they cannot say, "Where is now your God?"' At once came the assurance, 'Though a thousand fall at your side and ten thousand at your right hand, this calamity shall not come near you.'[6] Accepting this as from God she told her husband. But the flames were fast approaching before a driving wind, and he berated her sternly for her inaction. Then the incredible happened. The city Fire Brigade, baulked by the holocaust around the bridgehead, arrived instead by water at their very doorstep to make their home the headquarters for fire-fighting. Their skilled efforts combined with a fresh change of wind and some rainfall to stop the conflagration short two doors away. The two fires in one week had left an island of five riverside houses miraculously untouched amid the devastation. How could such mercy fail to strengthen the family's faith in God?

One day a little later, on her return from a preaching engagement, Huo-ping learned that the two ladies from White Teeth Rock had called seeking her. She had not so far met Margaret Barber and her colleague, though she knew that Watchman and his school fellows sometimes went to Pagoda for Bible instruction. She had in fact avoided contact since hearing that Dora Yu had stopped off there on her way home to Shanghai and had been baptized by them in the river. This, Huo-ping felt, had undone much of the good achieved by her revival meetings and she had not hesitated to speak out openly against it.

But now, a few days before Easter, Watchman came to her. 'Honoured Mother,' he said, 'tomorrow I have three days holiday from school. I want to go to Ho Sheo-ngen (their name for Miss Barber) for Bible study. Would you care to go with me?' 'Wait until I have asked the Lord,' she replied, and went upstairs. Kneeling, she prayed; then sat combing her hair. As she did so she felt God say to her, 'Go, and be baptized!' As a quite small child she had been baptized as a Christian along with her mother. Now God was asking her to do publicly the thing she had spoken against so strongly : to make a fresh adult affirmation of her faith. Clearly it was He and no other who was pressing her to this act of obedience. She remembered God's word to Jesus at His own baptism : 'Thou art my beloved Son; with thee I am well pleased.'[7] After some thought she went downstairs and called Watchman. 'I have decided to go with you to Miss Ho,' she said, 'and moreover I want to be baptized.' 'I, too,' he replied at once, 'am going for that purpose.'

For him it had been no less a matter of obedience—of giving to God 'the answer of a good conscience'. He had read in the New Testament Paul's words linking baptism with the death of Christ and Peter's linking it with His reign, and had glimpsed the fact of two mutually hostile worlds and the impossibility of serving their two masters, the prince of this world and the Prince of life. He knew now he must express in this public way his complete break with the one and committal to the other. 'I go out,' he was saying, 'I make an exit from the Satan-governed system. I belong no more to this pattern of things. I set my heart instead on that upon which God's heart is set. I take as my goal His eternal purpose in Christ, and I step into that and am delivered from this.'[8]

Hearing of their plan, Watchman's brother George expressed too the desire for baptism, and thus it came about that next morning the three of them set out by river boat for Ma Wei. Miss Barber greeted Huo-ping delightedly : 'Have you eaten your rice? What good tidings bring you to us?' and was amazed to hear from her own lips how, without human intermediary, God had spoken to her of baptism. Since learning through Dora Yu of God's dealings with her they had not ceased to pray for her. Now they all knelt and thanked God together.

Easter Sunday came and they went out to the riverside at White Teeth Rapid. The tide was slack and shipping in the anchorage was quiet, but the day was dull and the sky overcast with a light rain falling to damp their spirits. That morning one of Huo-ping's occasional bouts of tachycardia had assailed her and Miss Barber had offered to postpone the event. But she was insistent. 'I would rather die in the will of God,' she said, 'than live any longer in my own will.' She tells how, as the aged evangelist Li Ai-ming waded with her out into the shelving Min, she asked God for a sign of His good pleasure. Li immersed her, and just as her eyes broke water the Easter sun burst through the clouds. As Watchman and George followed it bathed them all in its golden light.

By this act Watchman had declared where he stood. 'Lord, I leave my world behind. Your Cross separates me from it for ever; and I have entered into another. I stand where you have placed me in Christ!' They returned to the meeting hall with a song in their hearts.

ACROSS THE GRAIN

WANG TSAI and Watchman Nee now grew very close together, sharing as they did a common zeal for the spread of the gospel among young men and women of the town and of the local schools and colleges. The street preaching went on and was carried into neighbouring villages. The long Chinese New Year holiday was devoted, partly to this and partly to a Convention for the scattered believers, to guide them in their spiritual growth. In this latter work Watchman's diligent study of the Word began to bear fruit, for very quickly he displayed a gift and clarity of exposition that was to prove most helpful to his hearers.

In Wang Tsai's home there was a room large enough for meetings and a few would gather there for prayer and Bible study. One Sunday evening in 1922 a small group of just four persons, Wang Tsai and his wife, and Watchman and his mother, remembered the Lord together in the breaking of bread. They found such joy and release in thus worshipping Him without priest or minister that they began frequently to do this, and after a few weeks they were joined by others, including Simon Meek, Wilson Wang, Faithful Luke, and a second ex-Naval officer John Wang, unrelated to the other Wangs.[1]

Near the end of 1922 another woman of character who has a major place in this story visited Foochow to conduct an evangelistic mission. Ruth Lee (Li Yuen-ju) was small but full of fire, a native of Tientsin and employed now as teacher in a Nanking college. She had once been a convinced atheist and an avid reader of Chen Tu-hsiu's *New Youth*. She had gone to Nanking first as principal of a government normal school, arriving there with the boast: 'Though the whole world turn to Christianity, I will never believe!' Learning that there was already some religious interest among the girls, she searched for and publicly burned the New Testaments that several of them were reading. Two pupils, joined by a part-time teacher in the school named Christiana Tsai, set themselves therefore to pray for her conversion. Then one term an epidemic of plague closed the school and Ruth had to accompany some of the students back by canal to their villages. Somehow that quiet trip through the fields of spring wheat brought her face to face with God as Creator. A new hunger awoke in her heart which secret reading of the Bible began to satisfy, and at length she found Jesus Christ as her Saviour. She then resigned her government post to find mission employment as a full-time Christian worker.[2]

Because Wang Tsai had met her at the time of his own conversion in Nanking, he invited Ruth Lee to stay on and conduct a further four days of open meetings in his home. They were remarkable meetings, crowded with men and women, old and young folk, and it was a time of great blessing. To at least one student, Faithful Luke, they were a spiritual landmark. He had attended all Dora Yu's meetings with a heart hungry for God and had eagerly participated in the two years of activities that followed; yet to him the full assurance of salvation only came through Ruth Lee's fiery preaching. Others too found the Saviour at this time and it became necessary to prolong the meetings after the special speaker had left. So, while young men went out and gathered people in off the streets, Wang Tsai, Watchman Nee, and John Wang in turn preached Christ night by night to increasing numbers.

That winter was exceptionally cold with the hill-tops white with snow, a thing rare on the Fukien coast. People were going about hugging to themselves their little baskets of glowing charcoal as though they contained their own very spark of life. Simon Meek had gone thirty miles down river to the narrows and across the coastal range for a brief holiday at his home town of Lieng Chiang. He was there scarcely a week when a post-card arrived from Watchman. 'Most urgent,' it read. 'God is doing a big work here and we need your help. Please return quickly.' Though the weather was appalling, and though rival armies were active in and near the city, Simon Meek at once made the hazardous journey back over the hills to Foochow.

What he found amazed him. God's Spirit was at work, and the student boys and girls who had repented of their sins and believed on the Lord Jesus were quite transformed. Moved by the spirit of joy and humble thanksgiving manifest among them, he too dedicated himself afresh to follow the Lord in singleness of heart. 'On earth as it is in heaven,' are the words he uses to describe the days they had entered upon.

The meetings continued in strength each evening and over the week-ends, and when term re-started they just went on after school. Bands of young men with gospel shirts and banners proclaiming 'Jesus is Coming' and 'Believe in the Lord Jesus Christ' went out with music, gathering people in to services that quickly filled with attentive listeners. As the days passed and enthusiasm increased it became clear that more space was needed. The young men therefore put together their resources and rented a house in Chien Shan, knocking up rough plank benches for seating. Simon and Watchman went into residence, to be available when not in class to serve the needs of inquirers. Each evening a band of boys came from school, washed their clothes and ate, and then went out preaching.[3]

More ambitious outgoings for village witness occupied such public holidays as the Dragon Boat Festival. Once freed from their studies the band of young men would set out, sixty or eighty strong, by one or other of the granite-paved roads through the rice and sugar-cane, where peasants clad in the same blue cotton as themselves trod endlessly the squeaking wooden water-lifts or waded deep in mud behind buffalo ploughs. Anyone literate whom they encountered on the road or at the rest-houses was given a gospel tract. Men of all classes from scholar officials to coolies and soldiers were readily engaged in conversation, for these boys were 'educated' and could anywhere command a hearing. Arrived in their chosen village they camped out in a borrowed church building, setting apart a room for 'prayer without ceasing' where they took turns to maintain a twenty-four hour watch. In the evening when the labourers were home from the fields they set out in orderly groups through the streets inviting the villagers to their gospel preaching.

Simon Meek affirms that Watchman was the planner and ringleader of these ventures. As he strode out smiling and cheerful with the singing bands or guided the less experienced in their personal contacts and witness he was always looking ahead, always concerned for the future of these dedicated lives and excited by the potential they offered to God. For this reason he insisted that the time not spent in evangelism be given up to Bible instruction designed to unfold to them the purpose of God and the high standards of discipleship set for them by Jesus Himself.

For his own spiritual renewal he would take the launch to Pagoda, where often up to two dozen young men and women attended the Bible classes run by the English ladies at White Teeth Rock. Margaret Barber did most of the teaching that from now on was to prove increasingly fruitful. Watchman found himself valuing more and more her counsel and friendship. Invited one day to join her in prayer he discovered that she was herself in the throes of a controversy with God. God wanted something of her and she knew it, and in her heart she wanted it too. Yet it was costly and she could not bring herself to give in. He listened as she pleaded with Him nevertheless not to reduce His demands. 'Lord, I confess I don't like it, but please do not give in to me!' All she asked for was time. 'Just wait, Lord, and *I* will give in to *Thee*!' She was so evidently sincere that he began to see in her one to whom he could safely bring his own problems, which were many.

For relations among the brothers were not always free from strain. With all his zeal and devotion to God, Watchman, as we have seen, was impatient of injustice. 'In my early days,' he recalls, 'I set myself to avoid all that was evil and to do what was good, and I seemed to make splendid progress. At that time I had a fellow-worker two years my senior, and we two were always disagreeing. Moreover our disagreements were about public matters, so our disputes were public too. I would say to myself: If he insists on doing things that way I must protest, for it is *not right*. But protest as I would, he never gave in. I had one line of argument: right and wrong. He also had one line of argument: his seniority. He justified his every action by reasoning that he was two years older than I, a fact I could not refute, so he always won the day. I resented his unreasonableness and inwardly I never gave in, but in practice he gained his point every time.'

One day Watchman took his grievance to Miss Barber and appealed to her to arbitrate. Was that other brother right or was he? But she, knowing God, and hating pride and jealousy in herself, ignored the rights and wrongs of the situation and quietly answered, 'You had better do as he says.' Watchman was thoroughly dissatisfied. 'If I'm right,' he protested, 'why not acknowledge it? Or if I'm wrong, say so! Why tell me to do what he says?' 'Because,' she replied, 'in the Lord, the younger should submit to the older.' Watchman was still a high-school student and, knowing little of self-discipline, gave vent to his annoyance. 'In the Lord,' he retorted, 'if the younger is *right* and the older is *wrong*, must the younger still submit?' But she simply smiled and said once more: 'You had better do as he says.'

The trouble was that this cast a shadow over their brightest days. That Spring of 1923 a first group of those newly born again had asked to be baptized. To the brothers this was a most significant time. 'Anyone who has seen men turn to Christ in a pagan land,' Watchman points out, 'knows what tremendous issues are raised by baptism.' But the solemn expectancy with which they faced the occasion was somewhat marred for him by this tension in the background. Three of them were to bear responsibility together, Watchman, the brother two years older, and one seven years older than he. What, he now wondered, would happen when they discussed arrangements? Would he who always bossed his junior by two years submit in turn to his senior by seven? They met, and the unyielding brother remained unyielding, dismissing every suggestion put forward by his senior. Finally he sent them both away with the remark: 'You two can leave things to me; I shall manage them quite well.' What kind of logic is this? thought Watchman, disgusted.

The day itself was in fact a high-light in their history, with eighteen young men, mainly students, bearing joyful public testimony in the river to their union with Christ in death and resurrection. To the watching crowd the gospel was plainly preached. Afterwards he once more sought out Miss Barber with his problem. 'What annoys me,' he protested, 'is that that brother has no place for right and wrong.' But she, always strict with herself, could therefore be most candid with others. Rising to her feet she looked him frankly in the eyes. 'Have you,' she asked, 'right up to this present moment never seen what the life of Christ is? Do you not know the meaning of the Cross? These past few months you keep asserting that you are right and your brother is wrong. But do you,' she went on, 'think it *right* to talk as you have been talking? Do you think it *right* for you to come and report these matters to me? Your judgement of right and wrong may be perfectly sound, but what about your inner sense? Does the life within you not protest against your own resentful behaviour?'

By meeting him thus on his own ground she had touched him on the raw. Dumbfounded, he had to admit to himself that even when by human logic he was right, the Holy Spirit within pronounced his attitude a wrong one.[4]

Margaret Barber often scolded Watchman in this way, yet to Faithful Luke she one day observed, 'He will become a great preacher.' And he in later years repeatedly acknowledged her influence upon the course of his life. 'I always thought of her,' he says, 'as a "lighted" Christian. If I did but walk into her room, I was brought immediately to a sense of God. In those days I was very young and had lots of plans, lots of schemes for the Lord to sanction, a hundred and one things which I thought would be marvellous if brought to fruition. With all these I came to her to try and persuade her; to tell her that this or that was the thing to do. But before I could open my mouth she would say a few quite ordinary words—and light dawned. It simply put me to shame. My scheming was all so natural, so full of man, whereas here was one who lived for God alone. I had to cry to Him, "Lord, teach me to walk that way." '

About this time she gave him to read the life of Jeanne de la Motte Guyon (1648–1717) the French mystic imprisoned by Louis XIV in the Bastille for her faith. In Mme. Guyon's writings the note of acquiescence in the will of God greatly moved him and was to have a strong influence on his future thinking. This book somehow deepened his awareness of the things in the unseen that are eternal. Another fruit of his access to Miss Barber's bookshelves, and to the writing of G. H. Pember, Robert Govett and D. M. Panton, was a quickened eschatological sense. The near return of the Lord Jesus became to him a real prospect, to be looked forward to and prepared for with a feeling of urgency. Faithful Luke recalls how at this time he expounded the books of Daniel and Revelation with enthusiasm and great effect, firing his hearers with a readiness to pay any price that would make ready the way for the coming of the Son of man.

But not everything was going smoothly for him. At about this time, he tells us, God showed him that he was to go during the college vacation to preach the gospel on an island that was known to be infested with pirates. It was, he says, quite a struggle for him to be willing to do so, but he took the call seriously. What might not God do if he obeyed? After much prayer he paid a visit to the island which was far out in the Min Estuary. To his joy he found the people willing to receive him, and with some difficulty he rented a house, got it repaired and had everything ready. The project had caught the imagination of the brothers and one hundred of them were praying for him and had contributed toward the expenses. All this time his parents raised no objection. Then, five days before he was due to set out and when all was ready packed up, they suddenly stepped in and forbade him to go! The house was prepared, the money was spent, the will of God was burning in his heart: what was he to do? His parents said No, and God had said, 'Honour thy father and mother.' In deep distress he sought light from God. 'Yes,' God told him, 'it *is* My will that you go. On the other hand it is no joy to Me when you force that will through to its fulfilment. What I want *you* to do is to be subject to your parents; so you will just have to wait and let Me work out My will another way.' The trouble now was that Watchman found he had no liberty to explain to others the reason for his change of plan, namely, that it was his parents who had stopped him. 'All misunderstood me therefore,' he says, 'and the one whose opinion I valued most said, "It will be difficult to trust you in future." '

He pondered long and bitterly on this problem, until one day he came on Jesus' words in Matthew's Gospel about the temple tax: 'The sons are free: however, not to give offence to them, take and give it for me and for yourself.'[5] All at once he felt the weight of that 'however'—and he understood. Even Jesus could accommodate himself to those who would be offended by the liberty that was His. Years later he could interpret the experience objectively in the light of the crucifixion. The will of God may be clear and unmistakable, but for us His way to it may sometimes be indirect. 'Our self-esteem is fed and nourished because we say, "*I* am doing the will of God!"

and it leads us to think that nothing on earth should stand in the way of that. Then one day God allows something to fall across our path in order to counter that attitude. Like the cross of Christ it cuts across—not our selfish will but, of all things, our zeal and love for the Lord! That is most difficult for us to take.' At the time indeed he couldn't take it. All he could feel was resentment at his parents' attitude, which he largely blamed on his mother. It would take him a while to get over this.

He asked Miss Barber if she could not lend him something to read on the subject of the Cross. Yes, she said, she had two books, but she would not give them to him at present; she would rather wait until he was mature enough to read them. 'I could not understand the reason for this,' he says, 'and I wanted those two books very much, so I obtained them by guile. I inquired from her the titles and author without her realizing what I was doing, and I wrote off to Mrs. Penn-Lewis, who sent them to me as a gift and wrote me a nice letter as well! One was *The Word of the Cross* and the other *The Cross of Calvary and its Message.*[6] Well, I read them most carefully, but though I received help of a kind, to my disappointment they didn't settle my biggest question. That, I find, is not God's way, to give us quick answers.'

For the last month of the summer term of 1923 a strike closed the school, and Faithful Luke with four others took this opportunity to testify in baptism to their break with the world and their union with their Lord. Luke's experience was typical. An influential uncle hurried from Ku-tien in hot anger that, having been brought up an Anglican, his nephew might by his action have forfeited his prospects of a grant to enter St. John's University. He urged him to repent of the step; but Luke replied, 'My repentance is toward God and for my sins. I am at peace.' Even his Principal had thought him out of his mind when he made his intention known. Trinity College was a doorway to State or Mission employment and boys went on from there to positions often of great influence. 'Do you mean, then, that you will not go on to further study?' he asked. 'No,' was the impetuous answer, 'I am going to preach the gospel.' The missionary was sincerely troubled. Nee, he feared, was becoming a disruptive influence in the student community. 'Go and pray,' he said, 'and come back to me after three nights.' But on his return Luke's mind was unchanged. 'I have decided,' he said, 'to serve the Lord Jesus only'; and through life he never went back on this decision.

The two boys who completed the year with Faithful Luke entered the Department of Customs, whereas he himself went to Pagoda. The English ladies were understandably full of praise for the flood of answers in recent months to their long praying and Miss Barber invited him now to act as host for the young men coming to her for instruction, while her colleague took care of the women. He was to be there for six years.

Now it was Watchman and Wilson who were in their final year at Trinity in a somewhat larger class. In the college through the winter months the evangelical fervour burned steadily on, and there were three daily prayer meetings among the boys, one in the early morning and two at night. In the city too the gospel witness flourished as Wang Tsai and John Wang preached night by night in the little rented hall. Sunday worship there with the breaking of bread was now a regular thing. Meanwhile Watchman gave what time he could to the spiritual growth of the converts and young workers, and even published for them a few issues of a mimeographed paper, *Revival*, embodying some of his Bible studies. The New Year conference took place again in February and with the Spring vacation the gospel bands went out once more into the villages. The summer term was disturbed by severe floods that put a heavy strain on the low arches of the ancient bridge and brought cholera and plague to the riverside homes, but the boys were able to complete their college year. In the final examinations Wilson Wang came out top with Watchman Nee a close second; in fact it was virtually a dead-heat.

Watchman was now twenty-one years old. For graduation he wore a new ten-dollar gown bought for him by his paternal grandmother, the Cantonese lady with the caustic tongue, now happily reconciled to her daughter-in-law. But to him far the most gratifying thing of all was the fact, for which the students now met at term-end to give thanks together, that within the past twelve months God had won to Himself scores more new converts in the Foochow colleges and city and the countryside around.

6

THE PROOF OF FAITH

FROM time to time during these years the Chang family returned to Foochow from Tientsin where Chang Chuen-kuan was now employed as a pastor with the Christian and Missionary Alliance. They and the Nees remained firm friends, and the general relaxing of strict social custom meant that the growing children could still meet freely in the home. Not surprisingly these encounters had awakened in Watchman an interest in his one-time playmate Charity who was both intelligent and extremely pretty.

But then Watchman had found the Saviour and had undergone, as we have seen, a total revolution of outlook. Moreover with his graduation he had made, like Faithful Luke before him, another radical choice. He would not proceed to St. John's College nor pursue further his formal education, but from now on would direct his life to the task of preaching Jesus Christ. The decision was a far-reaching one and appears to have been made from personal conviction alone.

It was now that he realized how much Charity Chang had occupied his thoughts. There had of course been no hint of a match, yet at some stage the idea had certainly found lodgement in his mind. Their next encounter however brought him up short. What he already feared was all too evident from their brief conversation. Her worldly tastes and passion for stylish clothes were the mark of something deeper. She in no way shared his love for the Lord with its new scale of priorities, but had goals of her own, ambitions for success in the world's eyes that he could no longer entertain. Clearly they were headed in different directions.

For a while he shelved the problem, until one day he was reading Psalm 73. 25, 'There is none on earth that I desire beside thee,' and the Spirit of God arrested him. 'You *have* a consuming desire upon earth. You should give up your attachment for Miss Chang. What possible qualifications has she to be a preacher's wife?' His reply was an attempt to bargain. 'Lord, I will do anything for You. If You want me to carry Your good news to the unreached tribes I am willing to go; but *this* thing only I cannot do.' How could he, just coming up to twenty-one, finally detach his mind from one who had so pleasurably engaged it?

He threw himself therefore into the work of the gospel. There were many doors open to him, and after participating acceptably in the New Year Conference in Foochow he gave himself to village work and especially to the instruction of new believers. Here he soon learned new lessons. 'For a year after my conversion,' he tells us, 'I had had a lust to preach. It was impossible for me to stay silent. It was as though there was something moving within me that drove me forward and I had to keep going. Preaching had become my very life.' He had had a good education and was well-versed in the Scriptures, so naturally he considered himself thoroughly capable of instructing village folk, of whom the women in particular were most of them illiterate. But after several visits to one group to help to confirm them in their faith his self-esteem was sorely deflated. These women had come, he discovered, despite their illiteracy, to an intimate knowledge of the Lord. 'I knew,' he says 'the Book they haltingly read; they knew the One of whom the Book spoke.' He was beginning to learn humility. There was no flagging of his zeal, but he was having his first encounter with a divine principle of fruit-bearing, that 'apart from Me you can do nothing'.[1]

At this time also, with his college grant ended and no paid employment in prospect, he began to face what it was going to mean to trust God for his material needs. From among the books he had drawn from the English ladies' shelves he was greatly influenced by accounts of the faith of George Muller of Bristol and Hudson Taylor of the China Inland Mission.[2] These men had shown their confidence in the Unseen by putting to proof God's sufficiency for the seen and tangible needs of His work. Nearer at hand Margaret Barber herself was to him a living example of this. She had started from Britain with no guaranteed backing beyond the assurance of a faithful Hebrew Christian: 'If God sends you, He must be responsible.' Often, Watchman knew, she had been down to her last dollar, but God had never yet failed her. In 1923 she had spoken to the brothers of her prayer for a ten-room hostel for expansion of her work at Customs Point, with no idea whatever of how this might be provided. Watchman was astounded when a little later a neighbouring industrial school ceased operation and God caused its *twenty* rooms to become available to her at a paltry rental.

Such faith was infectious. He was there one weekend when a friend of his with $2 in his pocket was in urgent need of $150 by the Monday morning, and the mail boat did not run on Saturdays or Sundays. After committing the matter to God this brother went out preaching and met a man who reminded him of a $1 debt, which he paid. The coin remaining in his pocket now assumed a new value, and when he met a beggar he thought of changing it into brass cash before making a gift; but God checked him and he gave the whole coin to the beggar. As that dollar went out, God came in. He returned home and slept peacefully, and on the Monday morning received by telegram a wholly unforeseen gift of $150.

To Watchman this divine principle of 'give, and it will be given to you' was to become a rule of life. If we would concern ourselves solely with the needs of others, then God, he believed, would make all our concerns His own. But he went further. We should never, he held, divulge to others our own financial needs, even when such secrecy might lead our friends to misread our poverty as wealth. Moreover, aside from brief hospitality, we should 'take nothing from the Gentiles' for God's work, and so avoid placing Him under obligation to sinners.[3]

He was soon to put these principles to the test. A classmate of his, K. H. Weigh, had earlier left Trinity to go on to Nanking University, and just now was at home in Kienning where his father was a doctor in the C.M.S. Hospital. Kienning (or Chien-O) is situated some 150 miles up river from Foochow, deep in the mountains at the confluence of several streams, and is a centre of the paper industry and an emporium of inland trade. From the Mission there Watchman now received an invitation to address a series of evangelistic meetings. His expenses would, he felt sure, be met, and after prayer he wired in reply that he would set out on the Friday.

The problem was to get there. He had only some $30 in hand and the fare by motor boat would cost $80 at the very least. What was worse, he became aware that here in Foochow another brother in Christ was in at least as much financial need as himself. When, that Thursday, God reminded him of this he knew he must take action, and with much trepidation therefore sent him a gift of $20 by the hand of Wang Tsai.

Next morning no one gave Watchman anything before he left, and as he crossed by ferry to the anchorage with a mere $10 in his pocket he prayed in desperation, 'Lord, I am not asking You for money; only to be taken to Chien-O!' Arrived at the landing-stage he was accosted by the owner of a small steam-launch who asked him, 'Are you going to Yen-ping or to Chien-O?' 'To Chien-O,' he replied. 'Come with me, then. I'll take you.' 'For how much?' 'Only seven dollars.' Amazed, he asked the reason as he carried his baggage on board. The boat, he learned, was under county charter, but the owner was free to earn a little extra by letting a seat to one passenger if it was not required by the hirers. Thus Watchman made the long journey unmolested by brigands and free of endless delays from *likin* tax collectors at Shui-kow and Yen-ping and other points on the route.

It was a scenically beautiful trip, the first section through a fertile half-hilly country where here and there the slopes were clothed with groves of *long-iens*, lichees, and pomeloes, and of the green and golden oranges that Watchman had loved from childhood. He was expressing a widely held view when he used to say with pride, 'I think there are no oranges in the world to equal those of Fukien.'[4] Farther up river the pine-clad mountains drew in closer and there were jagged rocks and floating timber to negotiate in the swirling waters as the chugging boat wound its slow way beneath frowning cliffs towards their destination.

At Chien-O Watchman preached throughout the two weeks with much liberty in the Word and a balance of $1.20 in his pocket. His messages were well received, and his friend K. H. Weigh was one who entered into a new blessing and dedicated himself afresh to God. At the end there was a farewell meal at which Archdeacon Hugh Phillips took the young preacher aside. He was a man of long experience and the survivor of incredible hardships for the gospel. 'We have been much helped by your preaching,' he said. 'Please may I share in your expenses?' Impetuously Watchman replied, 'There is no need. All is fully provided.' Truth to tell he was uneasy about accepting missionary help. God, he felt sure, would work in His own way. But next day on his road to the river with many new friends come to see him off, he found himself praying, 'Lord, You can't just bring me here and not take me home again!' Half way to the boat a messenger overtook him with a note from the missionary: 'Although you have someone to pay your fare, please by accepting the enclosed let this aged brother play a small part.' Recognizing God's hand in this he accepted the token of fellowship. It proved to go far beyond his expenses, for the same chartered boat was there ready to return, with the same seat vacant at the same cut-price. On the exhilarating run down the Min rapids his heart was at peace. Back once more in Foochow he discovered too that his own gift before starting out had met a really desperate need. It was an experience he would not forget. As he put it later, the way of God is not 'Save and you shall grow rich,' but 'Give and it shall be given to you, good measure, pressed down, shaken together, running over.'

In Nantai however a change had come about in Watchman's relationship with the fellow-workers operating from the rented hall. It is by no means clear in detail what led to the decision of the older brothers, Wang Tsai and John Wang supported by a few more, to put him out of their fellowship. True, he had disappointed them over the pirate island venture. Yet not this, but one single issue of principle is quoted by those involved at the time, and it seems a surprising one to have arisen in so young a group.

In his search for a fresh break-through in the work of the gospel Watchman had sought to return to fundamentals. God Himself, he saw, is the Originator of any work truly to be called His, and God too must be its Goal. But what of the task between? Was He not also, in a sense, its Agent—the One who must empower it all? Here, he felt, was something Christians generally overlooked. He put it this way: 'When we see a man of keen intellect, eloquent and energetic and with administrative flair, we say, 'What an asset that man would be to the cause of Christ!' But this is like saying that, while the beginning must be of God and the end for Him, the middle is within man's power to accomplish.' Notwithstanding the evangelical zeal with which Watchman drove himself so unstintingly, he was haunted by the statement of Jesus that 'the Son can do nothing of himself, but what he sees the Father doing', and by God's no less explicit words to Paul, 'My strength is made perfect in weakness.'[5] This essential element of divine miracle seemed to him the mainspring of all true achievement for God.

Watchman had tried to express this view in talks to the believers during the previous New Year's holiday. The Old Testament expositions he had given then were on the theme of the testimony of God as expressed in Israel's ark of the covenant. (Their theme may serve to illustrate for us his occasional excursions into allegory.) At Jericho, he reminded his hearers, the ark's presence had accomplished that city's downfall. Later on, in a day of defeat, whereas the priestly ritual might still linger on at Shiloh, it was that same ark in exile that God stood by, to the discomfiture of its captors.[6] The question Watchman asked was, How might God today have a work and workers to which He could so commit Himself?

For answer Watchman pointed to the ark's contents: the table of the law, the hidden manna, and Aaron's rod that budded. The last of these was set there as the memorial of a dark night and a resurrection morning.[7] This hinted strongly, he believed, at the one sure way of fruitfulness for every servant of God. We do not accomplish God's work merely by yielding to the appeal of open doors and great opportunities. There is also very often a dark night to be endured with patience for the sake of a new life (illustrated by the rod's budding) beyond man's capacity to produce. That resurrection life in its fullest sense was in view when Jesus Himself went to the cross; and in no way is the servant greater than his Lord.

These studies had appeared in print in the occasional magazine he edited, one issue of which had been paid for with Archdeacon Phillips' gift at Kienning. It was not yet Watchman's practice to compensate by careful editing for the preacher's licence to overstate,[8] and it may have been his too quietistic approach to Christian service that met with the brothers' disapproval.[9] But aside from differences of outlook among them, there were also external pressures. With the Anti-Christian Movement at high pitch in the cities, some in mission circles would certainly have preferred the student witness to take less uncompromising forms. Few could deny the stature of Wang Tsai and John Wang, both strikingly converted ex-Naval officers, and hopefully men such as these might be 'contained' within some part of the establishment. Indeed Wang Tsai had lately received formal ordination in Shanghai at missionary hands. Watchman, by contrast, may have seemed less pliant and a potential source of division, just at a time when any appearance of disarray in the Christian cause must be viewed with caution. Attempts were being made by some of the colleges to forbid students to attend the revival meetings, and one missionary at least had categorized him as 'a devil and a deceiver of many'. This may have represented a widely held view.

For one or more of these reasons Watchman was asked by the Wangs to discontinue worshipping with the group. Many soon regretted the step taken and by most the decision was later reversed. 'We did a very silly thing,' one of them observes, 'but maybe we were influenced too by jealousy, for brother Nee was so much more gifted than the rest of us.' Yet for a while the reservations about his preaching remained, and to his great sorrow the breach with a few of the brothers was never completely healed.

Watchman went down to Ma-hsien, the village between Pagoda Island and Ma Wei, and there rented a tiny hut with a window looking out over the anchorage. This he now made his base for his preaching tours, and here he began to study and to work more seriously on the magazine he had tentatively issued. One or two young brothers stayed with him for fellowship, and Faithful Luke was not far away at White Teeth Rock across the water.

About this time the doctor in charge of a C.M.S. Hospital down river, a Miss Li, approached Watchman. She had adopted and brought up a boy whom she had named Kuo-ching, but he had turned out a disappointment. At the age of sixteen he had had to be expelled from school, and in desperation she brought him to Ma-hsien and appealed to Watchman for help. So he took him in and gave up time to teaching him the Bible, and before long the lad was soundly converted. To his mother's delight and that of her whole family his conduct bore convincing witness to the change.

With January 1925 the Lunar New Year approached and with it the usual holiday convention in Foochow, drawing together believers from in and around the city. This year Wang Tsai sent

Watchman a message asking him not to attend. Criticism of the work was focussing on him and they would be easier without him.

The request, Watchman admits, shook him from his rest in Christ and plunged him deep in discouragement. In his extremity he took the ferry across to Customs Point to seek out his friend and counsellor. 'It's come to this!' he exclaimed, and outlined to her what had happened. She said very little in reply, indicating by her silence how much she felt with him in his sorrow. Nevertheless he went from her with his courage renewed.

Next he found Faithful Luke, who, while remaining loyal to the elder brothers in Foochow, had been deeply grieved by their break with his friend. Together they sought God in prayer. Watchman was realistic enough to value criticism from any source and he put his question humbly. Notwithstanding the many real conversions they had witnessed this very year, had he displeased God in some way? Had he given the brothers ground for their attitude? As they prayed the answer came clearly in their hearts: 'Leave your problem with Me. You go and preach the good news!'

It happened that Faithful Luke's adoptive mother was working just then as midwife at a village name Mei-hwa, out on the southern arm of the island-studded estuary. It was a place of pagan darkness, its people wholly ignorant of the gospel. He and Watchman, with four others, resolved now to spend the holiday there preaching Christ to the villagers. At the last minute the newly converted Li Kuo-ching came along too, making the party up to seven. They wrote ahead to an old Trinity student who was head teacher of the school, but when after nightfall they disembarked at Mei-hwa he refused them the use of the empty school premises as a base for their witness. Eventually they bedded down on planks and straw in the loft of a kindly herbalist.

For the first few days the fisherfolk and farmers were occupied with the usual noisy celebrations: ceremonial visits, vegetarian meals, ancestor worship, gambling, displays of fireworks, disbursement of charity, and, on the fourth day, entertaining with offerings their several household gods. No wonder they would not listen. But when by the ninth day there was still no response to the preaching, young Li Kuo-ching became frustrated. 'What's wrong?' he demanded of the crowd, 'Why don't you believe?' and was told of their wholly dependable god Ta-Wang (Great King) whose day of festival, made known by divination, was fixed this year for the 11th. Through the past 286 years he had, they affirmed, provided unfailing sunshine for the day he chose. 'Then I promise you,' exclaimed the headstrong Li, 'our God, who is the true God, will make it rain on the 11th.' At once his hearers seized on the challenge. 'Say no more.

If there is rain on the 11th, then your Jesus is indeed God. We will be ready to hear him.'

Watchman had been preaching elsewhere in the village, and when the news, spreading like wildfire, reached his ears he was horrified. The Lord's honour seemed put to hazard, for they had lightly committed Him to something He might well be unwilling to support. (All seven of them, he knew, and not just Li himself, must share responsibility for this.) Yet if God did not support it, what future could His gospel have in the islands? Had they sinned? he asked himself, echoing the question he had put to God but a few days earlier. Should they leave now, and let this Great King reign supreme? Back at their lodging they sought God in deep humility, ready for His rebuke.

Then to Watchman came the word: 'Where is the God of Elijah?'[10] and with it the assurance that rain would indeed fall on the 11th. So clear was this that they went out now and broadcast the challenge widely.

That evening their host alarmed them by confirming the villagers' testimony. Ta-Wang, the neighbourhood god, was a true guardian of peace and tranquillity, protecting his worshippers from sickness, their fields from pestilence, their women in childbirth.[11] On his festal day he could be counted on to reward their zeal with cloudless skies. Moreover, the man reminded them, half the natives were fishermen who spent months at sea and could at least be relied upon to forecast accurately the weather for some days ahead! Hearing this the brothers were sorely tempted to pray for rain then and there, but again they were met by the prophet's words, 'Where is the God of Elijah?' Next day therefore they crossed to a nearby island—the pirate island of Watchman's earlier disappointment—where at once three families turned to Christ, confessing Him and publicly burning their idols. They returned late that night, tired but rejoicing.

Next morning they slept late. Watchman tells how he was awakened by the sun's direct rays through the single attic window. 'This isn't rain!' he exclaimed. It was already past seven o'clock. He arose, knelt down and prayed: 'Lord, please send us that rain!' But once again the words rang in his ears, 'Where is the God of Elijah?' Humbled, he walked downstairs in silence. At length they sat down to their breakfast, the seven brothers and their host, all very quiet. There was not a cloud in the sky, yet they knew God was committed. As they bowed to say grace before eating, Watchman observed, 'I think the time is up. Rain must come now. We can bring it to the Lord's remembrance.' Quietly they did so, and once more the assurance came, but now with no hint of rebuke: '*Where is the God of Elijah?*' Even before their Amen they heard a few drops on the tiles. As they ate their rice there was a steady shower. On being served with a second bowl, Watchman exclaimed, 'Let us give thanks again,' and now he asked God for yet heavier rain. They began on that second bowl of rice, and the rain came down in buckets-full. By the time they had finished, the street outside was already deep in water and the three steps at the herbalist's house-door were covered.

Already at the first hint of rainfall a few of the younger villagers had begun to say openly: 'There is God; there is no more Ta-Wang! The rain has kept him in!' But his worshippers were not to be put off. They carried him out in a sedan chair, for surely he would put an end to the shower! Then came the downpour. After only a few yards the bearers stumbled and fell. Down went the chair and Ta-Wang with it, fracturing his jaw and his left arm. Still determined they carried out emergency repairs and put him back in his seat. Somehow, slipping and stumbling, they dragged or carried him half way round the streets of Mei-hwa before the floods defeated them. Some of the village elders, old men of 60 to 80 years, bareheaded and without umbrellas as their faith in Ta-Wang's weather required, had fallen and were in serious difficulties. The procession was stopped and the idol taken into a house where fresh divination was made. 'Today was the wrong day,' came the answer. 'The festival is to be on the 14th with the procession at six in the evening.'

With this news there came to the brothers the immediate assurance that God would act again. They sought Him in prayer: 'Lord, send rain at 6.0 p.m. on the 14th and give us four fine days until then.' That afternoon the sky cleared, and now they had a good audience for the gospel. God gave them over thirty real converts in Mei-hwa and its vicinity during those three short days. The 14th broke, another perfect day, and they continued to have a good hearing. As evening approached they met, and again at the appointed hour brought the matter to God's remembrance. Not a minute late His answer came with torrential rains and floods as before. Satan's power manifested in that idol had been broken and never more would Ta-Wang be an effective god.

Next day their time was up, for the brothers in employment had to leave. In due course the Mission whose 'field' included the islands assumed care of the converts. Watchman, looking back at that experience, was to see in it spiritual lessons of lasting value.[12] For the present it was the incident's timing that to him and those with him was profoundly reassuring. If they would but press on humbly, keeping close to God, the care of all the consequences was surely His.

7

FOREIGN FIELDS

AT MA-HSIEN village Watchman's 'small hut by the river' looked out across the deep-water anchorage with its splendid scenery and its constant movement of river craft and ocean-going vessels. Up river lay the Ma-Wei shipyard and nautical training school. Downstream on Lo-hsing (Falling Star) Island in the elbow of the river stood the 90-ft high pagoda that gave the anchorage its name. Here where the two arms of the Min reunited that for eight miles had encompassed Nantai island the scour of the river's waters had produced depth enough for big freighters to lie in mid-stream. Above rose the hills, some cultivated in terraces almost to the summit, others so steep as to admit only a stunted growth of firs. About the shipping sampans and lighters bustled, their decks echoing to the gulls' cries and the rhythmic 'Woo-ho, woo-ho, woo-ho!' of perspiring coolies.

Here, living very simply, Watchman made his base from his 22nd to his 24th year for what was to be a period of transition and of immense spiritual development in his life. He began to set himself goals. While at school he had once tried to ride a bicycle by fixing his eyes on the bicycle handles with the idea that if these were steady he would ride straight, whereas all that happened was that in the narrow streets he constantly ran into walls and bruised his knuckles. Then a friend who could ride showed him where the fault lay. 'Look off at the road,' he said. 'Keep your eyes fixed on the way ahead.' He now sought to apply this principle to his work for God.

One area in which he saw the need of this was in the matter of self-preparation and he set himself a strenuous study programme. But he seems already to have glimpsed the fact that the preacher matters to God at least as much as the thing preached. God, he saw, needed first to work out in him what He would proclaim through him. In fact for some of this time Watchman was in indifferent health, afflicted with a cough, and when this was so he gave himself to studying and meditating on the Word, and to wide reading that ranged from Alford and Westcott on the Scriptures to lives of Luther and Knox, Jonathan Edwards, George Whitfield, and David Brainerd. When he was fit he divided his attention between preaching tours and the editing of *Revival*, the small devotional paper which he had begun to publish as early as 1923. It consisted almost entirely of his Bible expositions, reproduced as spoken, supplemented by translated extracts chosen from a few Western devotional writers. *Revival* appeared at irregular intervals as God sent him the money in small gifts of a few dollars and cents, and was distributed without subscription to all who asked for it. With its helpful messages setting forth God's redemptive purpose in Christ the little magazine soon found its way farther afield and this led to further invitations for personal testimony and preaching.

Later that year family concerns took him on a visit to Shanghai and while there he heard news of Charity in Tientsin. It was some while now since they had met but he could not rid his mind of her. At Kean's College she was, he learned, doing brilliantly and hoped in due course to proceed to Peking and a place in Yenching University. Of her social interests however what he discovered merely deepened the conviction that if he would follow the Lord utterly he must abandon thoughts of her. Sorrowfully therefore he set himself to blot her from his thinking. He went to his room, knelt and committed the matter firmly and finally to God, and then wrote his poem 'Boundless Love'.[1]

Thy love, broad, high, deep, endless, is truly without measure,
For only so could such a sinner as I be thus abundantly blessed.

My Lord paid a cruel price to buy me back and make me His.
I can but carry His cross with gladness and follow Him
*   stedfastly to the end.*

All else I relinquish since Christ is now my goal.
Come life, come death, what can it matter? Why should I
*   look back with regret?*

Satan, the world, the flesh, seek if possible to confound me.
O Lord, empower Thy weakling lest I disgrace Thy name.

One morning in Shanghai Watchman's Bible reading brought him to the words of Jesus 'I must preach the good news of the kingdom of God to other cities also; for I was sent for this purpose.'[2] Shortly afterwards there came a telegram from his mother: 'I have been invited to preach the gospel in Malaya. Are you free to accompany me?'

A month or so earlier at a friend's birthday feast Huo-ping had met a visitor from Malaya named Chen, a man ethically much confused and in evident spiritual need. She felt the Lord say to her, 'I preached to the woman of Samaria. You tell the word of life to him!' He had heard, it appeared, of the wonderful conversion of the Nees, mother and son, and when she testified to him he responded eagerly to the claims of God upon his life. From Perak State he now wrote appealing to her on behalf of his home church in Sitiawan, few of whose members, he explained, knew the salvation in Christ that he had found. Would she come and preach to them? He would pay all travel expenses and they would be the guests of his sister and brother-in-law, a Mr. and Mrs. Ling Ti-kong, themselves sincere Christians. Huo-ping laid the matter before the Lord, and He gave her confirmation in the words from Luke's Gospel, 'I must preach the good news to other cities also.' With this assurance she had cabled Watchman who now joined her from Shanghai.

Travelling via Singapore and Ipoh they reached Sitiawan to find a warm welcome in the Ling home. Their reception at the Methodist church however was cooler. 'A month ago,' the pastor observed, 'two Americans held revival meetings for which we put forth much effort to gather in church members. The first day there were over three hundred present, the second sixty, the third only twelve. Now the situation is much worse for all are out tapping the rubber trees and we have no free time except on Sundays.'

When they arrived next evening at the church the door was locked. They sought out the pastor and found him calculating the day's yield of latex. He had, he explained, forgotten the meeting time. Showing no displeasure they took the key and opened up, setting to work to clean out the building with a borrowed broom, while an Indian believer stood in the street inviting folk in. The numbers at first were discouraging, until Watchman in his personal testimony alluded to the words 'I must preach' in Luke's Gospel. Then Huo-ping realized how God had used the identical scripture to call them each forth on this venture. Immensely encouraged, she proclaimed the word now with increased liberty and fire. Many repented with tears, confessing their sins, and there was much setting right of wrongs. Now the numbers rose steadily to a capacity three hundred and beyond, with overflow crowds standing listening at the windows. Only the pastor was cautious of so much emotion, and after sixteen days felt it right to terminate the meetings. Even then, at the Lings' invitation, they continued a while longer with Bible studies in homes designed to establish the new believers in the Word. Before leaving Sitiawan Watchman cabled Faithful Luke to come and follow up the work, but it was to be some years before the latter felt the call to make Malaysia and Indonesia his field of service.

During these weeks Mrs. Nee had found herself very much at ease in the Ling home, and was particularly taken with their eldest daughter Ai-king, a promising young Christian. In her she thought she saw the perfect match for her son. She spoke to the girl's parents about this and communicated with her docile husband, but with little reference to Watchman. Other preaching invitations held them in Malaya for a while longer and thus the families met again. Impetuously Huo-ping pressed the matter, forgetting her own bitter experience as a girl, while filial obedience demanded that Watchman suppress his doubts. In due course a formal exchange of cards and a small feast proclaimed a betrothal that was almost at once to prove a source of great unrest of heart to him. For while he and his mother were still in Singapore awaiting a passage home, a schoolteacher with designs of his own on Miss Ling came to Watchman with a false but plausible story defaming her character. He was most reluctant to believe it; yet the effect on him was to heighten his own sense of uncertainty. In a matter so deeply affecting God's purpose for his life he was desperate to take no false step. He spent some agonizing days in prayer, weighing before God what he should do, and eventually, on reaching Shanghai, told his mother that God was giving him no liberty to go on with the arrangement. He prevailed upon her to return the tokens of betrothal, while he himself wrote to the Lings as courteously as he could explaining his position. His mother found this hard to take, for she already loved Ai-king as a daughter. There was thus some strain between them as they ministered the Word at the Bethel Hospital at the invitation of Dr. Mary Stone (Shih Ma-yu); but then an invitation to Huo-ping to give her testimony at the Western Girls' School brought things into perspective by recalling to her her own unwelcome betrothal while a student there and she began to see things Watchman's way. On the boat home to Foochow she was ready to admit she might have been mistaken.

The appeal of Watchman's own preaching lay first of all in his gift of making so plain the way to God that relies solely upon Christ's finished work. All too many Christians were striving after a salvation based on good works of their own, a way little removed in principle from Buddhism. They had been told it was presumptuous to say confidently that they were saved. The preaching of new life as God's free gift startled them therefore with its novelty. Nor did Watchman stop with the good news of righteousness by faith. He was finding now much personal help from the writings of Andrew Murray and F. B. Meyer on the practical life of holiness and deliverance from sin. He read, too, all he could of Charles G. Finney, and of Evan Roberts and the Welsh spiritual awakening of 1904–5, and he delved into Otto Stockmayer and Jessie Penn-Lewis on the questions of soul and spirit and of triumph over Satanic power. His own New Testament study supported the view that here were great issues of Christian experience that must somehow be brought in simple terms to his fellow believers.

As such themes began to appear in his addresses, and over the years were reproduced in the magazine, they met with a warm response from readers throughout Fukien Province and beyond. No doubt much that he proclaimed was but the fruit of diligent study by an acute mind, and needed still to be worked out in his own experience. Nevertheless with the enthusiasm of youth he was soon turning over the idea of writing a compendium of the spiritual life of the Christian. So much of what he had read and rejoiced in found no mention at all in the mission churches around him. He would be called as speaker to a convention and would tell his hearers it was not enough to receive forgiveness of sins and the assurance of salvation, for these were but the starting-point. A man must come to know the risen Saviour as his very life, for only so might he hope to display conduct pleasing to God.

They would listen eagerly. These were fresh ideas to folk who thought of the gospel as designed only for sinners—a promise of heaven which, once trusted in, had no more to offer them in the present than comfort in adversity. 'Receive the Saviour,' was the theory, 'and then forget about the Saviour and turn to a human philosophy of life.' This explained why the ideas of Confucius and Mencius carried equal weight with the Bible in so many nominally Christian homes.

How infinitely far removed was this from the fruits of the new birth! It gave so little place to the indwelling Spirit of God, upon whose role as teacher of the unlearned, Watchman was coming more and more to lean. He had discovered one day a humble tailor named Chen who, months before, had picked up and read the detached last page of a Mark's Gospel. This man, lacking any Christian whatever to counsel him or to warn him of the dubious attribution of these verses to Mark, had selected from verse 18 what he concluded was the least of the signs, namely that of healing, and set off down the village to put it to the proof. Then, convinced by the outcome in a neighbour's dramatic recovery, he simply went back to his tailoring to witness there faithfully for Christ.

Experiences such as this helped to overcome one difficulty that had troubled Watchman. He tells us that in the early days he was very much afraid of meeting an atheist or a modernist higher critic, lest such a man should demonstrate to him that the Bible was untrustworthy, and as a result he might lose his faith. But as, personally and in the lives of others, he came face to face with the living Christ he knew he had the answer. To all their arguments he could safely reply: 'Yes, there is a great deal of reason in what you say—but I know my God. That is enough.'

In another village a newly believing farmer had faced a crisis. His strip of rice-field lay close above an irrigation stream on the terraced hillside, but once and again he had been defrauded of his laboriously pumped water by a neighbour beneath him on the slope who at night breached his retaining bank and ran it off on to his own land. In desperation the farmer went to his fellow-believers. 'It is not righteous!' he exclaimed. 'What shall I do? Tell me what should be my right conduct in this situation.' They knelt with him in prayer, and then the others suggested that he try going the second mile. 'If we only do the right thing,' they said, 'surely we are unprofitable servants. We should go beyond what is merely right.' So next day he carried forth his wooden trough with its 'dragon's backbone' water-lift and went to work once again on his treadmill. In the morning he pumped water for his neighbour's two strips of wet land below him, then in the afternoon he pumped sufficient for his own field.

The neighbour was dumbfounded. After weighing the matter he called on the Christian farmer and with every show of sincerity asked for the explanation. Soon he too was drinking in the Word of life.[3]

It was devotion of this kind to God and His Word that in the ensuing years Watchman felt called to foster and serve. Here were people who took the Bible seriously. Here was a true fellowship of new-born souls. In it he began to see both the essence of Christ's Church on earth and the spearhead of His Spirit's witness to paganism. Every least child of God should be such a testimony to the gospel's transforming power. Every fragile group of His own should become a centre of worship and witness where the will of God was discovered and where Christ might be encountered in living presence.

8

THE OLD WINESKINS

IN THE mere ten miles distance from Trinity College chapel with its elegant liturgy to his thatched riverside hut where two or three young believers met informally to pray with him, Watchman had travelled a long way in his thinking. Here, as at Nantai, the extremes of East and West forced themselves upon him. A settlement of comfortable foreign bungalows clothed the hillside behind, while across the water the coastal liners and freighters from Europe and America lay at moorings in the fairway or slipped out on the tide: but criss-crossing between them and bobbing and lurching in their wash were the tiny sampans and 'slipper-boats' of the local folk, worshippers of the goddess Ma-zu, and here on the shore around him their simple dwellings huddled alongside the sounds and smells of the native bazaar. It was a mixed-up world. How, he continually asked himself, did his Christianity fit into so complex a setting?

In Foochow it was the Anglican 'stone church' (or its U.S. red-brick counterpart) that symbolized the Christian faith. There once a week, as a contemporary describes it, the 'community' of consuls, port officials and merchants condescended to join the missionaries in a brief hour of religious exercise formally conducted by the port chaplain. That completed they went back, the representatives of Jardine Matheson or Gillman & Sassoon to their traditional after-church task of fixing the week's price of tea, the rest to the British Club and their Sunday relaxations.

Of course the smaller town and district congregations built up with such devotion over many years were more nearly Chinese in membership and ministry; yet even they partook of a structure and ethos that was essentially Western. Their laity was largely passive, dependents of a cumbersome ecclesiastical organization with at its apex a dedicated foreign bishop. Poor man, weigh he heavy or light, he must always rank four bearers to his palanquin! And, too, there was a chronic shortage of ordained clergy. The proportion of pastors qualified to administer the sacraments was often considerably less than one man to seven congregations. As another Fukien missionary describes it to us later, 'the inevitable result followed. A sacramental system that is exalted but practically unusable falls into contempt. The indigenous sects spread their influence.' (In the years of Watchman's youth it had been the True Jesus Church, *Chen Yeh-su Chiao*, founded by Barnabas Tong that had drawn many Fukien pastors and church members into its fellowship.) 'If your own Church cannot provide you with an effective ministry and frequent sacraments, and is not organized in such a way that you feel you are a member of a spiritual fellowship, you will, if you mean business, more often than not join some other which can provide these blessings.'[1]

So speaks an Anglican missionary by hindsight twenty-five years after these events. Let us hear Watchman himself, also some years after them, tell an incident from his own experience on the same theme of the sacraments. 'I know one man who hated another. The other had deeply sinned against him and so great was the injury that to have killed him would have seemed scant revenge. The one sinned against was saved, and for a few years saw nothing of the other man. Then he paid a visit to a certain city and on Sunday went to the local church assembly hall for the Communion service. Just after he was introduced he suddenly saw there his former enemy. 'He is here!' he said to himself. 'I did not know he was saved. What shall I do? What folly to have let myself be introduced!' During the next prayer he quietly got up and went out. He began to walk away, and as he walked he thought on the one hand of his salvation and on the other of his grievance against the man. The further away he got the worse he felt at having thus left the meeting, and on the other hand the more incensed against his enemy. He thought back ten years to the time when he was saved and how the Lord had blotted out all his past: yet all the same he felt that he *could* not forgive his enemy. Then at length the Holy Spirit brought to his mind the word, 'By this shall all men know that you are my disciples, if you love one another.'[2] Now he broke down and gave in. 'Lord, I forgive him,' he exclaimed, and turned and went back to the meeting with tears streaming down his face. When now he entered they had ceased praying and were about to break the bread. He got up, asked permission to speak, and confessed the whole thing, telling how God had brought him to the point of forgiving the man.

Such a movement of the Spirit of God in His gathered people was what Watchman continually looked for, and he believed it could not come to pass in the narrow context of a sectarian group. So we find him, again a little later, telling a congregation: 'If, as we gather round the Lord's Table today, our horizon is bounded by our own company we are not qualified to break bread, for the possession of Christ's life has brought us into relationship with the whole Church, not merely a section of it. Oh, we need to be enlarged so that our hearts embrace all the children of God; otherwise we shall eat this bread unworthily. We proclaim here that all the children of God are brothers and sisters; therefore we do not harbour any divisive thoughts. Let us remember that the same Holy Spirit who has come upon us has also come upon them.'

Here, in developed form, was his attempt at an answer to the imported problem of denominational divisions whose history and value were, he felt, nearly impossible for a new convert to appreciate. By afflicting the potential Church in China with their sectarian differences the missions were tending only to divide it. Among young Christians at this time Watchman was not alone in asking himself whether a return to a simple New Testament obedience might effectively reaffirm that organic unity of believers for the creation of which Jesus had prayed and then laid down His life.

He well knew that for any movement away from the established churches the danger lay in its tendency to be nationalistic and anti-missionary and to end in denouncing all other Christian bodies as false. But among the Westerners whose writings he was now enjoying there were some, such as Govett, Panton, and the much earlier J. N. Darby, who for conscience sake had resigned their Anglican orders and whose search for a more primitive pattern of worship and ministry God had evidently honoured. Such obedience to God's voice in Scripture should be enough. And his stand should be for spiritual quality of life. 'In God's work,' he says, 'everything depends upon the kind of worker sent out and the kind of convert produced.' If he made quality his goal there would be no need for a crusade against the missionary establishment. He dare not confuse his own spiritual pilgrimage with the current mood of nationalism.

This period from 1925 to 1928 was witnessing a fresh wave of nationalistic feeling among students. For years past their teachers had told them they were their nation's hope, destined some day to be its saviours. Yet with the passing of the ancient system of civil service entry their postgraduate prospects seemed not more but less secure. Moreover, being young they were idealists, impatient with the old and eager for the new, ready enough to assume the role of leaders of any hopeful mass action.

One event was to bring this home with tragic force to the Nee parents. Their third son, Sheng-tsu, brought up under the influence of his worldly and indulgent grandmother, had taken early to politics. A source of constant anxiety to them, he was seldom out of trouble. Ostensibly 'to save the nation', but in fact to evade study, he had joined first the Iron and Blood Volunteers and then the Dare to Die Corps, two revolutionary societies. At length the family's sorrow was complete when one day word came that he had lost his life in a revolutionary demonstration.

Already at the New Year of 1925, while Watchman and his friends were away witnessing in the islands, an anti-missionary riot had broken out in Foochow old city in which the Roman Catholic sisters and some C.M.S. ladies were roughly handled and narrowly escaped with their lives. On 12 March that year the death in Peking of Dr. Sun Yat-sen left a power vacuum that was not at once filled, and on 30 May there occurred the historic Nanking Road Incident in which the Municipal police of the Shanghai International Settlement opened fire on a student demonstration. This aroused a surge of anti-British feeling and led to further violence in the cities of the south.

The Foochow missionaries in their summer hill-retreat swiftly re-signed their remaining administrative posts in favour of nationals in the hope of reopening Trinity College for the autumn term. The revival of ancient superstitions about the pale-eyed foreign devils was placing severe pressure on Chinese in Mission service and there were some examples of immense courage for Christ's sake on the part of these 'running dogs of the foreigner'. So widespread indeed were the disturbances promoted by the Anti-Christian Alliance of the following year that by the spring of 1927 all up-country mis-sionaries were evacuated temporarily to the coast. That summer the junior school was burnt down, while January 1928 saw the destruc-tion by fire of the splendid dormitory building of the high school at the hands of a Marxist enthusiast. The honeymoon period of Protes-tant missions seemed to be ending.

Yet Watchman himself must continue to respect as servants of God those many missionaries who shared his living knowledge of the Saviour. Early in 1926 he was invited by some of them to Amoy in southern Fukien to address students of the Talmage College and Seminary of the American Presbyterian Mission. Here in the gradu-ate class he met two keen Christian students, Daniel Tan, and a pastor's son, James Chen, who in later years were to become close colleagues in his work.

This visit led to an invitation to help in the Spiritual Light Pub-lishing Society, a mission enterprise operating at Nanking, capital of Kiangsu Province. His friend Miss Ruth Lee was on the editorial staff of their magazine *Spiritual Light* and he was invited to share for a time in their work. He was not in the best of health and the change of climate might be beneficial. Above all the Lord seemed to say in his heart, 'Go and gain some experience in the publishing field.' He decided that God would have him make the trip.

The journey there by way of Shanghai was valuable in renewing old friendships and cementing new ones. Some he met now he speaks of with warm appreciation. Many readers of his new magazine *The Christian* (which from January 1926 had succeeded *Revival*) lived in Shanghai and the northern cities, as well as up the Yangtze, and he saw afresh Shanghai's potential as a base of operation for the country as a whole. With its atmosphere of cut-throat competition and political intrigue it was a stimulating if dangerous city, while its morals were often condemned with the remark that 'if God spared Shanghai He owed an apology to Sodom and Gomorrah.' But it was established as the main commercial, industrial, and financial centre of China. By contrast Pagoda Anchorage, remote and linguistically provincial, gave small room for manoeuvre; and since the dispersal of the original Foochow band of brothers, it offered less prospect of fellow workers. Should he, he found himself asking, transfer his headquarters to Shanghai?

In Nanking with its vast missionary community and many institutions he met men whom he rejoiced to work with as brothers in Christ and from some of them he gained some useful experience in editorial and publishing techniques. It was the fellowship with Miss Lee however that was most valuable to him. She was ten years his senior and of greater spiritual experience than himself, and he felt the need of such an 'elder sister'. He shared with her something of his vision for reaching China with the Word of life and found in her a wise counsellor and kindred spirit. She confirmed his feeling that the present unrest was awakening a new spiritual hunger among young Chinese turning to Christ but dissatisfied with Christianity as they found it. Could he not minister to this need? She gave support also to his view that Shanghai was the strategic place from which to work and said she felt called to resign her Nanking post and join him there, especially to set forward his written ministry.

Watchman's own Presbyterian connection lasted a few months only. He had no sense that God was calling him to serve permanently within its administrative system; but more seriously, in Nanking he was not just out of place: he was sick. He knew he must return. He set out again down river, spiritually refreshed but downcast in mind and weakened in body. Once more he had developed a cough, and the cough persisted. In the evenings he felt chilled and at nights he perspired freely. He longed for his warmer home climate. But on his way he sought medical advice.

The Shanghai physician who examined him ordered an immediate chest X-ray. It showed, we are told, heavy tuberculous involvement of the whole of one side and of part of the other. While the doctor viewed the wet film and Watchman awaited the result he overheard him say to the staff nurse in English, 'Poor fellow: just look at that! Do you remember the last case we had with a picture like his? He was dead in six months.' Watchman was called in. 'You've got extensive T.B. in your lungs,' he was told. 'Go home and rest and eat nourishing food. That's all you can do. You may recover.'

On the ship home Watchman was in an agony of mind. He had been so full of plans, so hopeful of great things. Now God had said 'No' to them all. He began to examine himself, his actions, his motives, his ambitions. One desire was uppermost with him now: to be pure before God. He confessed his sins, seeking where he might have given God ground for displeasure. The question that still troubled his conscience concerned the girl Ling Ai-king of Sitiawan. He had long ago discovered how his informant had deceived him. Had he himself sinned therefore in not showing filial obedience right from the start? Had he wounded her and her family in giving ear to lying tales? Had he misread God's guidance in the whole affair? He was willing to remain unmarried all his days for the work's sake. There seemed nothing else he could do to make amends.

It was on a day in the early autumn of 1926 that the coastal steamer sailed up through the Min narrows on the tide and dropped him off at Pagoda Anchorage. His hut at Ma-hsien when he reached it seemed a bleak place to return to. His whole way of life there suddenly seemed so ineffective. He wanted to cry out in protest to God. He wanted to question everything.

He tried to settle down to work. From a box in the hut he took out the outline of the book it had earlier been his plan to write. As much as three years ago he had sketched a first draft of two and a half chapters on the subject of the man of God, his spirit, soul and body. He had then shelved the project as too theoretical, for at so many points it lacked the proof of experience. But much had happened in the interval. In his own Christian life he had tasted new realities and he had seen many other souls liberated from the power of darkness. If God was soon to take him to Himself, Watchman felt he must somehow set down for them in writing the precious things God had given him. He sat looking out over the river, and took up ink and brush.

But even as he did so the fever took him. He could not write; he could not even compose his thoughts. So he gathered up his Bible and the manuscript pages. He knew now he could not get through alone. Shutting up the house once more, he went down to the wharf at Lohsing-ta and took a sampan across the mile of river to Customs Point. At the hostel door Faithful Luke welcomed him and gave him a room in the men's quarters. There he lay down on the little cot and let himself fall into the hands of God.

It was some comfort to him that the hostel was still there. His father had earlier warned him that the industrial school whose premises it occupied and of which he was a director was about to reopen with new engineering staff from the United States. Yet Miss Barber had set out for the hot summer weeks to Kuliang mountain above Foochow, wholly at rest in God, there to receive news that the school's finances had been suddenly liquidated and it would not after all be opening. The accommodation was still hers to use.

The ladies now supplied him with milk and good food and such medicines as were available and the brothers waited on him. The dark days dragged on into weeks as he continued to lose weight and feel his strength ebb away. 'He was so humble,' Luke recalls, 'so desirous to be healed. He asked me every day to anoint him in the Lord's Name and pray.' When he was too exhausted to read his memory of Scripture came to the rescue: 'Humble yourself under the mighty hand of God'—but he dared not yet complete the sentence.[3] 'For two months,' he observed, 'I lived daily in the very jaws of Satan.'

Miss Barber came regularly to visit him with the message 'Christ is Victor.' Yet while he knew the value of the precious blood for sins and could claim healing over sickness from One who has borne our infirmities, he truly believed he was at fault and had given Satan ground to withstand Christ in his life. She had Scriptures for him however that brought home the all-embracing effectiveness of the Lord's resurrection, until at length he was able to assent in faith: 'Christ is Victor!'

Slowly, in answer to their united prayers, God took a hand and the diet and rest began to work a change. With the access of a little strength he was soon asking again for paper and ink. Now, for as long as God might permit, he set his whole being to the task he felt so urgent. Like some reporter hounded to a newspaper deadline and doing his best work in the last desperate hour, he poured out his heart in a detailed setting forth of the Christian's spiritual life and the strategy of the heavenly warfare.

Eventually after months the first volume comprising four parts of *The Spiritual Man* was ready. It was very analytical and set out the believer's salvation, spirit, soul, and body, in exhaustive detail. In his Preface he described it as a work of Biblical psychology, but warned his readers that to use it merely as a tool for self-analysis would only hinder them from losing themselves in Christ. As a fruit of suffering it was rich in insights, but lacked the illustrative lighter touches that so enlivened his preaching. It owed much to his extensive reading, more to the keenness of his mind, but most to his profound knowledge of the Scriptures and his transparent openness to the impact of their message.

By the month of May, though still very weak, he was well enough to travel to Shanghai with the manuscript. Ruth Lee had already

moved there from Nanking where pro-Communist riots had caused
some missionary deaths. With her excellent literary Mandarin she
had volunteered to tidy up the final draft and prepare it for press.

Nanking was to become the headquarters now of the new régime
of Chiang Kai-shek whose armies, moving northward through
Hunan, had taken Changsha and Hankow and then turned east to
gain control of Shanghai. Here, with careless disregard for civilian
life, Chiang now put down the Communist movement among Shanghai workers by a ruthless coup on 12 April in which a certain Chou
En-lai barely escaped the massacre. Peace, of a sort, had now returned to the city.

It was while Watchman was in Shanghai putting finishing
touches to his project that he had an experience which was profoundly to affect his future exposition of its theme of deliverance
from sin. Words in the Epistle to the Romans he had preached on
many times suddenly came to life. He 'saw' the priority of divine
fact over the personal experience that flows from faith. Let him tell
it in his own words.

'For years after my conversion I had been taught that the way of
deliverance was to reckon myself dead to sin and alive to God
(Romans 6. 11.) I reckoned from 1920 to 1927, and the trouble was
that the more I did so the more alive to sin I clearly was. I simply
could not believe myself dead, and I could not produce death. Sin
was still defeating me, and I saw that something was fundament-
ally wrong. So I asked God to show me what was the meaning of
the expression, "I have been crucified with Christ." It had become
clear to me that when speaking of this subject God nowhere says
"You must be," but always "You have been." Yet in view of my
constant failure this just did not seem possible, unless I was to be
dishonest with myself. I almost turned to the conclusion that only
dishonest people could make such statements. Yet whenever I
sought help from others I was sent back to Romans 6. 11. I appreciated its teaching, but I could not make out why nothing resulted
from it. No one, you see, had pointed out to me that "knowing"
(verse 6) must precede "reckoning" (verse 11). For months I was
troubled and prayed earnestly, reading the Scriptures and seeking
light. I said to the Lord, "If I cannot be brought to see this which is
so fundamental I will not preach any more. I want first to get clear
on this."

'I remember one morning—how can I ever forget it!—I was sitting upstairs reading Romans and I came to the words: "Knowing
this, that our old man was crucified with him, that the body of sin
might be done away, that so we should no longer be in bondage to
sin." *Knowing* this! How could I know it? I prayed, "Lord, open

my eyes!" and then, in a flash, I saw. I had earlier been reading 1 Corinthians 1. 30: "You are in Christ Jesus." I turned it up and looked at it again. "That you are in Christ Jesus, is God's doing!" It was amazing! Then if Christ died, and that is certain fact, and if God put me into Him, then I must have died too. All at once I *saw* my oneness with Christ: that I was in Him, and that when He died I died. My death to sin was a matter of the past and not of the future. It was divine fact that had dawned upon me. Carried away with joy I jumped from my chair and ran downstairs to the young man working in the kitchen. "Brother," I said; seizing him by the hands, "do you know that I have died?" I must admit he looked puzzled. "What do you mean?" he exclaimed, so I went on: "Do you not know that Christ has died? Do you not know that I died with Him? Do you not know that my death is no less truly a fact than His?" Oh it was so real to me! I felt like shouting my discovery through the streets of Shanghai. From that day to this I have never for one moment doubted the finality of that word: "I have been crucified with Christ; it is no longer I who live, but Christ who lives in me." [4]

FRAGILE CLAY

WATCHMAN felt strong enough now to remain in lodgings in Shanghai and work on the further sections of the book he was sure God wanted him to complete. Slowly, under Ruth Lee's literary tutelage, the truths he had learned through so much suffering and failure found written expression. He was well pleased too to take a quiet look at the missionary scene. Here for the first time he came into close contact with the great interdenominational China Inland Mission, founded by Hudson Taylor, that for sixty years and more had extended its evangelical witness far into the country's interior. Its testimony to God's faithfulness was given fresh point by his friendship now with a missionary in its accounts department, Charles H. Judd, a man of long experience in the field to whom he quickly warmed in spirit. Watchman went often to his home where they would share their common interest in the Scriptures. To him Watchman spoke too of his own hopes of reaching China with the gospel, and when his strength permitted they would sometimes go together with a few young men preaching in the city's lanes and suburbs.

Ruth Lee now introduced to him a dear friend Peace Wang (Wang Pei-chen) the daughter of a wealthy magistrate, who had been one of her pupils and whose faith Ruth, as a determined atheist, had once sought to destroy. When as a young girl Peace had found the Saviour her parents had tried every means to make her renounce Him, first bribing her with jewels, then urging her to suicide, and finally driving her from home. After graduating from the Nanking seminary she had worked as an independent evangelist and was in special demand in the schools where her striking testimony was used to bring many to Christ. Now, years later, she had had the joy of leading her own mother to Him.

It was in Peace Wang's home that one Sunday late in 1927 four of them, Watchman Nee, Charles Judd, Ruth Lee, and she herself, met first to worship God together in the breaking of bread. They continued meeting thus for some weeks but Watchman already felt he must take a step of faith and rent suitable premises for Bible teaching and witness. 'Start from a little' was the Chinese saying, and it matched well with the prophet's 'Who has despised the day of small things?'[1] At length, early in 1928, he found a property on Wen Teh Li, a lane turning east off Hardoon Road in the International Settlement. It lay above flood-level to the north of Bubbling Well Road and some three miles west of the Bund. Several others had by now joined them and they moved in, meeting upstairs until the shop-space below could be cleared as a preaching hall. Early each Sunday Judd cycled right across the city from the C.I.M. centre at Woosung Road to be with them at the Lord's Table before returning to his own responsibility at the mission's Free Christian Church. But the association was to be short-lived for scarcely a year later the man in whom Watchman had such confidence was called back to Canada. In the light of subsequent history one may perhaps regret that so potentially valuable a link between this new work and the missionaries was thus abruptly removed.

In June 1928, the month in which Chiang Kai-shek's armies occupied Peking, the remaining six sections of Watchman Nee's *The Spiritual Man* were ready for press.[2] He had completed the book under the same sense of compulsion with which he began it. It was the first and last book he ever sat down and wrote, the rest of his publications all being transcriptions of his preaching and teaching. Its third volume contained a chapter on 'Sickness', and though like the rest this came out of experience, yet as so often happens to God's servants he soon found himself plunged into a fresh testing of what he had written. For this reason in later years he often stated that he felt *The Spiritual Man* was too 'perfect'. It gave the illusion of providing all the answers. 'It will not be reprinted,' he said in 1941.[3] 'It is not that what I wrote was wrong, for as I read it now I can endorse it all. It was a very complete setting forth of the truth; but just there lies its weakness. When a man has read it he ought not to have any questions left. But God, I have discovered, does not do things that way, and much less does He allow us to do them. For the danger of systematizing divine facts is that a man can understand without the help of the Holy Spirit. It is only the immature Christian who demands always to have intellectually satisfying conclusions. The Word of God itself has this fundamental character, that it speaks always and essentially to our spirit and to our life.' It must be clear from this that *The Spiritual Man* is to be read today not as a textbook but as a staging-post in the author's pilgrimage. He was, after all, not yet twenty-five when he wrote it.

The Wen Teh Li meeting-room on Hardoon Road could accommodate a mere one hundred, but later in 1928 there took place here the small but significant first Shanghai Conference, bringing together believers from various connections in the city for a time of exposition of the Word. Watchman was the speaker and his messages met with a warm response. But the effort, coupled with the constant demands of counselling those many who came to him, sapped his strength. With the chill winter weather his cough returned and he began once more to lose weight. Some family business claimed his attention and early in 1929 he seized the opportunity to sail away south to Foochow for what was to prove his last meeting with Margaret Barber.

With some hesitation Miss Barber had earlier lent him a few expository writings of C. A. Coates and J. N. Darby. Finding them to his taste he had written off to a London publisher for more of these, and as a result had enjoyed for a year or so some happy correspondence with a Mr. George Ware in England who belonged to this strictly Darbyite persuasion of the London Brethren. His own search for a more primitive pattern of Christian worship, free of the accumulated debris of tradition, had, he now discovered, led him to follow lines rather similar to theirs. The central act of every Sunday's worship was the evening meeting around the Lord's Table at which anyone present was free to express spontaneous adoration and thanksgiving to God, before all partook together of the bread and wine.[4] Other main features of the church's life were the baptism of believers, the exposition of the Word among them, their mutual care for one another and for the work of God, and their constant public witness to His saving acts in Christ. But also, like the Brethren, Watchman had begun to apply most rigorously the apostle Paul's restrictions upon women, forbidding them to preach publicly in the presence of men and enforcing upon them the wearing of headgear in church meetings.[5] Since no Chinese woman normally wore veil or hat, these had to be specially designed and took the form of a standard cap of black crocheted work. The Chinese sisters readily acquiesced in these regulations, and, except in meetings for women, Ruth Lee and Peace Wang gave up their widely acceptable preaching for the counselling of individuals.

But when, back at Pagoda, he harangued Margaret Barber on the wrongfulness of her taking Bible classes for young men she listened politely but kept her counsel. She in fact had misgivings about the doctrinaire position of these London Brethren, which she had divulged to Faithful Luke before he left her to start pioneer work down the coast near Hinghwa. They were, she felt, just one of several mutually exclusive such groups of meetings each claiming purity of doctrine and practice over a century past and each refusing communion on that ground to all other Christians. To Watchman she said little. She introduced to him however some publications of another English preacher and expositor, T. Austin-Sparks, whose messages on the Cross, owing something to Jessie Penn-Lewis, had in the past year or so brought blessing to her.

The brief visit to her enriched him, but in his uncertain health he could not again impose upon her hospitality. He took the river launch to Nantai, but on the two-hour journey his fever returned, and with it the devil to assail him by using the depressive effects of the tuberculosis to draw out his inner resentments. 'You had a bright future, full of possibilities, and you gave it up to serve God. That was splendid. But then you had a promising ministry in which, with your gifts, you were assured of success, and that too you threw away. For what? You relinquished so much; what have you gained? Sometimes God hears your prayers. Often enough He is silent. Compare yourself with that other fellow out there now in the big evangelical system. He too had a bright future, and he has never let it go. He is spiritually prosperous and God honours his ministry. He gets souls saved and they go on with God. And moreover, he *looks* like a Christian, so happy, so satisfied, so assured. Do you? Take a look at yourself!'

Disembarking, he went to his parents' home on the waterfront to pay them his respects and attend to the business that had brought him. Making light of his own indisposition he asked after their welfare. In his heart he was ready to say or to do anything God required if only he might recover his health. Next day he ventured out into the town, sorrowfully avoiding the two meeting places of the long divided local church. Below the bridge the cormorant fishers were at work and he paused to watch them as he used to when a child, marvelling at the patience of the captive birds. He walked slowly, leaning on a stick.

All at once, there on the street, whom should he encounter but one of his former Trinity College professors. He greeted him with a bow, and the man took him into a teashop where they sat down. After a few sharp inquiries he stopped and looked Watchman up and down. 'What is this?' he exclaimed with evident dismay. 'We thought a lot of you at high school and had hopes that you would achieve something great. *Do you mean to say you are still like this?*'

Traditionally the Chinese student holds his teacher in high regard, returning to him formal thanks for each scholastic success, so the very pointed question struck cruelly home. Here was one whom Watchman instinctively honoured and who saw him merely as an educational drop-out. He quailed before the man's penetrating gaze. For it was true: his health was broken, his prospects gone; what had he to show? And here was his old teacher of Chinese law asking 'Are you still not an inch further forward? No progress, no career, *nothing?*' In that moment Ni To-sheng, grown man as he was, was

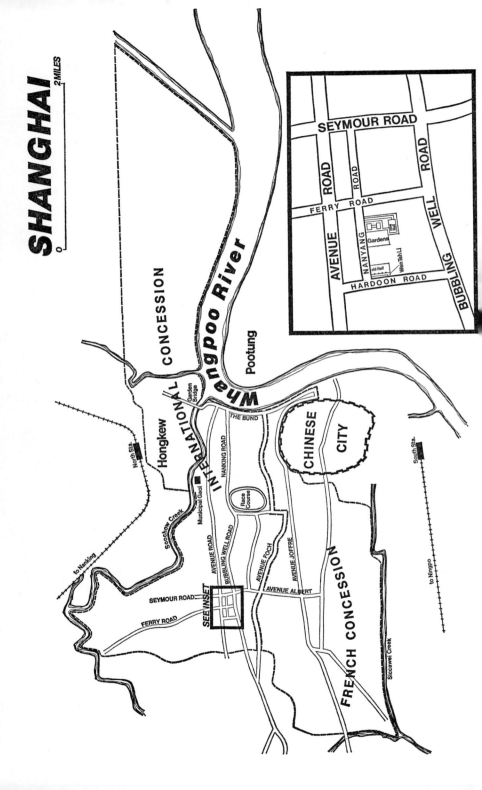

close to tears.

And the very next instant (as he tells us), 'I really knew what it meant to have the Spirit of glory resting upon me. I could look up and say, "Lord, I praise you that I have chosen the best way." To my professor it was a total waste to serve the Lord Jesus; but that is the goal of the gospel—to give everything to God.'

He remained at home for a while, glad of the renewed contact with his parents and happy to share news of the other members of the family, most of them now married. Huo-ping was still her energetic self, out wherever doors were opened for prayer and witness. She had had the joy of leading her aged father, the merchant, late in life to a living knowledge of the Saviour. At his death her brother arranged a Taoist funeral from which she absented herself, sending to follow the hired bands and white-clad mourners a curtained sedan chair, empty save for a huge stone. When her mother learned this she threatened to hang herself, but eventually she too, who had been worldly all her years, responded to her daughter's pleadings and found the Lord.

Huo-ping tells us she feared at this time that Watchman had not long to live. She worried over him, but because she tended at the same time to assert her disapproval of much that he did he resented her ministrations, and said so. He rested however, and he prayed again and again for strength for the work to which he felt so certainly called. At length God seemed to say to him, 'This is my affair. You trust Me and drop it!' Yet so insistent was he that God's will should be safeguarded that, try as he would, he could not relax and let the matter go to Him. He still found himself pursuing it obsessively in prayer.

One day he was out walking on the beach meditating on his predicament. Abruptly he came to a halt. Driving his stick clean under the sand he stood upon it and proclaimed, 'Lord, I trust in You. I have dropped the matter of my healing here!' Then he walked away. But scarcely had he gone any distance before the old anxiety overwhelmed him again and brought him out in a cold sweat. Involuntarily he began to pray once more, arguing with God that his healing was an absolute necessity. All at once he stopped short in his tracks, aware of what he had done. This temptation was from the Adversary and to pray now thus was to submit to him. He turned and walked back to the place where he had driven the stick into the sand. Pointing to it as a witness he declared, 'Lord, I dropped the matter of my healing here. I refuse to take it up again!'

His business completed, he set out again for Shanghai. At Wen Teh Li once more, nursing his strength, he preached the gospel each Sunday morning, urging on his hearers separation from the world and total dedication to Christ, while in the evening he met with the believers at the Table of the Lord. Several devoted brothers had joined the group, two of whom, John Chang and a hospital ophthalmologist Dr. Yu Cheng-hua, were now able to take care of things in his absence. Soon an adjacent property became available, 15ft by 30ft like the first, making when opened up a larger meeting-place where sisters sat one side and brothers the other of a line of pillars. With more space upstairs the publishing work went ahead fast. *The Christian* (renamed for a while *Revival*) grew rapidly in circulation and a new but short-lived periodical *The Bible Record* joined it.[6] The magazine was to continue to play an important part in the outreach of the work.

A growingly effective adjunct to the gospel witness was the steady flow of excellent booklets and tracts reproduced from Watchman's evangelistic addresses. Clearly reasoned and couched in simple, straightforward terms they presented the way of salvation plainly and could be easily read and understood by the man in the street. And to meet another need that was increasingly felt Watchman translated hymns for their use in worship, some by Miss Barber, others from a Brethren hymn book he had received from England. He wrote too some original ones of his own. His health now was improving. The doctors confirmed a change for the better in his lung condition and now advised a spell of rest in the healthier climate of Kuling Mountain.

Kuling lies in Kiangsi Province six hundred miles up the Yangtze and just south of the river port of Kiukiang. The sides of this high valley in the Lushan range were studded with western-style bungalows where the staffs of Shanghai and Hankow business houses sat out the hot summer season or weary missionary families took turns to recuperate. Tall lilies bloomed in shaded gardens, and enticing trails led out to vantage points among the rocky hills. Lower down, outside the wooden barriers that bounded the ceded territory, there huddled the Chinese market-town of 'the Gap', itself 3,500 feet above sea-level.

Advised not to attempt the hill stairway Watchman was compelled to submit to a sedan chair. Nor, at ten taels a day, could he afford treatment in the well-equipped Mission Sanatorium, so a lady from Nanking had arranged sleeping accommodation in her unoccupied house No. 103 at the Gap and he found mealtime hospitality in a neighbouring home with a mechanic and his wife. Even here in Kuling Mountain friends sought him out for conversations in the mornings, but he gave out that he was 'otherwise occupied' in the afternoons—flat on his back.

He had been asked also while there to visit a young man from

Amoy, C. L. Yin, lately returned from engineering studies in Boston, Mass., who was spending his U.S. dollars on treatment of a sudden chest infection. His mother was concerned for his spiritual welfare, but when Watchman called on him in the Sanatorium ward Yin did all the talking, enumerating at length his intellectual objections to his mother's faith. Rebuffed, his visitor could only smile and ask as he rose to leave, 'Are these questions genuinely yours, or have you borrowed them to build a fence against your soul's salvation?' The question clung. Back in Amoy, unable to shake it off, Yin sought out another Fukien man, John Sung, himself lately back from Ohio with a Ph.D., and this man of God led him to the Saviour.

Watchman now became very friendly with his mealtime hosts, but for two weeks, apart from silently asking a blessing before food, he said nothing to them about the gospel. Then one day, in answer to a question, he told them what the Lord Jesus had done for him. They listened eagerly for their hearts were hungry, and soon came to the Saviour in simple faith for the forgiveness of their sins. With their new birth a fresh light and joy entered their lives. Watchman now read the Bible with them and explained how God's Holy Spirit indwelling them would henceforth open to them the Scriptures.

For many weeks he recuperated in Kuling, taking occasional walks to a viewpoint from which he could see far below him the brown Yangtze, dotted with motionless sails, winding its way across the patchwork plain. He was rethinking his Christianity and discovering where lay his real rest of heart. 'When first I came to the Lord,' he says, 'I had my own conception of what a Christian was, and I tried my utmost to be that kind of Christian. I thought a true Christian should smile from morning to night. If at any time he shed a tear he had ceased to be victorious. I thought, too, that a Christian must be unfailingly courageous. If under any circumstances he showed the slightest sign of fear he had fallen short of my standard.' But his serial reading of the New Testament had brought him back and back again to Paul's autobiographical letter, 2 Corinthians, where he read 'as sorrowful . . .' and the words arrested him. A great Christian who shed 'many tears', who could be 'perplexed', and who could even 'despair of life itself' must be very human.[7] Is it possible, he asked, that Paul *despaired*? This was just where he himself had been! 'I discovered,' he says, 'that Paul was *a man*, and the very sort of man I knew.' There began to dawn on him the secret of Christianity that is summarized in the words: 'We have this treasure in earthen vessels, to show that the transcendent power belongs to God and not to us.'[8] Now, as he learned to trust God hourly for his very life, he came to a new place of rest in Him.

But the season was changing and the weather turning colder. The

day arrived when he must bid farewell to his new friends and return
to Shanghai. This time, taking it slowly, he walked down the stone
stairway beside the headlong torrent framed in jungle. At the mountain's foot the road with its hire vehicles brought him again to
Kiukiang and the river steamers.

One day at Wen Teh Li some months later word was brought to
him that a caller was downstairs asking to see him. It proved to be
his host from Kuling Gap. In Shanghai on business he had come to
recount an experience he had had. During the winter months he had
been in the habit of drinking wine with his meals, often to excess.
With the return of the cold weather the wine appeared on the table
again, but that day when he bowed his head to return thanks for the
meal no words would come. After one or two vain attempts he
turned to his wife. 'What is wrong?' he asked. 'Why cannot we
pray today? Fetch the Bible and see what it says about wine-drink-
ing.' But she turned the pages in vain seeking for light on the
subject; and of course it might be months before they could consult
Watchman who was many miles away. 'Just drink your wine,' said
the wife. 'We'll refer the matter to brother Nee at the first opportunity.' But still the man found he just could not return thanks to
the Lord for that wine. 'Take it away!' he said at length; and when
she had done so, together they asked a blessing on their meal.

The man told Watchman his story, and then exclaimed in wonder, 'Brother Nee, Resident Boss (*li-mien tang-chia tih*) wouldn't let
me have that drink!' 'Very good, brother,' Watchman replied. 'You
always listen to Resident Boss!'

One day in May 1930 Watchman received a cable from Pagoda
Anchorage: 'Margaret Barber passed to her rest, gloriously carried
through by the Lord.' Serene Loland, the Norwegian nursing super-
intendent at Kutien Hospital, had hurried down river to nurse her
through what was to be her last illness. She was sixty-four. Of the
old team of seven brothers only John Wang was present at the end,
but Faithful Luke and Simon Meek hurried back to join him in giving her a suitable burial on the hillside above the river. She had died
nearly penniless.

As he thought back over her life, Watchman could only give
thanks to God. He had often been troubled at her isolation there at
White Teeth Rock, concerned that with her living knowledge of the
Book and of its Author she was not used more widely. Yet subsequent years were to prove what was already becoming apparent,
that many young men and women of promise in evangelical work
traced their spiritual wealth to her instruction. In particular Wang
Tsai (Leland Wang), now in Hong Kong, was moving widely as an
evangelist among mission churches and in due course was to found

in Indonesia the China Overseas Missionary Union. 'In those days when I was associated with Miss Barber,' Watchman was to observe later, 'she was used by the Lord in a very real way.' He recalled now one of her songs[9] that he had grown to love:

> If the path I travel lead me to a cross,
> If the way Thou choosest lead to pain and loss,
> Let the compensation daily, hourly be
> Shadowless communion, blessed Lord, with Thee.

Her care was always to see that from her side there were no shadows, and when there arrived from Foochow the much-thumbed Bible she had willed to him, he found in it the prayer, 'O God, grant me a complete and unrestrained revelation of my own self.' And on the fly-leaf she had long ago written words he would henceforth make his own: *'I want nothing for myself, I want everything for the Lord.'*

DISENCHANTMENT

FOR ten days in December 1930 Watchman Nee and John Chang enjoyed some happy Christian fellowship with a visitor from England. Mr. Charles R. Barlow of Peterborough was a believer associated with the 'London Group' of Brethren, and his travels for a British engineering firm had brought him to Shanghai. After talks with them and others he observed in letters home: 'Some of these dear brethren are very sincere and thirsting for truth. Watchman Nee is undoubtedly the outstanding man among them. He is far beyond all the rest. He is only 28 but has had a good education and is possessed of marked ability. He is a hard worker and reads much. He is, too, a great student of J. N. Darby and has evidently been greatly helped by his writings.' For Watchman this visitor met briefly a need he had felt since the departure of C. H. Judd, of a mature and wise Westerner—and this one was not a missionary but merely 'a beloved fellow Christian'—in whom he could confide as a friend. He speaks warmly of the help he received from him. Very soon Mr. Barlow was invited to address about forty believers, including a sprinkling of university students, at their usual meeting time of 4.0 p.m. daily. On Sunday afternoon the numbers rose to eighty or ninety. The report he carried back to his Christian friends in England was warmly encouraging.

What most impressed this visitor was Watchman's knowledge of the Biblical text. 'When remarking,' he says, 'that he had not noticed a certain expression anywhere in the New Testament, he casually added, "and I reckon to get through the New Testament once a month".' We have no details of his plan of Old Testament reading, but a similar impression is preserved by Faithful Luke. In Shanghai with his wife Eunice some months later, he tells how Watchman called on them late at night with his Bible in his hand. 'Where are you going to preach at this late hour?' Luke asked. 'Nowhere,' was the reply, 'but for today I still have some chapters to complete.' It is certain too that the diligence of these first ten years was preserved far into those ahead, and Witness Lee could say of him long afterwards, 'I have never met a man so well-versed in the Scriptures as he.'

Late this year in the enlarged Wen Teh Li premises they held their second Shanghai conference. A C.I.M. observer reports of these 'young Christians carrying on a great work apart from the missions' that this conference lasted twelve days and that they spent up to four hours daily in prayer. Huo-ping, on a brief visit to Hardoon Road at about this time writes: 'What my son preached was too deep and I could not understand it; and I was too proud to ask questions so could receive little from them; but beholding their life I was bowed to the ground in respect.' For this occasion the hymns that till now had appeared only in pamphlet form were collected and published as *Hsiao Chun Shih-ko (Little Flock Hymns)*.[1] Many of its 134 translations and original songs, sung often discordantly but always with enthusiasm,[2] were to find wide acceptance in homes and churches and to carry their Biblical ideas to distant places. But the publication was to have an unforeseen side-effect.

Watchman had a horror of denominational labels such as Anglican, Lutheran, Baptist, with their national, personal, or procedural connotations, and tried very hard to limit himself to the simplest Biblical terms. The Christian life he spoke of was 'The Way' and the believers as Christians, the local meeting place was a Church Assembly Hall, the periodical was *The Christian*, the literature office was The Gospel Publishing House. For the translation of hymns Watchman's source had been the Brethren book *Hymns for the Little Flock*.[3] Its title too had appealed to him as Biblical, memorable, unpretentious, and effective in Chinese. It caught on however all too well, and within a year or so the Hardoon Road congregation was to be nicknamed by mission adherents *Hsiao Chun*, 'the Little Flock'. Although the book's title was quickly changed simply to *Hymns* the harm was done; the label stuck. As Watchman's work spread across China all associated local groups of believers were thereafter dubbed by observers with a name their members deplored and never themselves used: 'the Little Flock Churches'.

Scarcely was the Shanghai conference over when trouble erupted in the city. The Japanese occupation of the Three Eastern Provinces (Manchuria) had aroused Chinese anger which now found expression in a country-wide boycott of Japanese goods. In Shanghai the Japanese demanded action by the Municipal authorities to counter this, and then, to protect their nationals, they landed marines who did much damage. Hostilities ceased in May but it was a brief foretaste of things to come.

Miraculously Watchman's health was at last improving. God had lifted His hand, and he was free not only to teach the Word but to travel more widely. These were years of devastating floods and much loss of life in the Yangtze basin, but in many small riverside towns work was growing up, as well as in the national capital of Nanking and in Hankow farther up the river, and all of these were included in his tours. On another occasion he visited Peiping ('northern peace', the new name for the one-time capital, Peking) and there had his first friendly touch with the courageous fundamentalist pastor Wang Ming-tao.

At Tsingtao on the Shantung coast he encountered the so-called Spiritual Gifts (Ling En) Movement which was very active in the Province. He viewed with caution its uncontrolled emotionalism and extravagant methods of arousal, and in the summer of 1932 published in his *Revival* magazine a series of articles distinguishing between the divinely given baptism of the Spirit and the external accompaniments thought of as essential by some of its exponents.[4] He quotes with approval Miss Barber's observation: 'There is no need for people to *feel* the power which comes from the Holy Spirit. It is not given for that purpose. Man's duty is to obey God.' At the Shantung resort of Chefoo he met also for the first time Witness Lee. A native of that city, Lee came of Buddhist parents and had been converted in 1925 at the age of 20. Since 1927 he had received Watchman's magazine and was himself developing fast a gift of preaching and Bible exposition. God was now speaking to him about the testimony of baptism, and late at night on one of the holiday beaches Watchman Nee baptized him in the Yellow Sea.

The effect of this new freedom of movement was to bring fresh people in touch with the editor of the widely read little paper. While the Hardoon Road meetings were viewed cautiously by some as sectarian, others in fresh circles were soon to discover Watchman's striking gifts of presenting Christ. At Tsinan on the Yellow River, the capital of Shantung Province, some of the staff of Cheloo University were accustomed to invite an evangelist or Bible teacher each year for special meetings. Cheloo was a Union University that drew its students from many provinces and was noted for its advanced thinking and liberal theology. For several years however a small group of evangelical staff had met weekly in the home of Dr. Thornton Stearns and his wife Carol to pray for spiritual revival. At holiday seasons they would take groups of students on a Retreat in the hills to which they would invite as speakers the best Chinese Christian leaders and evangelists available. Dr. Stearns of the Presbyterian Mission, Professor of Orthopaedics in the Medical School and a most humble man, took the lead in these arrangements.

In December 1931 Dr. John Sung of Hinghwa chanced to pass through Tsinan during a preaching tour, and after a meeting in the Stearns' home at which he spoke, some forty or fifty students found Christ within a few days.[5] God's Spirit began to work among the student body in conviction of sin, and the Stearns to whom they came for counselling were greatly exercised about whom to invite for the forthcoming Spring Retreat. The unanimous choice was Wang Tsai but due to engagements in Java he was found not to be available; and then a student from Foochow suggested the name of Watchman Nee as a man with a satisfying message. This little-known Shanghai preacher didn't make bookings and was said to be difficult to pin down, but after prayer Dr. Stearns wrote inviting him, and he felt free to accept.

He came, and God was with him as over a weekend in the Medi-cal·School auditorium he proclaimed the way of life to exception-ally crowded meetings. The longed-for revival spread as more and more of the students found the Saviour. Among many of them the experience was to become a legend, for heaven itself seemed to open to their hearts. Afterwards a group of more than a hundred students gathered at a mountain beauty spot in the Tai-Shan range above the city of Taian, traditional site of Confucius' grave. They studied the Bible and prayed, and before the end a large group of them were baptized in the cold pool of a mountain torrent, publicly confessing Jesus as Lord.

Meanwhile the enthusiasm felt by Mr. Charles Barlow on his visit to Shanghai had been conveyed back to the circle of meetings with which he was associated in the English-speaking world. His account created a sensation. It was felt among them that here in China was an original work of the Spirit of God, in its beginnings surely, yet parallel with their own. The fellowship in which it found expression seemed to them to be based on the truth as they saw it and to reflect principles which they had inherited from their own beginnings a century before. Accordingly they resolved to send a deputation to Shanghai to meet the Chinese brothers, and from May 1932 corres-pondence with Watchman Nee and those with him was designed to prepare the way for such a visit in the same autumn.

The Chinese responded warmly and arrangements were made to receive the visitors at Hardoon Road for meetings in November. The eight foreign guests, six men and the wives of two of them, arrived in Shanghai on 23 October and were accommodated in a suitable hotel in the Concession. Mr. Charles Barlow and a Californian who joined him in Vancouver carried the good will of believers on the Pacific coast and in Britain, and besides another British couple there were also four delegates from Australia.[6] They were much moved by the warm Chinese hospitality to which they responded with sin-cere affection. Watchman himself was indisposed on their arrival but was soon able to take part in the two weeks of friendly talks. The first week the visitors asked to be excused from breaking bread with the Chinese on the Lord's Day, while they prayed and debated, weighing carefully what they had seen and learned in conversations, lest there should be some flaw. How could they associate their friends at home with something God might not approve? But there was so much to reassure them: the attitude of worship and of obedience to the Scriptures, the prayers, the evident authority of the brothers, the meekness and silence of the women—and their seemly head-covering.

It had been planned that a week's conference should follow the Sunday gatherings on 6 November and to this some forty representative brothers from distant places were converging to join the Shanghai workers. In addition there were to be some public meetings. Watchman had written earlier to his father asking him to purchase and ship from Foochow two hundred wooden chairs at $3 Mex. each to supplement the existing backless benches. He had earlier, with his return to health, felt moved to write and apologize to his mother for his coolness towards her when he was so ill and she had responded with a stern letter enumerating his crimes, forgetting, she admits, her own failures as a mother. Now she resolved to make amends. The purchase of chairs being somewhat outside Nee Weng-hsiu's field she had placed the order herself and had entrusted them when ready to a shipper. At this point they were nearly lost when a rapacious customs examiner tried both to have the chairs impounded and to embezzle a $50 fee. Her husband got them released, but once at sea she had to fight impossible charges imposed by the ship's captain whom John Wang had persuaded to load them as deck cargo. Then off the Yangtze mouth on the morning of the 5th the ship was becalmed in fog in the Steep Island passage and she despaired of delivering them in time. But joined by two friends she prayed publicly to God for its dispersal, visualizing, she says, the chairs all set in position at Hardoon Road. The fog lifted, but then on the ship's arrival in the Whangpoo River the customs once more blocked their unloading at the Bund. Late at night the brothers had to retrieve them from the Pootung shore. Yet next morning they were all in place when the meeting opened, and Huo-ping had herself had a hand in dusting and arranging them!

By now the visitors felt sure before God that there was nothing to debar their home assemblies from identifying with these in China and had cabled their feelings to representatives in Vancouver and Brisbane, 'two neighbouring meetings'. Being assured in reply of their fellowship with them in so doing they now on Sunday evening 6 November joined with the Chinese in participation at the Table of the Lord. It was a time of unspeakable joy.

Next morning the special conference meetings got under way

amid mutual felicitations. The principle speakers were Charles Bar-low and W. J. House with Nee himself as interpreter. Faithful Luke was present with others from the south and there were a number from up the Yangtze and from farther north, including two brothers named Gih from Kiangpei, formerly with the Presbyterian Mission where they were known as 'the Moodies of north Kiangsu'. 'Some of the brothers from other parts,' the visitors observed, 'are men of worth, real gold. The work is spreading and they have much to encourage and much to exercise them.'

Several Kiangsu brothers present now invited them to visit their church groups but this northern area had been very disturbed earlier in the year and the risk of their guests' capture by bandits was felt to be too great a one to take. Two of the party however, W. J. House and C. R. Barlow, had expressed a wish to visit the scene of the work's beginnings. While therefore they took ship to Amoy for a gathering of the several groups in that area, Faithful Luke went ahead to meet John Wang and extend to them a welcome to Foochow. It was in the teeth of a monsoon gale that the visitors at length reached Foochow to be entertained by Huo-ping and her husband in their riverside home. The meetings there were large, numbering 250 souls, and they returned to Shanghai much encouraged and with their sense of history enriched.

The story they all took home was so favourable that in the Spring of 1933, invitations came to Watchman to visit Britain and America that summer, bringing with him Dr. Yu or Faithful Luke. Yu was sick with T.B. at the time and Luke now far away, but Watchman said nothing to either of their inclusion in the invitation. Did he have some presentiment of problems ahead and think of himself as the appointed watchman for his people? Anyway, after prayer with his brothers he resolved to go alone. The passage to Europe made possible a stop at Singapore, and he broke his journey there long enough to visit Sitiawan and pay his respects to the Ling parents,[7] an action that set its seal on the peace God had newly planted in his heart.

The long sea journey meant time for rest and study and he reached England late in June much refreshed. He was met by Charles Barlow who took him to his Peterborough home. He visited meetings as widely scattered as Scotland and Islington, Croydon and Ventnor, and tasted the warmth of love expressed within the group. He was shown tremendous hospitality everywhere, for his coming was such a novelty to believers in this very strict and circumscribed group of the Brethren[8] who themselves had no missionary outreach. He was invited to tell about the work and was of course welcomed to participate at the Lord's Table and sometimes to minister the

Word, though in this last his English must have limited him. He also had long conversations with senior men among them. The Chinese believers were regarded by his hosts as very immature Christians needing a lot of tutoring. Moreover he himself, though thirty years of age, had the looks of a mere student, and with his native respect for wisdom and seniority was ready enough to listen to advice. He astonished them however with the kind of practical questions he and his brothers in Shanghai had regularly to face, such as, 'I want to be baptized, but I have two wives : what shall I do?'

To younger friends he spoke light-heartedly of the simple Chinese rule for meetings : 'No Bible, no breakfast !' or regaled them with stories of the Fukien 'scissor-demons' who cut holes in your oiled-paper umbrella to let the rain through. But most of the time when not involved in discussions he was quietly listening and observing. He never ceased to respect the wealth of spiritual knowledge to be found within this group, but was very disturbed by the complacency that allowed them more than once in his hearing to say things like : 'Is there anything in the field of spiritual revelation that we Brethren do not have? To read what other Christians have written is a waste of time. What do any of them have that we have not got?'[9] Once at a conference at Park Street, Islington, when invited to add his comment to a long discussion of doctrine to which he had listened, he gave vent to his mounting impatience. Rising to his full six feet and stretching his arms wide, 'My dear brothers,' he said, 'your understanding of the truth is vast, but in my country it would avail you *so much*,' and he brought finger and thumb together, 'if when the need arose you could not cast out a demon !' He felt guilty afterwards at this outburst, but it reflected too his own awareness of the reality of the Unseen.[10] And as he left Britain he observed with frankness to his friend Charles Barlow, 'Your people have wonderful light, but oh so little faith !'

On his longer journeys in Britain Mr. Barlow or someone else accompanied him, as when he visited Aldeburgh to call on the veteran George Cutting, author of the widely used gospel booklet *Safety, Certainty and Enjoyment* which by that date had run to thirty million copies. Once however he excused himself for a week to visit London on business, during which, without telling his hosts, he broke briefly out of the very closed circle in which he was moving. He called, that Sunday, at the Christian Fellowship Centre in Honor Oak Road, South London, to worship with an independent evangelical group brought together through the ministry of T. Austin-Sparks, a former Baptist minister. This friend, whom he had greatly hoped to meet, was away in the north, but George Paterson and others welcomed him warmly and he enjoyed the fellowship and ministry of the Word, and received with gladness the bread and wine.

Two weeks later his stay in England ended. With this sole exception he had remained exclusively within the very close circle of a single group of Christians, and had made no contact whatever with the wider field of evangelical church life and witness in Britain. James Taylor of Brooklyn, N.Y., an older man whose word carried everywhere almost pontifical weight with this 'London Group' of Brethren and who had been for some weeks in England, planned now to accompany him back across the Atlantic. Taylor was a skilled and penetrating interrogator and was delighted to find Nee very open and free with him about the Chinese work, outlining its local conditions and spiritual needs and asking much counsel. When it came to doctrine however, and especially prophecy, he found that Nee entertained ideas of the second coming of Christ which he could not approve and which on further questioning he could only regard as glaring error.[11] They reached New York where Nee was received with the greatest affection, and he addressed a meeting at Westfield on the subject of deliverance from sin 'which by most was thought wonderful' but which in Taylor's judgement 'was defective doctrinally'.

Meanwhile in Britain a senior brother of the group chanced to find himself seated in a train to Glasgow opposite a teenage girl who was diligently reading the Bible. Conversation with her elicited the fact that she worshipped at the Honor Oak Road meeting. He probed further, and learned in due course that a very pleasant Chinese had been there at the weekend. Had someone failed to account for Watchman's movements? He resolved to investigate. That night George Paterson had a phone call from a stranger: 'Do you know a Chinese named Nee? Has he been in fellowship with you? *Has he broken bread with you?*' To each question he answered a matter-of-fact 'Yes', and then the phone cut off at the other end. 'Someone's in trouble,' he thought.

A cable went off to Taylor at Brooklyn, but by now Watchman was away at New Haven. His main reason for crossing the Atlantic had been to spend a few days with Thornton and Carol Stearns who were home with their family on furlough from Tsinan. That Sunday in defiance of Taylor's expressed advice he broke bread, as he had done in China, with the Stearns family and some others in their home. 'He made no admission of violation of principles,' Taylor wrote in sorrow. Pressed as to his position in the matter Watchman, who was by now under considerable stress, declined to say or write anything until he had taken counsel with his fellow-workers in Shanghai. The facts as Taylor saw them were forwarded to Van·

couver, where Nee was to attend special meetings.[12]

In principle the meetings of the 'London Group' were fenced off from all other meetings of Christians. Substantially anyone outside was debarred from fellowship with anyone inside it unless he agreed from that time forth to restrict his movements to meetings within the fence. This rule was carried also into ordinary social relations, and was later to be enforced with increasing rigour by James Taylor, Jr., until in the early sixties the movement was agonizingly disrupted on this issue.[13]

In Vancouver nevertheless Watchman was welcomed most warmly and invited to speak at the planned meetings. He seems to have enjoyed real liberty, for at least one young Canadian found the Lord, and as also by many in Britain, he is still fondly remembered. While there he renewed fellowship too with his dear friend C. H. Judd of the China Inland Mission, and called also on Lena Clark who, having worked for 23 years with the C.I.M. in Szechwan, had resigned from the Mission in 1929 and was now to return in fellowship with the saints meeting at Hardoon Road.

On the long, quiet voyage home across the Pacific, as if to set His seal on the way He was leading His servant, God gave to Watchman a fresh revelation of Christ as his life. For a long while he had been acutely aware of a failure in his conduct in the matter of pleasing God. Let him tell it again in his own words. 'When I was a young Christian I was commended by various people for the Christ-likeness of my life, but some years later I found to my consternation that my temper was often getting the better of me. Even when I managed to control it so that it did not actually flare up, it was seething inside; and to add to my distress and disillusionment, those kindly Christians who had commended me for the Christ-like qualities that formerly impressed them were not slow to tell me how unfavourably my present life compared with my past. I used to be so humble and so patient, they said, so gentle and loving—but now...! The worst of it was that their criticisms were not unfounded. I could have far outdone them with my own tales of failure. But how had this state of affairs developed? What was the trouble?'

He used, he says, to think of Christ as a Person apart, failing to identify Him in a practical way with the host of praiseworthy qualities such as meekness, patience, love, wisdom, holiness, that he felt so strongly the lack of. 'For two whole years I was groping in that kind of darkness, seeking to amass as personal possessions the virtues that I felt should make up the Christian life (rather as before my conversion I used to amass worldly things) and getting nowhere in the effort. The trouble was that I had been accumulating things, spiritual things, and God had taken in hand to relieve me of them in order to make way for the life of His Son.

'And then one day in 1933 light broke from heaven for me. Reading again 1 Corinthians 1. 30 I suddenly *saw* that Christ was ordained of God to be made over to me in His fulness. What a difference! O the emptiness of "things"! Held by us out of relation to Him they are dead, for God is not seeking a display of our Christlikeness but a manifestation of His Christ. Once I saw this, it was the beginning of a new life for me. He Himself is the sum of divine things, and thus He was the answer in me to all God's demands, and that, not as a matter for my future discovery but as a fact for my present acceptance. My daily life as a Christian would be summed up thereafter in the word "receive".'[14]

NEW HORIZONS

BACK in China immense tasks awaited him. Correspondence between the Shanghai brothers and their erstwhile friends in the West was to drag on for two agonizing years to its sorrowful conclusion, but it must not be allowed meanwhile to divert them from the gospel outreach or the instruction and training of God's servants. The strength of Watchman Nee's work lay in the fact that every believer was an unpaid worker, and everyone moving to a new city for business or in government service might make his home a place of prayer and a fresh centre of witness. China was fast opening up with road systems and new railways, and the rapid development of air services meant that travel about the country was becoming increasingly free. To the brothers to whom these new fields would open he gave talks in the New Year to guide their thinking on church formation.[1] He had observed many anomalies in the West and these had led him back to examine the New Testament again, where he saw confirmation of the simple principle he had found operating satisfactorily among his Exclusive friends, that a town or village should have one church, not several.

But he was restless. For some time he had wanted to visit the remote south-west provinces of Kweichow and Yunnan, to acquire a first-hand knowledge of the people and their spiritual needs. Now in the Spring of 1934 an opportunity for this presented.

A man named Ma had recently come to the Lord and at his baptism had taken the name of Shepherd Ma (Ma Muh). He had a successful business centred on the Yangtze port of Yochow in Hunan with interests extending into Kweichow Province. A very straightforward brother, he possessed a Ford car and an adventurous spirit, to which was now added a new-found zeal for the gospel. Together the two planned a tour to the extreme limit of the new south-western motor road. Watchman took ship to Yochow to join him for the project.

Loading the car with cans of petrol and Christian Gospels they set out on the circuit of the great Hunan rice bowl, first south to the provincial capital of Changsha and then north-west to Changteh. They took their time. Shepherd Ma did the driving, while at each

Watchman Nee 1938

Nantai Anchorage and the Bridge of Ten Thousand Ages, Foochow.

Right Boys in Middle School Uniform, Trinity College, Foochow, 1930.

Below The College chapel.

iew down river towards Kuliang Mountain and the coast.

Left Preaching band with Gospel shirts. (A later group in Taiwan 1952.)

Margaret E. Barber, Foochow, 1896, and (standing) with Margaret L. Ballord at Pagoda Anchorage, 1928.

Above Sitiawan, Mal-
aya, 1925. Watchman
is 3rd from right. His
mother is seated with
Miss Ling Ai-King
standing beside her.

Right The college
student.

Above In 193◼
during his long il◼
ness.

Above Nantai Island with a fire on the foreshore; shipping in the anchorage.

Below Watchman (in dark gown) with fellow-workers in Shanghai 1930. John Chang is 3rd from left.

Above Shanghai, The Bund, 1932.

Below Welcoming overseas visitors.

Chinese leaders with Brethren delegates, Shanghai 1932.

Above L to R: John Chang, Dr. C. H. Yu, Watchman Nee, W. J. House, Faithful Luke, Phillips, A. Mayo, and (seated) Charles R. Barlow.

Below Standing: Mayo, Phillips, Dr. Powell, Joyce, House. Seated: Ye, Nee, Chang, and Luke.

Above Local church group at Amoy 1932, with C. R. Barlow (*left*) and W. J. House, and (*between them at back*) Faithful Luke.

Below Left With Dr. Thornton Stearns at Chefoo University, Tsinan, 1931.

Below Right At Southampton 1933.

Shanghai street with shop signs, 1932.

Below Right Trainees in Manila, Philippines, 1937, with (centre L to R) Dr. H. S. Huang, Watchman Nee, Simon Meek.

Below Left Faithful Luke.

Above Trams and rickshaws, Shanghai 1932.

Below Marriage of Watchman Nee and Charity Chang, Hangchow 1934. On left bridegroom's sister (Mrs. Ling), mother, brother (Hong-tsu) and father. On right bride's sister-in-law and brother (Samuel Chang), and eldest sister (Beulah).

Above John Sung, Leland Wang, and Watchman Nee, Shanghai, 1934.

Below Kuliang Mountain, Foochow. The rest houses walled against typhoons.

Right Outside the Keswick Convention marquee, July 1938.

Below Left With T. Austin-Sparks, London 1938.

Below Right Elizabeth Fischbacher (seated) with Mary Jones, 1960.

Watchman Nee 1939.

Top Left Witness Lee, Taiwan 1956.

Bottom Left Mr. and Mrs. K. H. Weigh, Hong Kong 1955.

Top Right Simon Meek, Manila 1956.

Bottom Right Mr. and Mrs. Stephen Kaung in India, 1941.

Off duty.

品琤大姊：

　　收到你四月七日的信，知道你没有收到我通知你每次东西都己收到的信。你信上所提的东西，我都己经收到了，实在感谢你。

　　我身体性况，你是知道的，是慢性病，是器官病。发病就很难过，就是不发病，病依然在身上。只有发不发之分，没有好不好之分。夏天到了，多晒些太阳可以改变一点皮肤颜色，但不能改变病。但我维持饱满喜乐，请你放心。希望你们己也多保重一点，心中充满喜乐。

　　　　祝你好

　　　　　　　　　　　　　　述祖
　　　　　　　　　　　　　四月廿二日

Watchman's last letter, dated 22nd April (1972) and signed with his childhood name, Shu-tsu.

ferry crossing or wherever a few passers-by gathered Watchman stood up in the halted car and preached to them Christ.

The navigable Yuan River has traditionally been the route of trade with the south west, and their road now led up its broad valley to Yuanling, as rice terraces gave way to barley and wheat on the hillsides. This city lay within striking distance of the Communist Ho Lung's 2nd Army base at Sangchih, but all was quiet as they climbed on to the Hunan frontier. Here in many cities there were outposts manned by European missionaries; yet still much of the country was unreached with the gospel.

Kweichow was a province of rapid change as streets that hitherto had stopped at city gates were carried out into the countryside, and contoured roads replaced the stepped paths that wound across the hills. There were hazardous road-works to negotiate and even finished road surfaces were rough in the extreme. Shepherd was very short-sighted and wore thick lenses, and at the unfenced hairpins, where a precipitous drop awaited any false move, his arms 'turned to putty'. At such times Watchman, with less driving experience but steadier nerves, was compelled to take over the wheel.

At Kweiyang, the provincial capital, there was a group of believers meeting in a home where they were welcome and spent some days in fellowship. Watchman spoke to them several times, and Ma was amazed to hear him give one talk surveying Church History, packed full of dates and names and figures, without reference to a single note. Here however they began to realize how uncertain was their way ahead. Long stretches of the road to Yunnan were, some said, non-existent. But they had come so far, and padding themselves against the cold they pushed on with determination ever deeper into the mountains. Snow lay yet on the peaks as they climbed still higher passes among azaleas and rhododendrons, always conserving their scanty petrol by coasting on the downward slopes. Ma tells how the rhythm of the Ford's engine took up and drummed into his mind the teachings of Watchman's whistle-stop sermons, but at the higher altitudes Watchman found his heart giving him frequent trouble, suggesting that his earlier long illness had taken a toll. The rains of Kweichow were giving way however to strong Yunnan winds as they reached a point where laughing tribal folk gave them one more long push over some road works. At the end an engineer assured them that they were in fact the first long-distance travellers to come through. Exhilaration now overcame their cold as they began the long descent to the Kutsing plain, amid farmsteads and fields green with spring rice. There were wayfarers once again and this last stretch of the motor road was in fair shape. But approaching Kunming their fresh attempts at roadside witness were diverted by their hearers' inquisitiveness about the vehicle. With the discovery that it had come through by road all the way from Hunan it quickly acquired fame.

They themselves however had a special interest in coming so far. North of Kunming across the River of Golden Sand lay Tibet. In Shanghai there were brothers from Yunnan whom God was calling to evangelize the Tibetans and Watchman wanted to see the situation for himself. A trek of several days brought them to a market in the mountains to which Tibetans brought their wares. Here Shepherd Ma recalls their extreme hospitality, always refilling his plate before he had emptied it, while Watchman, helped by an interpreter, sensed their spiritual darkness and need of the message of salvation.

Their whole trip into the south-west was providentially timed. It would have been quite impossible in the two years of civil warfare that followed. For in the autumn of 1934 the Communists under Mao Tse-tung and his lieutenant Chu Teh, the opium-addict transformed by Marxism, were forced by Chiang Kai-shek's encircling armies to break out of their south Kiangsi base. Ever since 1929 these two had campaigned with success for a true peasant soviet in the villages. Now, driven out by overwhelming force, they began their historic six-thousand-mile trek, with bag, baggage, and archives, west into Yunnan, north up the Tibetan border, and east again into Shensi. Other groups from Hunan, Anhwei, and north Szechwan made similar long treks to join them. The whole movement, known to history as the Long March, was to be a critical and formative experience in the history of Chinese Communism.

But long before these events Watchman was back in the great commercial city of Hankow where he stopped to give to the believers a series of Bible studies on the Song of Songs.[2] These owed much to the Brethren commentator C. A. Coates and demonstrate an indebtedness to these writers he was always ready to acknowledge, whatever the strains that might afflict his relations with their successors.[3]

From Hankow he returned to Shanghai where in late summer he appears in a happy photo with John Sung and Wang Tsai. This meeting had been arranged by the Christian leader K. S. Lee with the commendable aim of bringing together in a single team the gifts, methods, and outlooks of these three so different men.[4] The encounter however was a passing one, each again going his separate way. Wang Tsai disagreed with Nee's reliance on unsalaried ministers of the Word, as well as with his work's independence of the missions which, he feared, could only bring division and loss to the Christian cause. Yet in the light of subsequent events he was in later years to speak with generous regard of Nee's unflinching stand for his principles.

John Sung and Nee unhappily never hit it off, though each reaped where the other had sown. Sung, who lived for only ten years after this, was a whirlwind evangelist who relied for effect upon emotional appeal. A friend describes him as 'cocksure and stubborn, constantly off at a tangent, a man whose every opinion was a conviction'.[5] Yet though Nee was the more talented evangelist, Sung was the one whom God used to sweep multitudes into the kingdom, and the revival that flowed from his preaching spread like a prairie fire.[6] In the words of one observer, when he preached 'the sheep woke up and were hungry, and because there was no one to feed them Watchman's teaching ministry was timely in filling the gap.'[7] But Sung was outspokenly critical of Nee, while Nee privately expressed his contempt for Sung's theological immaturity and the impermanence of his work. Can we however sense here a hunger for an anointing of God that he felt Sung possessed and he himself lacked?

There followed now the third Shanghai teaching conference at which he spoke on the centrality of Christ in the Scriptures and in the life of God's people. At this conference Witness Lee was able to be present from Chefoo, as well as believers from cities in Kiangsu and Shantung where assemblies were fast springing up since Watchman's 1932 visit. The brothers date the work's 'beginnings' in three four-year stages: Foochow 1924; Shanghai 1928; the North 1932.

At this point an unexpected and most welcome figure re-enters the story. On his return from England Watchman had learned that his schooldays sweetheart Charity Chang was back in Shanghai having achieved an M.A. in English at Yenching University. All this while she had remained the worldly girl he had known, accustomed to wear make-up and dress fashionably, but now she attended several meetings at Wen Teh Li and there met the Lord. She was soon asking for baptism, and the older sisters witnessed that she was completely transformed, a fact which, when he met her, Watchman's own observations fully confirmed. The meeting aroused too his own long buried feelings towards her.

Seeing this, Charity's sister Faith took a hand. She sought out Watchman, back once more from his wanderings. 'Now that Charity has become an earnest Christian, serving the Lord with steadfast purpose, would you,' she asked, 'consider marriage with her? I feel sure she would have no objections.'

But only after much prayer, concluding at length that it was God's will, did he yield to his heart's promptings. Then an urgent letter to his parents in Foochow appealed for their help with the wedding arrangements. Huo-ping was struck with panic, recalling her blunder over the Sitiawan betrothal, but they set out for Shanghai, only to be met there by a host of rumours. Charity's widowed aunt Chang Mei-chen was, it was said, strongly opposed to the match, resentful that her brilliant niece should be joined with a despised preacher. And there were corresponding doubts in the minds of those believers who idolized Watchman and who were shocked that he, a man of prayer, should think about sex and a family—and worse that he should consider marrying a college beauty from Yenching.

But his mother went to meet Chang Shui-kuan, Charity's uncle and the family's legal head, who to her relief gave his approval. She then invited Charity to accompany her to another city to take part with her in special gospel meetings. They shared a room for a week, living and praying together, and by the time they returned God had given her complete confidence that Charity was indeed His choice for her son.

Early in October nearly four hundred believers gathered at Hangchow, capital of Chekiang Province, an ancient city of picturesque beauty set amid steep hills and soft green lakes. A special conference had been arranged here by Philip Luan to consolidate the work in this very responsive region. Ever since Peace Wang had first visited the area for work among women small local meetings had been growing up in eastern Chekiang, and among those who now gathered were believers from such towns as Fenghwa, Wenling, and Chuhsien.[8] Others came from Soochow in Kiangsu and from many more centres. Here for ten days Watchman expounded the Word in what was afterwards remembered as the 'Overcomer Conference', and he was overjoyed to have both his parents present. The day following had been fixed for his wedding, and so slow was he to bring his mind round to the idea of being a bridegroom that Faithful Luke had to drag him that morning to a second-hand clothing store so that he might buy himself a wedding gown.

Thus on the afternoon of 19 October 1934, the anniversary of his parents' wedding, Ni To-sheng was united in Christian marriage to Chang Pin-huei in the presence of a large gathering of believers. They gave thanks to God, singing the hymn he had written for her ten years earlier; and afterwards they feasted at thirty tables of ten guests each.

Now the storm broke. They arrived back in Shanghai to find that Charity's aunt Mei-chen had given vent to her spleen in a public attack on Watchman that took the form of a harshly-worded advertisement, couched in scholarly Chinese, in a national daily. How, she asked, dare this poverty-stricken preacher carry off her beloved

Pin-huei? How could he possibly ever afford to support, let alone satisfy so cultured a young lady? If he could, it must be from foreign sources that he got his money. And there was a veiled attack upon his morals, offensive enough in this context and readily seized upon by those who disliked his influence. Not once but daily for a week the nationwide attack went forth, while handbills in the same vein were printed and distributed widely in Christian circles. 'The one I read was so vile,' one missionary remarked, 'that I burnt it, and then felt I needed a bath.'

Watchman became profoundly depressed. In their new home he retired to bed and would see no one. One strong-minded missionary lady called however. 'He'll see *me*,' she announced, 'because I have a message for him from God,' and she went in. 'No weapon that is formed against thee shall prosper,' she declared, 'and every tongue that rises up in judgement thou shalt condemn!'[9] And Faith Chang came and talked in lighter vein in an endeavour to lift his spirit. 'Does it matter what they say?' she teased. 'You have won a wife after your own heart!' For Charity was indeed a joy to him. Her Chinese was beautiful, and so was her English. She had a humble walk with the Lord and would be the greatest help to him in his work. And, as all agreed, she was beautiful.

In November they travelled south for special conference meetings in Amoy, but there followed a period in which he was beset with problems. The London correspondence was dragging on. His heart condition too that had appeared in Yunnan kept recurring. And in particular he had an inward problem concerning personal enduement with the Holy Spirit for service—both a sense of something lacking in his own experience and also some confusion of mind about the doctrine. On the doctrinal issue God gave him the light he sought while he was away for a month working in a remote place far out of reach of anyone qualified to answer his theological questions, and when therefore in desperation he enlisted the prayer help of some extremely simple village believers.[10]

And there were other rays of light to cheer him. One of these was the return of Thornton and Carol Stearns in January 1935. The formation of a 'separatist' group in the town following Watchman's 1932 visit to Tsinan had made things uneasy for them at Cheloo University and accordingly Dr. Stearns had resigned and taken a new teaching appointment in Shanghai. On another occasion quite by chance Watchman met Li Kuo-ching, the doctor's son who spoke out of turn at Mei-hua fishing village. He had gone on to Amoy University and was now a pilot in the airways. When Watchman asked him whether he still followed the Lord, 'Mr. Nee,' he said, 'do you mean to say that after all we went through there I could ever forsake Him?'

But the long interchange with London and New York, painful as it was, was helping the Shanghai brothers to formulate more clearly their ideas on church relations. The brethren in the West had charged Watchman Nee with having 'compromised the fellowship' extended to him by partaking at the Lord's Table (in Honor Oak and New Haven) with Christians who were governed by the principle that 'anyone claiming to be a believer was allowed to break bread without regard to the religious and other associations in which he was involved.' They sought therefore 'to enlighten the Shanghai brethren as to the principles of Christian fellowship and to help them to judge Nee's actions.' Occasion was also taken to call attention to Nee's unsound views on prophecy.

The harsh issue was one of separation from all other Christian associations prior to being received at the Lord's Table. In fact some in the Chinese meetings had long retained their links with mission congregations without any questions being raised till now. To the Western brethren however this kind of thing would not do, and the comparative immaturity of the Chinese movement was no excuse. The brethren offered to them a century of written 'truth' and, as James Taylor put it in a letter to Faithful Luke, 'You are obligated to the Lord to embrace it, profit by it, and stand firmly by it.'[11]

The Shanghai elders' eventual reply was a humble and gracious appeal to Christian reasonableness and the rule of the Holy Spirit. Their long letter dated 2 July 1935, addressed from 36/38, Lane 240, Hardoon Road, and signed by D. C. Du, Y. A. Wu, W. Nee, and K. Y. Chang, contains the following statement of principle:

'We must distinguish between "sins" (either morally or doctrinally) that hinder fellowship with God and "sins" which do not. We know definitely that sins like adultery, and disbelief in Christ coming in the flesh, would certainly put one out of fellowship, but as to the other "sins"—say that of "bad association" and wrong interpretation of prophecy, fellowship with God is not hindered.

'The fact remains that many a child of God in the different systems whom we have thought unfit for fellowship, is having a closer walk with God and a richer communion with our Lord than we.

'It is the Spirit, and the Spirit alone, who can decide the question of one's fitness for fellowship.

'The reason why we receive a man is that God has received him (Romans 14. 3). So the divine command is, "Now him that is weak in faith, receive" (14. 1). We must receive all those whom God has received. This command is clear, decisive and embracing.'[12]

This was a straightforward plea for open communion based upon awakened Christian conscience, but it was met only with an entrenched exclusivism. A representative meeting 'of assembly character' was called on 30 July 1935 at Park Street Hall, Islington, when the formal break with the Chinese brethren was announced. Several who were present registered a profound shock to their better sense, but it was an authoritative decision, binding by consent on every meeting of the 'London Group' worldwide. The letter conveying this to the Shanghai brothers was dated 31 August 1935. It called into question the sincerity of the Chinese brethren's love for Christ, it charged Nee with lack of uprightness, and it stated that, had the principles outlined been disclosed in 1932, fellowship then would have been impossible. 'We grievously failed in our lack of holy care in laying hands too quickly on those with whom we were insufficiently acquainted. We are unable to walk with you.... This, of course, applies also to all those maintaining links of fellowship with you.'

One of the letter's signatories was Charles R. Barlow, a deeply sorrowful man. The Chinese too were left in a state of shock by the whole episode, for the disappointment in the sphere of Christian relationships and grieved love was profound.

Watchman himself was with Charity in Chefoo when the reply reached him. Here Miss Elizabeth Fischbacher, much in demand as one of the C.I.M.'s gifted missionary speakers, was holding revivalist meetings in the town.

She had recently come to know Watchman, who, as we have already seen, was passing through a period of spiritual barrenness, and he had shared with her some of the churnings of his inquiring mind. He was still hungry for a new experience of God and now he sufficiently overcame his reservation about women preachers to attend her Chefoo meetings. She herself shared the Shantung predilection for ecstatic accompaniment of preaching and prayer and when her English would not hold out any more she would pray and sing in the Spirit in other tongues. But there was real power in her preaching and Watchman now came under its spell, responding to the appeal of the Word and entering into what was for him a quite new discovery of divine blessing. What is certain is that from now he found a new release that brought to an end this somewhat barren phase in his preaching. He sent a telegram back to Shanghai : 'I have met the Lord.'

To the autumn conference there he brought a message of the outpouring of the Spirit of God that led many into a similar experience of divine power. The effect of this was that over a period of a year or two a wave of spiritual excitement and a fresh emphasis on experiences swept southwards through the assemblies—groups that hitherto had been governed by an intellectual approach which never allowed the Christians to forget the Bible in favour of mere subjectivism. Nevertheless it had already been the custom to end prayer meetings with a brief period of simultaneous prayer when those whose petitions had been crowded out by the limit of time could unload their burdens Godward. This practice, said to have originated with John Sung, could be a most moving outlet for the Holy Spirit when under His control, as prayer rose in a crescendo and waned again to the silence of completion in the space of a minute or so. But now rein was given to extremes of excitement, with jumping, clapping, laughter, unknown tongues that conveyed no message to hearers or even speaker, and a flood of dramatic healings, some undoubtedly real but not a few mistaken.

Late in 1935 Watchman and Charity reached Amoy where, due to a hitch over accommodation, the planned special conference meetings had at the last minute to be redirected elsewhere. At Tsinkiang, between that city and Foochow, the dean of the Christian College, Lukas Wu, who had lately found the Saviour through acting as interpreter for John Sung, now came to the rescue by opening his large home for the ten days conference which nearly four hundred attended. Watchman spoke on the Victorious Life and the Outpouring of the Holy Spirit, and there was yet one more outburst of divine blessing. Thereafter Wu's household formed the nucleus of another worshipping and witnessing group, a pattern that was to be reproduced in coming days in one city after another.

Witness Lee affirms that Watchman 'never spoke in tongues'.[13] This may be so, but cannot now be proved and is in every sense an argument from silence. He certainly believed in the Holy Spirit's lesser gifts to the Church of healing and of speaking with and interpretation of other tongues. 'I have seen with my own eyes,' he said, 'cases of instantaneous divine healing. We do not oppose this; we only contend with erroneous ways of healing.' And again: 'Some ask me if I oppose speaking with tongues. Certainly not, though I do question tongues which are obtained through faulty means.' And to the writer he recounted from experience a telling illustration of how in one very confused village congregation God had used this means to convey to them unpalatable facts which they needed urgently to face, but which the only other informed person was under a promise not to divulge. This kind of thing, he maintained, gave meaning and purpose to the gift.

On the other hand he was equally strong in affirming that 'not all speak with tongues',[14] and his teaching on the theme was always balanced. Indeed a senior C.I.M. missionary who a few years later attended his lectures on the Holy Spirit in Shanghai describes them as 'the clearest teaching on this subject that I have ever heard'.

Some revival methods, Watchman held, worked like spiritual opium. Addiction to them compelled merely an ever-increased dosage. Elizabeth Fischbacher felt herself to blame for the loss of restraint that followed in the wake of these events and abandoned public preaching altogether, to discover in due course a richly rewarding ministry through her gifted pen. And three years later when the pendulum had swung back and the episode had run its course Watchman observed in a conversation with K. S. Wong, 'We find on looking back over this period that the gain has been rather trivial, the loss quite large.'

RETHINKING

IN OCTOBER 1935, with the first straggling survivors of the Long March, Mao Tse-tung emerged in northern Shensi to take up his new headquarters at Yenan as the undisputed leader of the Chinese Communist Party. Their year-long feat of endurance was to become an emotional high peak in the Party's annals. Some of its spectacular episodes were already legends of Communist heroism and invincibility: the break-out from the Kiangsi encirclement, the secret crossing of the River of Yellow Sand, the forcing under fire of the Bridge of Iron Chains over the Tatu River at Luting, the ascent of the Great Snow Mountain, and the nightmare traverse of the Szechwan swamplands. Sustained throughout by political formulae and iron determination, they emerged now at a key point on the fringe of the north China plain, welded by their ordeal into a disciplined nucleus for future operations. After so long under nearly continuous military attack they had acquired a new self-assurance as Chinese Communists in their own right, no longer answerable to Russia.

Chiang Kai-shek's attempt to exterminate them had, at least for the present, failed dismally and its abandonment in the south meant that the way was at last open for the Shanghai brothers who had felt called to the Tibetan borderlands to set out for Yunnan. In the next year or so six made their way there. Among the Tibetans they met with a heart-warming response, but seriously lacked literature. Tracts and Scripture portions in the Tibetan language were therefore printed in Shanghai and shipped to them via Hanoi, where to Watchman's disgust, the French government confiscated them. He arranged therefore for the plates to be flown to Yunnan and the printing done on the spot. Only thus after long delay was the problem overcome.

Elsewhere in China the expansion of the work was set forward by two factors. One was the increasing demand among converts of whatever mission allegiance for Watchman's sermon transcriptions. The magazine and the Bible-centred booklets found their way into Christian homes everywhere, providing food for many who had been aroused spiritually by revivalist preaching but now had none to feed them. Nee's gift of explaining Christian doctrines in simple words went far to meet their need.

The other factor was, as we have seen, the spontaneous use of believers' homes. A prayer group would spring up where a believer moved by transfer of business or official service and at once this would become a fresh centre of Christian witness, drawing people, some out of paganism but not a few from various mission connections, into a primitive church fellowship. They were men and women who had turned from their sins to the Saviour to give their all to Him. As each small nucleus grew it was given elders (*chang-lao*) in the New Testament pattern to guide its activities and make provision for its ministries. It might in due course require larger premises, but its meeting place must be functional and never monumental and there was no thought of buying land for church building or even renting halls that did not spring from the expansion of the Holy Spirit's work in the believers themselves.

The movement also had 'apostles' (*shi-tu*, an envoy). These were full-time workers with a roving commission to evangelize the unreached, to establish churches where there were none, and to build up the believers. They might move farther afield, perhaps hiring a public hall for some fresh outreach in a new situation.

This meant that the activities embraced two concepts, the churches and the work. The work he viewed (to use the English adjectives he himself coined) as 'platformic', the churches 'round-tablic'. To preclude if possible fresh sectarian divisions on grounds of doctrine or around personalities[1] the churches were thought of as local units corresponding geographically to secular administrative areas (villages, towns, municipalities) somewhat on the old Saxon 'parish' system. They were self-supporting, self-propagating, and locally autonomous, whereas the work had a loose central organization or fellowship in which Watchman and a few brothers acted as advisers to the apostles, training them and being responsible before God for the flow of financial support. When an apostle found himself in any local church situation (but not when engaged in his wider work) he subjected himself to the local elders. In 1938 Nee stated that there were 128 such 'apostles' out in full-time service.

The whole structure and procedure had grown up over the previous decade by extempore application of their reading of the New Testament to situations as they had arisen.[2] It was still in process of development, and it was thought of as secondary to the spiritual life and fellowship of the believers. Always conformity to Christ and witness to His saving power were the primary concerns.

The movement's strength lay in the quality of its man-power. Men and women joined it of their own free will, without the attraction of associated gain such as was offered, for example, by the

mission educational system. As Watchman has explained, what the
Chinese saw and the missionaries took longer to realize was that,
quite apart from the foreignness of mission patterns, they had un-
avoidably offered in the early days avenues of promotion in the
church to men who had begun life as missionaries' servants, and
who, despite the splendid dedication of many of them, nevertheless
constituted in practice a 'class' of Christians unlikely to inspire
esteem among more cultured and intellectual Chinese. In the sphere
of leadership, early missionary success could thus in the long term be
self-defeating.

But here in the 'Little Flock' meetings people met as believers to
learn to know the Lord and serve Him better, and some of the
assemblies began to show a high preponderance of educated men,
doctors, university staff, businessmen, army officers. Among the
students who in Peiping in 1936 'composed almost entirely the regular congregation of the Christians' Meeting Place in that educational
centre' there were 'top honor students of Yenching, Ching Hua,
Peiping Union Medical College, Peking University, and nurses in
training in the Methodist and Presbyterian Hospitals. The missionary doctors said of them, "They are among our finest nurses, and
they really seem to have something".'[3]

A quick survey of the extent of the work at this time suggests
that within the movement there were already more than thirty local
churches, some doubtless quite small, within China together with a
few overseas. But the feeling of observers about their spread was
mixed. In the north-west province of Kansu in the early nineteen-
forties an Alliance missionary found reason to suggest that 'the
further the movement got from its base the more it failed to distinguish between unfeigned love of the brethren and certain less
admirable emotional expressions'.[4] He felt, as did others, that its
adherents could be justly charged with spiritual pride, and that
though in the coastal cities the movement flourished among the
elite, there too it made 'unabashed efforts to prejudice members of
established churches and divert even pastors if it could.' An English
Baptist, writing of Shensi Province, reports how 'in 1942 a group of
earnest young men in Sian who studied the Greek New Testament
and read Madame Guyon left the older churches to form a purified
body called the "Little Flock", which re-baptized Christians who
joined and which met for the "breaking of bread" and the preaching
of the Word each Sunday. They were strongly anti-church and criti-
cised different denominations of the Church in China as foreign
accretions, yet do not see that their action in drawing away from
the Church was setting up yet another denomination.'[5] And in the
coastal province of Chekiang, whereas some of the China Inland

missionaries might speak with warm appreciation of their excellent teaching and of the true Christian fellowship to be found among them, to others the rapid leakage of believers into their ranks from among the flourishing Mission-related churches was a cause of growing concern. To them Watchman Nee seemed but a sheep-stealer and thus a most dangerous man. There is little doubt that he was at this time a thorn in many a missionary's side.

Of the Fukien brothers several had already gone overseas as workers and Christian witnesses, Simon Meek in 1931 to the Philippines, Faithful Luke, Daniel Tan, and K. S. Wong to Singapore and the Malay States, others also to the Dutch Indies. In July 1937 at Meek's invitation Watchman visited Manila, and there and in Baguio addressed meetings of up to a hundred for four weeks on the Christian life of victory, the fulness of the Holy Spirit, and the practical fellowship of the Church.

He left again for Singapore just as the full-scale Japanese invasion of China began with their seizure of Peking, and thus he was still away from Shanghai when on 14 August hostilities broke out there. Chinese planes struck at Japanese shipping on the Whangpoo and two jettisoned bomb-loads caused a massive death toll of their own civilians in a department store and on a neighbouring street. Marines landed to make a Japanese stronghold of the Hongkew suburb, while throngs of refugees swarmed into the Concession from the surrounding areas and set up 'straw villages' on every empty plot. Shanghai remained open from the south, and by this route within a month Watchman had found his way back to his wife. Their home was in an evacuated area but she herself was safe with the sisters at Hardoon Road, though still within earshot of the land-fighting at Chapei just a few miles to the north. Not for the last time their possessions had been ransacked, and when they found their way back there it was to miss, among other things, the Chinese Bible he had given her as a wedding present.

Satisfied that all was well he was soon off again, circumventing the battle area for a journey up the Yangtze to Hankow. Here he called together as many full-time workers as could be reached, and gave them a course of addresses with open discussion on the lines of a similar conference held the previous January in Shanghai. On these two occasions he abandoned for once his emphasis on the Christian's inward life in order to deal with more technical externalities. He had, he tells us, been led to see that Corinthian truths are just as precious as Ephesian ones, since the apostle who wrote the two epistles was inspired by one and the same Spirit, and that those who are acquainted with Ephesian truths cannot afford to make Corinthian mistakes. He set out therefore to crystallize and codify the practical principles derived from Scripture that together they had worked out and used in living situations in the conduct of the work and the formation of local churches. Until now the workers had relied on his personal counselling, but with the disturbed state of the country he felt he owed it to them to define more clearly the position reached. This task completed, he returned again past the battle area to Shanghai which by November was wholly under Japanese control, every house and junk and sampan flying a Rising Sun to show who was master. Barbed wire, sandbags and barricades were everywhere and commodity prices soared. In December the capital, Nanking, fell to the invaders amid unprecedented horrors. The Nationalist government had begun its long retreat westward that was to end in Chungking.

Full notes had been taken of the two series of lectures and were shared around, and this immediately led to a demand for their publication. With Charity's and Ruth Lee's literary help, therefore, Watchman prepared them urgently for the press so that believers and workers throughout the country might share the values of the two conferences. By March 1938 the book was printed, appearing under the title *Kong Tsoh-tih Tsai Hsiang (Rethinking the Work)*.[6] In his preface Nee quotes Margaret Barber's observation that 'God's Spirit will only work along God's lines'. The book is in fact an examination from Scripture of 'God's lines' of church life and expansion as revealed to these particular men over this period and in this historic setting, and herein lies its value. 'The truths referred to in this book,' Nee wrote, 'have been gradually learned and practised during the past years. Numerous adjustments have been made as greater light has been received, and if we remain humble, and God shows us mercy, we believe there will be further adjustments in the future.'

From his handful of missionary friends too there was immediate pressure for an English edition of the book, but of the wisdom of this he was not convinced. For his first title in English to be so untypical of his ministry as a whole seemed merely to invite misunderstanding. But anyway, in his search for the fellowship of older and wiser men he now had plans to accompany Elizabeth Fischbacher and two other missionary ladies on a visit to Europe. Before leaving this time he was overjoyed to be given by the doctors an absolutely clear report on his lung condition.

Taking Charity with them as far as Hong Kong to stay with the Nee parents out of reach of the war, they sailed by Anchor Line, and on arrival in the Clyde in July he went first to Kilcreggan to meet Mr. T. Austin-Sparks. Till now they had only corresponded, but Watchman had been an appreciative reader of his devotional magazine *A Witness and a Testimony* and they quickly found themselves on common ground. They travelled south together to the annual Convention for the Deepening of Spiritual Life in Keswick, Cumberland, where the C.I.M. ladies joined them. There on a morning of sunshine he attended the great missionary meeting chaired by the Rev. W. H. Aldis, Home Director of the China Inland Mission. As he sat with a Japanese speaker on the platform the war havoc in China was fresh in everyone's mind, and when his turn came he led the meeting in intercession for the Far East in terms that to many of us back there in the 'thirties were a revelation. It was a prayer that few who were privileged to be present forgot. 'The Lord reigns: we affirm it boldly. Our Lord Jesus Christ *is* reigning, and He *is* Lord of all: nothing can touch His authority. It is spiritual forces that are out to destroy His interests in China and Japan. Therefore we do not pray for China, we do not pray for Japan, but we pray for the interests of Thy Son in China and Japan. We do not blame any men, for they are only tools in the hand of Thine enemy. We stand for Thy will. Shatter, O Lord, the kingdom of darkness, for the persecutions of Thy Church are wounding Thee. Amen.'[7] While at Keswick he talked to mission candidates on 'The Necessary Qualifications of a Missionary', and, from the Epistle to the Romans, on 'The Lord's Work for our Salvation: the Lord Himself for our Life'. Most significantly, at the end of the week he partook at the Convention's vast united communion service under the banner 'All one in Christ Jesus', thus publicly setting his seal upon the position he and his Chinese fellow-workers had taken three years earlier.

Watchman now travelled to London and to the Christian Fellowship Centre at Honor Oak Road, where his single previous visit had precipitated so acutely the issue of open fellowship. At once he felt at home here with Mr. Austin-Sparks and the other responsible men in the church. He made this his temporary headquarters and it was here that the present writer spent with him some unforgettable weeks.

The church at Honor Oak was widely open to the Lord's people and had a clear missionary vision, but with an emphasis also upon the subjective work of the Cross in Christian lives[8] which, in the evangelical climate of the time, was felt to be somewhat negative and liable to divert active witnessing Christians to a too passive occupation with 'higher things'. Moreover, like Nee himself, Honor Oak was blamed for a drift of missionaries out of the historic missions in search of a more primitive or 'spiritual' pattern of life and testimony. Watchman had thus again chosen to swim in a current slightly aside from mainstream evangelicalism.

Those of us who as a result briefly enjoyed something of a

monopoly of his fellowship and ministry were immensely enriched by the experience. He was so easy to talk with, and his Eastern cultural background made discussion of our common heritage in Christ so stimulating. When he spoke in public, whether taking morning prayers or addressing a church meeting, his excellent English conspired with the charm of his mannerisms to make him a joy to listen to. But it was the content of his addresses that won us. He wasted no words, but brought us straight to grips with some problem of Christian living that had long bothered us; or confronted us with some demand of God that we had side-stepped, for on too many matters we Christians excell, as he engagingly put it, at 'dotching the itchue'. He displayed too the Chinese thinker's great care in his choice of terms and often gave back new meaning to our worn evangelical clichés.

Moreover he could see through us, and seeing, still be faithful. This was because always his object was to exalt the Christ he loved. Within a month of coming among us, skilfully, but with obvious concern, he put his finger right on our danger point, and that, sure enough, was our spiritual pride. God had shown him from experience, he told us gently, that 'Judge not, that ye be not judged'[9] is as surely a principle of His dealings as 'Give, and it shall be given to you.' No wonder, then, that notes of his talks to us have seemed, thirty years later, to leap from the tattered notebook with fresh and startling relevance.

At that time I was a serious young missionary recruit on the point of setting out for Asia, and with two other friends enjoyed long and valuable conversations with him on everything from missionary finance to the Book of Revelation. Never at any time did he so much as hint that I should leave, or not join, an established missionary enterprise. The best advice he gave me as the Lord's messenger in a foreign culture was to wear (metaphorically) for the first ten years one of the English learner-driver's L-plates that so delighted him when he first saw them in use. I came in due course to feel that for a Christian the ten years he suggested should be indefinitely extended.

We were passing just then through the Munich crisis in Europe and as a foreign guest in Britain Watchman observed our anxious digging of shelters and distribution of gas-masks, and then the outburst of emotional relief at Neville Chamberlain's 'peace in our time'. Because not directly involved he tasted, he says, that right kind of detachment that, on another level, the Christian rightly feels as a stranger and sojourner in this world.[10] But he had his own private sorrows. At around this time news reached him from Hong Kong that Charity, who was expecting a child, had suffered a miscarriage. When her own letter came it was a brave one, but he knew how deeply she must have felt this blow with him away half around the world, and he wrote as best he could to comfort her. In fact, as soon as she was fit to travel, his mother took her off on a tremendous journey by way of Hanoi to Kunming to visit the evacuated believers in Yunnan Province. Charity was not in fact to conceive again and the Nees had no children.

In October at the invitation of Pastor Fjord Christensen of Copenhagen Watchman was in Denmark for meetings at the International School at Helsingor (Hamlet's 'Elsinore') where he gave a series of ten addresses on Romans 5–8 entitled 'The Normal Christian Life'. These, supplemented with others on the same theme, were later to form the book of that name.[11] To Watchman 'the victorious life' was a wishful term used too often by the non-victorious for what in fact was real Christian living. Those who 'overcome',[12] he argued, are in God's eyes normal Christians; the rest are below normal! Moving on to Odense Watchman gave a notable talk on the key words 'sit, walk, stand' in Ephesians. It seems clear that he found, as have so many, much release of his spirit while among the Danes.

When coming to Britain he had planned to spend at most four months in the West, returning in November via the United States. However the visit seemed incomplete without a fuller exchange of views with his new friend and counsellor on the problem of what he saw as 'the practical outworking of the Body of Christ'. When he reached Paris by way of Norway, Germany and Switzerland, a letter from his Shanghai co-workers urged him not to return without this. It would mean the translation into English of his *Rethinking the Work*. Happily Elizabeth Fischbacher was free to join him there with a colleague, Phyllis N. Deck, to undertake this task, so for two months she translated while Watchman abridged and edited and wrote another preface. At last in January, the manuscript completed, he returned to London for a further four months based largely at Honor Oak, during which a mutually rewarding friendship with Mr. and Mrs. Austin-Sparks was cemented.

Here there were meetings once again, but not all the time. He found delight in tasting English family life, and where before he had been rather formal, now he would relax and play hide-and-seek with the children, folding himself easily out of sight into a cupboard in his long blue gown. Once, after preaching very effectively at a full conference, he joined a party of them for a picnic in the Surrey heathlands and is remembered by one as 'such fun to have around: not at all a "very spiritual brother"!' In the home he was astonished that everyone didn't stand up every time Grannie entered the room, and that on the other hand an adult would go so far as to apologize to a pet dog that had accidentally been trodden on. Out driving, with the frugality learned in Yunnan days, he insisted on switching off the car engine when descending hills. He took out the children too to Chinese meals, but himself found it necessary to support our bland English foods with soya sauce, of which he contrived somehow to keep a steady supply.

He had of course freedom to move around, and at Sheringham in Norfolk he sought out Margaret Barber's friend of Norwich days, D. M. Panton, whose writings he had valued and to whom he tried to demonstrate his appreciation by, it is said, preparing two eggs for his breakfast. At another local church of the Open Brethren he met Mr. (later Sir) John Laing the constructional engineer who recalls how Watchman graciously declined the offer of a gift from Western funds towards his work. And, most happily of all, he found opportunity for a private meeting of warm reconciliation with his long-time friend among the Exclusive Brethren, Charles Barlow.

In the month of May 1939, just before he left Britain, the English translation of *Rethinking the Work* appeared in London with the Witness and Testimony imprint under the title *Concerning Our Missions* and was avidly seized upon by many as a tract for the times.[13] This period, it must be remembered, was the heyday of interdenominational missions, some of whose long-established institutions seemed by now sacrosanct. But already a few missionaries were beginning to face honestly the system's in-built vagueness about what to do with converts. In some circles the view was gaining ground that only in fresh living churches could the results of their labours be conserved, and to these readers Nee's strong emphasis on the local church, answerable to God alone, came to them as a breath of fresh air. Moreover his distinction between 'the churches' and 'the work'—a reasonable deduction from Scripture—seemed a useful one. Besides this there were passages in the book of such evident practical helpfulness as his clear-headed chapter on finance.

When as a Chinese he rejected wholesale the plethora of overlapping Western denominations, sympathetic readers mostly nodded assent, but when they came to his strict emphasis on 'locality'—one city, one church, worldwide—there they stuck. It was a possible inference from Scripture and no more, since, as one Bible scholar shrewdly pointed out, in writing to the one city which in New Testament times probably had a million inhabitants, Paul does not address his letter 'to the church in Rome'.[14] Nee seemed to be asking believers in Western cities of many millions to return somehow to New Testament population figures in order to recover New Testament practice.[15]

Many had thought through this problem for half a lifetime and more, honestly, humbly before God, with the Bible before them and with the evidence of growing complexity arising from centuries of fresh beginnings. Was there, they asked, a way forward for us all that was not in essence a retreat backward to the 'ideal' social conditions of Asia Minor or Saxon England? Thus, for example, his friend T. Austin-Sparks had chosen rather to emphasize the mystical 'Body' of Christ, and the freedom of the Holy Spirit to give it today a variety of expressions on earth, each a 'testimony' to the Head who is in heaven. 'To understand the Church, the churches, Church order, the work of the church,' he wrote in his own copy of *Concerning Our Missions* 'it is necessary to start from God's inclusive standpoint which is Christ. To know Christ in all His parts and ways is to know what the Church should be. Everything is "in Christ".'

Thus, though the understanding and warmth of fellowship between the two men was profound, on this particular issue they took some time to find themselves on the same wavelength. They were in no disagreement about the new wine, but Watchman's concern was with the wineskin to contain it. His particular problem was one of accommodating to a sound, divine pattern the expanding and largely tradition-free work with which in the years to come he expected to have to grapple. But if in the West he did not get all the practical counsel for which he had hoped, it must be admitted that, at the period in question, what he sought was everywhere in short supply.

Some months after his return to Shanghai he wrote back to his friend words which express his loneliness as a leader: 'You know, with the brethren here, because of their juniority, everything I say goes, despite their seeking to know the mind of the Lord.' Of the fellowship therefore that in so short a time had grown up between them 'the Lord has been speaking to me,' he said. 'As a younger man, recognizing you as a senior brother in the same testimony, I think I need this fellowship in a very real way.' Yet in fact they corresponded but little, and still in China there never appeared a man of his own stature, Chinese or Westerner, to whom he could turn in time of need.

13

HEYDAY

As HE had done six years earlier, Watchman planned now to travel home via the United States. But when he made inquiries at his embassy they hinted that the Japanese at some Pacific ports were using compulsory inoculations as a means of liquidating certain Chinese returning from the West, so he decided that after all it would be wiser to travel all the way to the Whangpoo by British ship. The journey via Bombay and Colombo permitted a very brief stop-over in India, but July found him back in Shanghai, to the immense relief of Charity who had been dismayed for his safety in the war-threatened West. They were delighted to be together again. Some months later he told a newly-wed couple that 'a marriage is like old shoes, more comfortable with passing time'.

He arrived in a city that was a shadow of its former self, its gay life silenced under the miseries of alien occupation, its once prosperous trade strangled by the pressures of war. From the devastated areas across the Soochow Creek pestilence seeped into the foreign concessions. These were still kept open by the presence of British, French, and American warships but were packed now with destitute refugees. As Watchman, inconspicuous in old gown and battered felt hat, moved in and out among the homes he encountered a callousness of spirit even more tragic than the prevailing hardships, for in the struggle to exist unashamed self-seeking and opportunism prevailed to which not even the faithful seemed immune. 'I found many have already been hardened to protect themselves,' he said in a note to a friend, 'and some have even been praising the Lord because they are not feeling anything of the sufferings around. As for myself, I have to confess I am feeling every bit of them; only I am holding on to the Lord by standing into the Kingdom. What has been happening around us is enough, even if one has a thousand hearts, to break every one of them. But my Father is God! I have never learned to love the word "God" as much as today. *God!*'

A rift had appeared briefly among the brothers in his absence but the preaching gap had been filled by John Chang, and more particularly by Dr. C. H. Yu the eye-specialist. Dr. Yu, short of stature and with delicate, refined features, was also musical and sometimes accompanied the singing with his violin. As a speaker he showed promising gifts, for he loved the Lord and was sensitive to His Word.

On the first Sunday morning of September 1939 Watchman called the church to prayer about the tense situation in Europe. Asking that several brothers would join him in leading the congregation, he 'marched into God's presence taking the church with him', claiming that nothing but His will should be done in this crisis. At the end of this very impressive hour in which many more took part he concluded, 'Well, Lord, You can never say Your church hasn't prayed!'

Both the Monday prayer meeting and the Sunday evening breaking of bread were now being divided between several homes in the city and here believers began to intercede strongly with God that He would set a limit to Japanese inroads into the Concession. To help clarify their thinking therefore Watchman gave, early in 1940, a talk 'not to Chinese (or British or Americans) but to men and women in Christ', on the theme of God's use of world governments. All the way from Cyrus king of Persia to the Spanish Armada he showed how God's ordering of secular history is essentially in relation to His own people. 'We must know therefore *how* to pray. It must be possible for British and German, Chinese and Japanese Christians to kneel and pray together, and all to say Amen to what is asked. If not there is something wrong with our prayer. We may remind God of what attitude Japan takes to Him, but we must also remind Him that in China Christians and missionaries have too much intimacy with the State. In the last European war there was much prayer that dishonoured God. Let us not fall into the same error. The church must stand above national questions and say, "We, here, ask for neither a Chinese or a Japanese victory, but for whatever is of advantage to the one thing precious to Thee, the testimony of Thy Son." Such prayer is not empty words. If the whole church prayed thus the war could soon be settled God's way.'

Bible teaching at Wen Teh Li was seriously constricted by the still inadequate premises. An elderly sister in the meeting raised their hopes by offering a large building and land at only 40 per cent of current value, but then wished to dictate the form its development should take, and when the brothers put to her the principle that God Himself must lead them in how best to use a gift given to Him, the offer was withdrawn. Instead the upstairs of the old frame building was remodelled as offices and more hostel accommodation was found in the Lane. Downstairs the many wooden pillars of the three-property space (later extended to five properties) compelled various adaptations of the ground floor area for tight-packed meetings. The hall had no heating and the floor squeaked atrociously when walked on.

Lena Clark who had spent seven years among them describes the scene in 1940: On Sunday morning crowds gather quietly at 9.30 to hear the preaching of the Word, the women sitting on one side and the men on the other, the hall being wider than it is long. On the backless benches all must sit as close as possible to make the maximum use of the space, for outside the building on three sides more people sit at the windows and the big double doors or listen to the loudspeakers, and there is even an overflow upstairs. As well as the poor the educated and rich are here: doctors mingle with labourers, lawyers, and teachers with rickshaw men and cooks. Among the modestly clad sisters are not a few modern women and girls with fashionable hair-styles and make-up, short sleeves and daringly slit cheongsams of tasteful silks. Children run about, dogs wander in, hawkers enter the lane, cars honk in the road outside, and the P.A. system is erratic. But each Sunday the word of the Cross is faithfully preached. Sin and salvation, the new life in Christ and the eternal purpose of God, service, and spiritual warfare—all are expounded and nothing is held back. They are given the strongest food and the straightest challenge.

With Watchman's return to preaching an eager crowd hung on his every utterance. Standing there in his dark-blue cotton gown he held their attention with his gentle manner, his simple but thorough reasoning and his apt analogies. No one ever saw him use any notes for he remembered and could reproduce anything he read. To illustrate a thing visually he would draw a swift imaginary sketch in the air (which a young worker might reproduce on poster paper afterwards) and if to illumine some point he told a personal anecdote it was nearly always a story against himself. His keen sense of humour sent frequent ripples of laughter round the hall and 'you never got sleepy in his meetings'. But from start to finish he never strayed from his subject. 'What matters,' he used to say, 'is the effectiveness of the word proclaimed', and unfailingly at the end he had left a clear and deep impression on the minds and hearts of his hearers.

Always Charity was present, quiet and reserved and preferring to be a little separated from the throng but supporting him in all he did. Her sister Faith (Mrs. Bao) was, like the other women workers, more actively involved with the personal counselling, and so was Watchman's second sister Kuei-cheng (Mrs. Lin) who slipped away when she could from her other responsibilities in the town to give help behind the scenes with the sisters' needs. And always, too, in the background were Peace Wang, large, cheerful, and reassuring, and Ruth Lee, small and bird-like, wise-looking and infinitely kind.

In the spring of 1940 Watchman gave the congregation a series of down-to-earth studies on Abraham, Isaac, and Jacob under the title 'God's dealings with His People'[1] which was particularly telling in its later sections. With his return from Europe he also brought to his preaching on the Church a more 'spiritual' or mystical note. 'The Church, the Overcomers and God's Eternal Purpose' was the theme of his first Conference addresses, and these were followed by an extended course on 'The Church, the Body and the Mystery' for believers and fellow-workers.[2] Witness Lee was among those present and returned to his spiritually thriving Chefoo congregation greatly enriched. In order to continue with them he was shortly to reject an attractive invitation for Bible training in the United States.

This spiritual emphasis, which was not wholly characteristic of Nee, catered unwittingly to a taste among the dedicated women missionaries who had rejoined him from the West and who now, with others from various connections in Shanghai, constituted a growing body of foreign sympathizers. Some had already resigned from their missions to attach themselves to Nee's work and there was a tacit expectation among these that others would follow their example. In London, back in 1938, W. H. Aldis had expressed to Nee his 'sincere hope that on your return to Shanghai it may be possible for there to be more and closer fellowship in service between yourself and those associated with you and the C.I.M.'[3] This hope may have been realized in certain local instances, but it is hardly surprising that on any large scale it was destined to be disappointed. The field directorates of the C.I.M. and other missions continued to view Nee's work with caution, though the main ground for this was still perhaps his image as a sheep-stealer of converts in the field.[4]

Of the missionaries Dr. Thornton Stearns had lately been invited to participate with the Chinese as a church elder, but apart from him there were unhappily no foreign men associated with Wen Teh Li. This was a grave lack, for a few of the ladies were unquestionably carried away with adulation of Nee as something exceptional as a man of God. To them, not only was the church at Hardoon Road the supreme expression of the Body of Christ in Shanghai: the only person in China through whom they might discover God's will was 'our Brother'. They became preoccupied with the 'new teaching' of God's eternal purpose of dominion for His children and saw everything concerned with the mere salvation of unbelievers as digression from this. Service and witness, prayer and the Quiet Time could easily, in these terms, be mere 'exercises of the natural man'.

What this terrific revelation of the Body of Christ called for was the breaking of that natural man by a long probation. So, 'sit quiet and let God do everything!'

Such extravagances lent support to the charge that some folk left their missions and sat at Hardoon Road doing nothing. Whatever the element of truth in this, the impression given was of paralysing inertia, a fear to move lest they act 'out of the Spirit'. Visible activity for Christ seemed to be despised and abandoned in favour of something conceived to be higher. On such evidence the view has been expressed that Nee's effect on foreigners was unhelpful, but it might be asked rather, was it not the effect of some of these on him that was open to question? Certainly at one point, faced with an influx of Westerners, he confided in the Stearns that he feared some of these 'come-outers' from the missions and even discussed with Thornton the formation of a separate meeting for them. And in 1941, to two idealist but ill-informed young missionaries, eager on slender grounds to fling themselves headlong into his work, his counsel was psychologically sound: 'You have had a pretty disturbed time and need a good holiday. Go to the beach and find some children and wrestle with them!'—a prescription that proved both timely and rapidly curative. The mature conclusion of one of these is probably just, that since what Hardoon Road represented for China was Christianity without foreign strings, it was arguable that foreigners, with some notable exceptions, did not fit into this context. Those missionaries who appreciated the 'local church' witness in the field often did the work and themselves the greatest service by standing humbly alongside to pray over it in its growing-pains while themselves remaining in their missions.

Spiritual inertia was never in fact a feature of the 'Little Flock' work. If some groups, preoccupied with their growth in grace, made Bible study their first exercise, most were very vigorous indeed in their evangelistic witness and outreach. They supported it too with imaginative follow-up of converts for whose instruction Watchman now supplied a series of papers on the fundamentals of salvation. Even the Foochow 'gospel shirts' continued as a feature of the street and village witness. And in Wen Teh Li an extensive children's Sunday School work for which there was not space in the halls went on largely unnoticed in homes. Watchman's excellent gospel tracts have already been mentioned. Well-written and brightly coloured they invited distribution and discussion of their contents. Christian shopkeepers kept them ready at the cash desk or on display stands, like the one a visitor found in the midst of a long sales counter of glassware. Watchman's clear instructions to believers on how to introduce men to the Friend of sinners was supported by his own unremitting example, for though God might give to the church some to be evangelists, the instruction to Timothy to 'do the work of an evangelist' he held to be binding upon all.[5] Witness to at least one person a day, was his rule. He was thrilled therefore to discover how, when in a lane of twelve houses a maidservant believed, she decided to start work on the maid in the house on her right, and having won her to the Lord had worked on down the lane until, by the time the story reached his ears, six maidservants had found the Saviour.

Yet though these were, by general consent, some of the best years in the church in Shanghai its witness went on in the face of an astonishing amount of criticism. They were charged with fickleness because the layout of the hall and the character of the activities was so flexible, and because special meetings would be put on at short notice when there was a burden on the preacher's heart and not at some obvious fixed season. From another angle there were attacks on Watchman's doctrine, and one respected missionary, while acknowledging that 'so many in China today are turning to Mr. Nee as a teacher and leader to bring them back to the truths of the New Testament', felt it necessary to publish an attack upon his 'serious error' of usurping the term 'apostle' for his pioneer workers and charging him with 'drawing away multitudes of disciples after himself'.[6] And a Chinese who claimed to have inside knowledge published a pamphlet averring that Watchman had access to a steady flow of foreign funds with which to support his work, and even attacking his integrity in their use.[7] Stature as a leader seemed but to invoke the proverb 'He who raises his head above the heads of others will sooner or later be decapitated.' Or, in more Scriptural terms, 'All that would live godly in Christ Jesus shall suffer persecution.'[8]

In his private valuation of the missions it was the Christian and Missionary Alliance that topped the list, and for a while he was on very friendly terms with one of its missionaries, who however then disappointed him by writing a magazine article criticizing him and his work, as he felt, unjustly. He had however a philosophy of his own regarding self-vindication. 'If I proved myself right, my brother would be proved wrong; but what advantage would it be to me that my brother was proved wrong?' More seriously, he recognized that what we do to our brethren in the Lord will be the basis of his treatment of us in practical things. If we are gracious, He is gracious.[9]

For this reason he suppressed his feelings and, retiring from preaching, slipped away out of sight to Chefoo for some weeks. There a friend found him in the depths of depression and, sensing his need of emotional release, challenged him: 'Have you tried praising the Lord?' 'I'll try it,' he said, and going out on the tennis court and summoning the full power of his now healthy lungs he bellowed 'Hallelujah!' The prescription worked and he was shortly back on the platform again.

Someone in Shanghai had given him a baby Fiat which spent most of its life shut away in a garage, but into which he occasionally folded his long limbs and drove off on ministry with some fellow-worker. Once, with Faithful Luke who was on a visit from Malaya, he drove to Hangchow to enjoy the ministry of a young worker, Stephen Kaung whose gift as a Bible teacher, they agreed, held great promise for the future. Stephen and his wife were shortly to be sent by the church to help forward the work in Singapore, narrowly escaping from there before the invading Japanese.

There were happy tokens too of God's personal care of them. One day the Nees were invited to tea by a lady who surprised Charity by handing her a parcel. She opened it, to find Watchman's wedding gift to her, the Bible that had disappeared from their home after the Japanese landings. This was the story. A China missionary speaking at a meeting in Ireland had exclaimed during his talk, 'If only I had with me a Chinese Bible I could expound this passage so much more clearly!' To his surprise one was produced. 'How did you come by this?' he asked. A friend's son, it appeared, had been in the British forces in the Concession, and yielding to the looting instinct had entered their empty home and picked up a book. On the fly-leaf he read in English: 'Reading this book will keep you from sin; sin will keep you from reading this book.' This must be a Bible he thought, and kept it as a memento. The missionary looked at the inscription and found there names in Chinese that he recognized: 'Charity from Watchman'. He asked and was readily given permission to return it.

Mother Nee, ever on the go, had left her husband in Hong Kong with the eldest daughter Kuei-chen (Mrs. Chan) and was staying for a while with Watchman and Charity in Shanghai. Though in the church she was just one of the sisters, she was still the dominating mother in the home. She was constantly out preaching, praying for the sick, witnessing to anyone from professional men to opium addicts. Yet she fussed over her son, concerned lest, when he himself was out visiting, nobody would think to give him anything to eat. This could have irked him, but he had by now come to terms with his ancestry and parental upbringing. 'Sometimes we feel we must have been born into the wrong family!' he had told his fellow-workers in June 1940, 'but God determined whose child we should be. Joseph, with a special work to do for Him, might well have wished for different brothers; but "*God*", he could say, "sent me before you to preserve life". Our whole life right through, and not merely since our conversion, is prepared by God to fit us for fulfilling His highest purpose. Samuel, Isaiah, Jeremiah, Paul, all were God's men, prepared long, long before the need arose. "It is not of him that willeth, nor of him that runneth, but of God." '[10]

On Sunday, 7 December 1941 the Japanese attacked Pearl Harbour in Honolulu. At 8.00 a.m. next morning in a gentle drizzle of rain, as though heaven wept for Shanghai's five million souls, the Japanese sank the American and British gunboats at anchor in the Whangpoo and entered and occupied the International and French concessions. The action was swift and complete. Barbed wire barricades were flung across the roads, cars were commandeered, bicycles were at a premium, buses disappeared, food prices quickly soared. As the death-rate increased among the refugees warehouses were piled high with coffins, since none who died in the city might be carried forth to burial. Crime grew fast, and the Japanese did not care. Fear of their terrible retaliation protected them.

On 18 December 1941, in Hong Kong, Watchman's father died suddenly of a heart attack just one week before the Japanese occupation of that city. He was 64. Not long after Watchman was able to travel there and make the funeral arrangements. Ni Weng-hsiu had died a true child of God.

14

WITHDRAWAL

ONE advantage the revivalist preacher enjoys is his freedom to move on, leaving to others—and to God—the care of the fruits of his labours. By working as an apostle, planting churches and concerning himself with their upbuilding, Watchman had assumed a far weightier spiritual burden and one that told heavily upon him during these years of political crisis and the breakdown of communications. Most serious of all was the moral responsibility he felt for the young full-time workers who, without assured salary of any kind, were scattered throughout the country faithfully serving in the gospel. His own early experiences in proving God for his practical needs had given him some understanding of the testings they went through in their costly service for God. As he had put it after observing one of them passing through a severe trial of faith, 'to keep our hand on the plough while wiping away our tears—that is Christianity'.[1] So he could write to a colleague, 'Affairs of the churches, and things of this part of the world, are weighing heavily upon me. I am not buoyant, but treading on with trust in the Lord.'

It may be asked how this fast-expanding work, with some two hundred full-time workers, extensive travels, a publishing programme, rented premises and plans to own property, was financially supported. The main principle was the tithing of personal income. This was at no time legalistically enforced since the 'tenth' was seen as a token of one's giving one's all to God; but the principle of giving was taught and sedulously practised, and as a result all local Assembly Hall churches were self-supporting. There was, however, as we have seen, a distinction between the churches with their eldership and the work with its fellow-workers who were not necessarily answerable to any local church. These when out breaking new ground with the gospel might be involved, over and above their family's livelihood, in such outlays as the temporary hire of halls and the printing of Scripture portions and tracts. They might receive gifts from the churches and from individual Christians, and were taught the life of faith, but for spiritual counselling and material support they were in some degree the personal care of Watchman Nee himself. Some forty of them were in practice his direct responsibility. The Work's finances were handled therefore as a fund separate from the church offerings, controlled by him and two or three senior fellow-workers.

The Chinese have a special flair for commerce, and the saving Good News had brought many successful businessmen into the church. Some of these expressed their love for the Lord in generous financing of the extensive outreach of the work. In a penetrating talk on 'the mammon of unrighteousness' given at this period Nee shows how, if Egypt is to be 'spoiled' in God's favour, our money must be brought, not sent, across the boundary that divides the world's currency from God's; that is, we ourselves must come across that line.[2] Accordingly he did not discourage secular employment, rather he followed the apostle Paul's instructions to Titus: 'Affirm confidently that those who have believed God should be careful to apply themselves to honest tasks.' 'Let our people learn to enter honourable occupations, so as to help cases of urgent need, and not to be unfruitful.'[3]

But with the earlier disruption of the Yangtze trade by the Japanese occupation of the eastern seaboard many Chinese commercial interests were crippled, and in as far as it depended on these the whole financial structure of the Lord's work had been hard hit. Twice at a critical time, soon after his return from overseas, Watchman had received gifts from Britain for the work. Now with the outbreak of hostilities between Japan and the United States inflation rocketed still further and Chinese commerce in the Concession almost reached a standstill. Any release and movement of funds for Christian enterprise became well-nigh impossible. So it was that he now saw many of these loyal young 'apostles' and their families hungry, physically sick and financially destitute. For ordinary church members were not much better off, and neither they nor he had funds left with which to come to their aid.

Thus it comes about that Watchman Nee's story now takes an unexpected turn and one which some may feel to be out of character. Dismayed at this mounting problem he had for some months sought God for a solution. Now, early in 1942, he took a step to which he felt sure God had led him, but which was to raise big questions in the minds of some of his friends.

His brother George, with a BSc in Chemistry from St. John's University, had set up as a research chemist with his own laboratories. He had also built up in Shanghai a manufacturing and distributing pharmaceutical company, Nee Brothers, in which some of the family had part shares. It was not thriving because George was a teacher and a scientist rather than a business man. Watchman saw, however, that here was something with potential. While non-military in character, it could yet remain viable because it met a war-time need.

As long ago as 1938 while in London Watchman had sought advice for his brother on securing a licence to manufacture sulphanilamide. Now he conceived the idea of floating an associated company for the manufacture of high quality synthetic drugs, employing his brother's experience as a chemist and turning over the excess profits to the work of the Lord. So was born the China Biological and Chemical (CBC) Laboratories, 9 Kiaochou Road, Shanghai. As manager he invited from Hong Kong C. L. Yin, who years ago as a young patient at Kuling Sanatorium had rejected his witness, only to be captured for the Lord by John Sung. To begin with as Chairman of Directors Watchman left things to the management and merely kept a helpful eye on the project, slipping into a modern-style gown to attend a business appointment and then returning to informal dress for visiting the saints, his old slouch hat on the side of his head making him, as one remarked, look like a brigand. Faithful Luke tells how with David Tan and Philip Luan he visited the simple home at 13 Yu-Hua Villas where Watchman and Charity lived, and as they sat in the almost unheated room with the blackout curtains and the windows pasted with anti-shatter strips, he put the question many were asking: Why have you left the work of God to go into commerce? 'I am merely doing what Paul did in Corinth and Ephesus,'[4] he replied. 'It is something exceptional, and it is part-time. I give an hour a day to training company representatives; after that I do the Lord's work.' And the representatives were his hard-pressed 'apostles' who were encouraged now to mingle their gospel witness with their paid employment. But when pressed he added ruefully, 'I am like a woman who has lost her husband, and must go out to work from financial necessity.'

Significantly however he later admitted a contributory reason: his growing boredom. As a brilliant man he perhaps felt beset with the mediocre, starved of the stimulus of interchange with bigger minds. His trouble then may be recognized as the mediaeval sin of accidie, 'a contempt of holy exercise, a hatred of one's profession ... so peculiar that when the psalms are being sung it causes its victim to interrupt the verse with an untimely yawn'.[5] His reaction, therefore, at first of rebellion and then of stedfastness in adversity, can be interpreted in the light of Chaucer's remedy: 'Against this rotten sin of accidie and the branches of the same there is a virtue that is called fortitude. This virtue maketh folk to undertake hard and grievous things of their own will, wisely and reasonably.'[6]

But his new way of life very early raised questions with the four Shanghai church elders, Chu Cheng, Tu Cheng-chen, Dr. Yu, and another no longer named. Their image of him had become tarnished and he was now in their eyes a renegade, or to change the metaphor, a ploughman who had looked back from the furrow. How fit, they asked, was such a one to minister the Word? Already towards the end of 1942 they asked him to discontinue preaching at Wen Teh Li, although it is possible that Dr. Yu, a sensitive man, demurred for he himself retired forthwith from preaching. Watchman was downhearted and did not know what to do. 'I envy you,' he said to C. L. Yin as they sat together sharing a bag of his beloved Fukien oranges. 'You are free to do what you like in the factory, and if then you go and say a few words at the meeting they will acclaim you a very zealous brother. No one will question you. But me? Twenty-four hours a day they want to know exactly how I spend my time. I am a marked man.'

The shock to the rank-and-file believers of their elders' action was very severe, and not unnaturally it raised speculation that there were more serious grounds for it than the ones given. Ill-wishers pointed to his business lunches with people of the world, the kind of people to whom in the past his witness had often been most fruitful. Since the responsible brothers remained silent he felt his whole testimony to be in question; yet because of the many workers dependent on him he had no freedom to abandon the course he had adopted. There is no evidence that in the following two years they made any approach to him. For his part he recalled Margaret Barber's meekness in the face of his own tirades and once again he made no attempt at self-vindication but accepted their action as a discipline from God who would in His own way justify Himself.

Understandably Charity who was actively helping him in the business did not at once appreciate this attitude. One day she heard Watchman answer a phone call in which the voice at the other end went on and on at a high volume. Watchman simply listened to it all, answering now and again with 'Yes ... yes ... thank you ... thank you.' 'Whoever was that?' she asked, when he had rung off. 'It was a brother telling me all I have been doing wrong.' 'And were you guilty of all that?' she asked. 'No,' he replied. 'Then why did you not give him an explanation instead of just saying "thank you"?' she exclaimed impatiently. 'If anyone exalts Ni To-sheng to heaven,' was the reply, 'he is still Ni To-sheng. And if anyone tramples him down to hell, he remains Ni To-sheng.' God was righteous, and to him that was sufficient. Characteristically he is known to have ministered secret financial help to some of the brothers who were opposing him.

By the early months of 1943 the Japanese had made ready their internment camps or Civil Assembly Centres and to these the foreigners were led off in batches. Watchman did all he could for his friends, turning up thoughtfully with articles likely to be of value in the difficult days ahead, and was especially concerned for Dr. Stearns who was in hospital and in fact too ill to go with his family into camp. On 16 March, the night before Elizabeth Fischbacher and Phyllis Deck were due to enter the Lunghua camp south of the city, the Nees entertained them in their little home with the single stove and the red and black curtains. Over a simple meal they prayed to God, proclaiming together His faithfulness; then the ladies returned late to their flat at 17 Bedford Terrace. Finding she had left the key inside Phyllis Deck climbed, as they sometimes did, on to a shed to reach a window at the back, and while doing so suffered a stroke and fell to her death. One of the most sane and godly of the missionary friends of the work, she died, it is said, still smiling.

For the C.B.C. Watchman had coined the Chinese name 'Sheng Hua Drug Manufacturing Company', enshrining it, as a sales gimmick, in a clever couplet proclaiming the drugs' efficacy. Besides producing such basic antibacterials as mercurochrome they began to manufacture sulphathiazole, sulphaguanidine, vitamin B concentrates, and Yatren. Of course there were problems he had not foreseen, and the demands of the project soon began to make inroads on his time, for in a business you are not your own master. There was commercial jealousy and cut-throat competition with the other big concerns who were each fighting to come up with the first output of a new drug. There were complaints from shareholders, and accidents reported from sensitivity to the Vitamin B injections. Moreover the family business was a weak link, bringing him into suspicion because it claimed as distributor the first batch of a new product. His organizing and conciliatory gifts were called into play in handling what would at any time be a delicate operation, aggravated now by the conditions of war. As a result Watchman was frequently absent from Shanghai.

Now, having made arrangements with his brother George for the flow of remittances to the workers, he planned a longer absence. With the Japanese armies thrusting westward against Chiang Kai-shek's stronghold, it was nevertheless possible for a Chinese civilian, by using air travel and choosing his route, to cross the war front. He now set out for Chungking whence reports had already reached Shanghai of spiritual awakening in the still free provinces. There the finest refugee Universities and the shrewdest commercial and banking speculators in the land were bringing the far west swiftly into the twentieth century, and as it was no part of Watchman's plan to be marketing drugs to the Japanese army, he began to investigate alternative lines of distribution in areas where the need was greatest. In this he was highly successful, soon obtaining government contracts that by degrees brought C.B.C. up from one of the least to a place among the foremost of China's pharmaceutical importers and manufacturing wholesalers. If the people of Foochow are famed for their inability to do business, this one gave no support to the legend. He was to spend two and a half years in frequent travel between Shanghai and Chungking, where he rented a small dwelling and Charity joined him, her young brother Samuel also having business interests in Szechwan. The meeting of believers in the city had been augmented by the influx of displaced Christians and was thriving under the ministry of Stephen Kaung who, with his wife Mary, had escaped via India from the Japanese occupation of Singapore. Watchman laid himself out to help some of the refugee brothers with employment in the pharmaceutical industry. From time to time he preached the Word with his accustomed clarity and vigour, and in 1945 gave a series of talks on the Seven Churches in Asia, equating these with the subsequent phases of church history in such a way as to reinforce his own views on the special place of the local church in God's missionary strategy.[7]

Thus in his dual role he was intellectually extended as never before, and enjoyed it, but his physique, fragile at the best of times, began to show marks of the stress imposed upon him. For a while the demands of the business were so great that he had little or no strength remaining for any direct work for the Lord. His eldest sister's son Stephen Chan, who was a student at Fu Tan University, met them both one day in a Chungking Restaurant in 1945 and found Watchman so preoccupied with secular cares as almost to have lost his old rest of spirit.[8] Evidently it was time for a change.

Meanwhile in Shanghai the Hardoon Road meetings had struggled on for a while with diminished numbers and then, partly from discouragement and partly to avoid joining the Religious Union sponsored by the Occupying Power, had dispersed altogether to meet in believers' homes. This was also a wise precaution. The Japanese had instituted a blockade complex of road barriers at every city block which, at a signal, would suddenly be closed for hours or even days. In cases of severe reprisal they might even remain shut for weeks, causing unspeakable suffering since none might move out of the section in which he was trapped. Like other Christian groups in Shanghai therefore the Hardoon Road church survived, if at all, in private houses where those whom the Spirit moved took what lead they could.

But the eight-year-long war was dragging to its conclusion. A final

Japanese thrust southward from Hankow, by cutting China in two, nearly brought down the Chungking government, and then Japan, with her own home islands heavily bombed and the U.S. land forces poised for invasion, accepted on 16 August 1945 the allied terms of capitulation. Armistice with China was signed on 9 September at Nanking.

With travel no longer a hazard Watchman left Chungking. At Christmas he was in Hong Kong and he soon arrived back in Shanghai, but still not to preaching, nor yet to a restored church. The saints were in spiritual need, but remained confused by rumours about him. It was hinted that he had misused church funds, or alternatively that he had collaborated with the Japanese. Even his close colleagues admitted to an unease about his secular employment. Clearly he himself could not interfere. 'I have put it,' he told a friend, 'into God's hands.'

In the months that followed he began quietly making plans to detach himself from C.B.C. Having satisfied the shareholders, he and George, as agreed, set aside a large accumulation of profits for transfer to the work and for future provision for the workers. Next he travelled to Foochow, where the family home at 17 Customs Lane in Nantai had fallen vacant. It had a large garden and outbuildings and would adapt ideally as a centre of training for workers. As head of the family he now took steps to reoccupy it and with Charity's help to bring it into use for the Lord.

Back here in his boyhood surroundings he sought to adjust his thinking with fasting and prayer and the Scriptures open before him. Throughout those difficult years he had not ceased to study the Word and to plan ahead for the extension of the gospel. The problem now was where to begin. The confusion in Shanghai required that he wait quietly to see how God would move. The faithful Dr. C. H. Yu had returned to preaching there and in face of odds was slowly drawing the believers together, appealing to them on the ground of Christ indwelling to be reconciled one to another. Progress however was pathetically slow. Something more seemed needed.

Watchman bethought himself now of his friend Witness Lee. Behind the Japanese lines in Shantung war conditions had not been so hard, and meetings in the coastal cities had grown rapidly in numbers. Particularly was this so in Chefoo where Lee had been preaching the Word with great power and remarkable results. Now in mid-1946 Watchman wrote from Foochow presenting to him the needs of Shanghai and appealing to him to come to their aid. Finding God confirming this in his heart, Lee moved south with his family to

Nanking and from there as base gave himself to the overdue task of recovery in that city and in Shanghai.

The message he brought reinforced that of Dr. Yu. The living Christ indwelling them was His people's hope of unity, even as He was their source of life. But Lee was an activist and where Watchman as a profound Bible student had laid doctrinal foundations Lee's more volatile temperament introduced something of the Shantung excitement and fire. This brought quick returns and in a matter of months confidence was restored and people were flocking again to the meetings which soon began to snowball.

Lee is energetic and authoritarian, thriving on large numbers, and has a flair for organizing people. This gift he now brought to bear on the confused situation in Shanghai. Early in 1947 the growing numbers attending were grouped on a district basis, and the pattern which developed in the ensuing twelve months was as follows. Twice a week they met at Wen Teh Li as the one 'church in Shanghai', at 10.0 a.m. on the morning of the Lord's Day for the ministry of the Word (the first Sunday of each month being evangelistic, the others for edification) and on Saturday evening for fellowship. Three times weekly they met as *chias* or 'families'[9] in fifteen separate locations for the breaking of bread on the Lord's Day evening, for prayer on Tuesday evening and for instruction of new believers on Friday evening. In addition there was a Wednesday evening evangelistic meeting centred in four *chias*. The elders remained in over-all charge of the whole church, but each *chia* had a leading brother and a leading sister with several others, designated 'deacons in training', to help them with the charge of duties and to instruct inquirers.

It was soon found that people tended to wander from one district to another, so by June 1948 people were allocated to their districts with the injunction 'obey them that have the rule over you',[10] and had to apply for permission to change. By this date also, because of the rising numbers, the problem of pastoral care had become acute. The groups of from 40 to 200 believers in the *chias* were therefore subdivided again into sections or *pais*[11] of an average of 15 persons, often comprising those in a single street or lane, with two persons in responsibility for each *pai* to watch the believers' attendance at meetings and care for their spiritual condition. This system conserved some values discovered during the church's dispersal under the Japanese, namely the intimacy of smaller meetings in which more can participate in prayer and discussion, and the development of spiritual gifts in those compelled to take a lead. It is to be noted that there were no men's or women's meetings, no special meetings for students or other classes of the populace, since the church was without class. But the existence of gifted women preachers seems to have created a problem. Occasional women's meetings would be arranged for them, but a young Christian in the Canton meeting recalls one day finding men suspending a large white sheet across the width of the hall. He asked what it was for and was told that Ruth Lee and Peace Wang were visiting the local church. Since they must not preach to men, the brothers would therefore sit behind the sheet and listen to their messages from there!

Evangelism was not the task of the preacher alone but of the whole church. All believers were trained as 'counsellors'. At the end of a gospel address everyone turned and counselled the person sitting beside him, noting his name and address, asking him questions, letting him talk, and if possible, but without pressure, getting him to pray calling on the name of the Lord, for sometimes in that very act he would be saved. Missionaries who saw this in action were understandably impressed.

On Friday evenings there was exposition of the Word specially geared to those who had newly believed. In 1948 Watchman was asked to supply fifty-two lessons of systematic instruction in Christian fundamentals, ranging from justification by faith to the practical principles of church life.[12] These lessons were followed by each Shanghai group leader and came to be widely used in most churches. The year's course was virtually compulsory for those who meant business with God, absentees being followed up and taken through the lessons personally at home. If you came to the Lord for salvation you soon knew what it was all about.

The effect of so much energetic organization however meant that something of the earlier freedom in the Spirit began to be lost. A clock-in system was soon to be introduced at meetings which, together with a full index of believers' addresses, employment, family, etc., meant that your failure of attendance could be quickly followed up.[13] The Lord's Table was 'fenced' and you were formally introduced and wore a badge with your name. No longer might you be accepted simply on your own testimony that you were born again and loved the Lord. In the past the Table had always been a place where conscience and the Holy Spirit's conviction were given full play in a man's heart. Now however your detachment from other Christian connections and committal to the Meeting Hall churches was first carefully examined. And Watchman's advice to a brother in 1940: 'Don't expect the Holy Spirit to be doing the same thing in Tsingtao as in Shanghai: give Him liberty', was soon to give place to regimentation imposed by a strong authoritarian hand at the centre of the work. Witness Lee was careful of course to disown the concept of 'organization', explaining that, like a cup containing drinking water, these arrangements were merely the vessels for communicating spiritual things. But he exhorted everyone in the church to be submissive. 'Do nothing without first asking,' he urged. 'Since the Fall man does as he pleases. Here there is order. Here there is authority. The Church is a place of strict discipline.'[14]

15

RETURN

DURING the latter years of the war the Chinese Communist Party had been conducting from their headquarters in the loess caves of Yenan a single-minded campaign against the occupying power. One of the legacies of their 1935 Long March had been the development of technical skill in guerilla warfare based on mobility and the absence of fixed bases. This they had put into effective operation to confine the Japanese to the cities and establish close contact with the ordinary Chinese villagers behind their lines. They had successfully applied their agrarian policy of land reform in considerable areas around the Yellow River and these of course remained effective after the allied victory.

A second consequence of the March had been the emergence of Mao Tse-tung as undoubted leader and ideologist whose 'thoughts' were now established as infallible guide-lines as the Party thrashed out its ambitious policies for the future. And the third legacy was an impressive self-discipline that bound together the disparate elements of the C.C.P. into a unified force, frugal and abstemious in its way of life by contrast with the luxury of Chiang's Kuomintang leaders, and wholly convinced of the validity of its goals. As a result, while during hostilities many Chinese business men and intellectuals had chosen to migrate to Chungking and the south-west, the more idealist thinkers, eager for a clean-up of the country's internal disorder and corruption, had gone to Yenan for inspiration. It was thus known in Shanghai that in the northwest was an impressive body of men with clear-sighted plans for the future.

Since the war's end and Chiang Kai-shek's return to Nanking, distrust between the Nationalist government and the Communist Party had developed into a hostility which even the skilled and sincere diplomacy of General George C. Marshall had failed to allay. Chiang's extreme hatred of the C.C.P. led him once again to launch a massive campaign of extermination which overran much of the area where land-reform had taken root, and by March 1947 he had even captured Yenan. For a moment the Nationalists seemed to have triumphed. But it was an empty victory, for the Communist guerilla ethic made such a success largely meaningless. Mao Tse-tung's armies had merely stepped aside and were in fact poising themselves for a spring.

In the hearts of those bearing responsibility in the Assembly Hall churches the concern occasioned by Watchman Nee's prolonged absence from their ministry was very great. Already in 1946 Witness Lee had challenged the Shanghai elders: 'Were you in the Spirit when you made the decision to reject him? And what was the effect? Can you say it brought life?' 'No,' they had replied sorrowfully to each question. The remorse felt among the fellow-workers and their patient search for a way back is well expressed by one of them in April 1947. 'Brother Nee's case was a mortal wound to us, and words cannot tell how far the consequences go. The charge that he collaborated with the enemy is entirely groundless and much else that has been said was not based upon pure facts. This was the work of the devil and shows our own spiritual deficiency at that time, but we hope we may have learned our lesson. Objections to his coming back to our midst have been gradually eliminated. He is ready, and there is a growing desire for his return. The brothers here at Shanghai repeatedly visit him in his home, and through such fellowship hearts are bound together and barriers are cleared away. So we are waiting for the right moment.'

At Watchman's request two Christian businessmen had been found to relieve him of his remaining responsibilities in the drug company, and in April he was free to leave again for Foochow, expressing before going his readiness to return to the church in Shanghai at any time. In Fukien as elsewhere missionaries had been thronging back to their stations and rounding up their scattered flocks, but the number of foreign staff was less than before. The missions therefore had superfluous holiday properties in the Kuliang hill-station east of the city. Two of these were for sale, spacious one-storey stone cottages protected with typhoon-walls on their ocean-facing sides. These Watchman purchased for use as a long-term training centre for men and women workers.

Here in the summer of 1947 a small group of workers from Fukien, Chekiang, and elsewhere, including his old school friend K. H. Weigh on leave from Hong Kong, joined him for an intensive course of studies. In an initial series of ten addresses Watchman returned to his spiritual starting-point, the foundation principles of his message of the Cross. Widely read since then under the title *The Release of the Spirit*, they are concerned with the principle of 'brokenness' as a condition of the release of divine power, and with the pivotal words of Jesus, 'Unless a grain of wheat falls into the earth and dies, it remains alone; but if it dies, it bears much fruit.'[1] They formed a fitting basis for a new beginning. But this was not all.

In Shanghai God had greatly used him in recent meetings for newly converted students at a national university. Now in Foochow some-one hired for him the large hall of the American Mission and im-mense crowds came from the area around to hear the former Trinity student. God seemed to be placing His seal afresh upon His servant's evangelistic witness.

Towards the year-end Witness Lee, who had till now concen-trated his energies on Shanghai and Nanking, yielded to pressure and paid a visit to the local churches in the famine-ridden southern prov-inces, ending in February 1948 with a series of meetings in Foo-chow. When these were over he and those with him, who included Miss Peace Wang, came for counsel to Watchman in his home in Customs Lane, Nantai. Since the Allied victory the wider work had been left to care for itself and Lee had observed with concern the weakness and isolation of its scattered labourers. He strongly ap-proved Watchman's training programme and looked forward to discussing further with him the revolutionary methods of evangel-ism he himself had been free to develop in the Japanese occupied north.

Churches in the coastal cities of Shantung had grown in size dur-ing the mid-forties and Lee had conceived the plan of evangelism by migration, though it is not certain whether this idea originated with him or from Watchman's observation of the remarkable fruitfulness of the war-time migratory movement to the south-west. Certainly for reasons of population and trade the Chinese had constantly emi-grated, north across the Wall into Manchuria, west into Sinkiang, south and east into the Southern Ocean. 'Now,' said the respons-ible brothers in Shantung, 'we have vast meetings here on the coast, and it is both impractical and unrewarding to maintain lonely pioneers indefinitely in the distant regions. Let a whole group of believers uproot themselves from Chefoo and settle as a self-support-ing economic unit in an unevangelized area. There let them become a nucleus of Christian life and witness.'

For precedent they found in Acts the statement that 'There arose on that day a great persecution against the church which was in Jerusalem; and they were all scattered abroad throughout the re-gions of Judaea and Samaria except the apostles. They therefore . . . went about preaching the word.' And again, 'They that were scat-tered abroad travelled as far as Phoenicia and Cyprus and Antioch . . . speaking the word and preaching the Lord Jesus.'[2] 'As yet,' said the brothers, 'we have no such persecution, but even without one we can follow their example and disperse.'

Lee made a study of the matter and carefully worked out the details. Groups of families, selected as to personnel and representing a suitable cross-section of trades and professions—gardeners, shoe-makers, teachers, nurses, barbers—were chosen and carefully pre-pared for their venture. (The barber's trade was popular. It required little equipment and gave ready scope for witnessing.) All these gave themselves to the church who supplied their travel expenses and three months' living costs at their destination. At the end of that period they were expected to support themselves in the new setting.

Back in the spring of 1943 two parties left the Chefoo church, one of thirty families going northward into Manchuria, another of sev-enty families to towns westward up the Paotou railway across Shansi into Sui-yuan, far beyond the Wall. Some in these groups suffered great hardships and the scheme was not wholly a success. Moreover as a result of this plan in May 1943 Lee himself came under Japanese suspicion for espionage activities and underwent with great courage a month's interrogation with flogging and the 'water treatment'. Nevertheless there was real spiritual fruit from the migratory experiment. A letter in October 1944 to Dr. C. H. Yu in Shanghai from a brother Sun of the Swatow assembly, writing from a town on the upper reaches of the Yellow River, tells how they started meetings there on 5 December 1943 with a nucleus of seven brothers and three sisters and then goes on to recount the baptism on 19 February 1944 of six men who had newly believed. 'There were no indoor arrangements to baptize them, but they were so anxious to obey the Lord that they just could not wait. So the only thing possible was to break the river ice which was two foot thick. Every day was extremely cold, but on the day chosen it be-came suddenly twenty degrees warmer. We set up a changing-tent by the riverside, and no one was frostbitten or taken ill.' On 2 March they held a second baptism of four brothers and of one sister aged 66 who normally never went out of doors in winter for fear of catching cold. This time there was more difficulty from lack of water under the ice and they had to search down the river for a deeper place. Again there were no ill-effects but only great joy, and the letter ended with words of exhortation to the Shanghai be-lievers.[3] And this was a single one of many known centres where fresh life began to spring up by these means.

Now in February 1948 in Watchman's Foochow home they dis-cussed the application of these experiences to the scene of confusion that Lee had found in the south. Might not a region like Kwangtung or Fukien, Lee suggested, be evangelized best by collective effort from a centre such as Foochow?

Watchman agreed. Jerusalem, he pointed out, was just such a centre. God's method was to concentrate His workers there, save many souls, establish a church, and thereafter disperse men from

there to Samaria and to the ends of the earth. 'What we saw at
Hankow in 1937 regarding Acts 13 and the principle of apostles
going forth from Antioch was right as far as it went; but the Book
of the Acts begins not at chapter 13 but at chapter 1. Our failure in
these few years is that we have had no structure of the work corresponding to the principle of Jerusalem. We should concentrate
fellow-workers for ministry in regional centres until local churches
are fully established and thereafter transfer whole communities to
other parts—*unless the Lord arranges a persecution to scatter them
abroad.*'⁴

Somehow this came as a flash of new light to them all. They had
come to him, Lee says, seeking to restore fellowship, but through
him God gave them something more. Just as they had earlier come
to see the churches in a strictly local city-by-city context, now they
saw the Work afresh in this broad geographical setting. It would
mean for the 'apostles' or workers an end of individualistic enterprise. 'We fellow-workers then present,' says Lee, 'willingly laid
down our work, and we decided upon Foochow as our Jerusalem
and starting-place.' Several leaders were also present from the local
church meeting at Tsin Men Road, Foochow. These called their
whole company of brothers and sisters together on 3 March, when
'they formally handed over the church and we fellow-workers
formally took it over. Thus,' says Lee, 'the work and the church in
Foochow had a new beginning.'⁵ This statement appears a startling
reversal of Watchman's earlier insistence on the local churches'
complete independence of apostolic (that is, worker) control.⁶ It is
from this point in fact that the tighter authoritarianism makes itself
felt throughout the movement, and not least in the churches outside
China. But initially this gesture by the elders in Foochow was perhaps in the main a generous act of reconciliation towards Watchman himself after twenty-four years of exclusion from its fellow-
ship.⁷

Lee was the bearer also of a conciliatory move from the Shanghai
elders. Watchman was now invited to lead a Conference at Hardoon Road in April, and felt able to accept. He arrived there to find
sixty workers from all over China and over thirty elders and others
from the Shanghai local church awaiting him. They included some
from Shantung who had seen the Communist land-reform in operation at close quarters and who entertained no illusions as to the
hostility of the Party cadres to the Christian faith.

Watchman went aside first of all with the Wen Teh Li elders and
in the presence of God made full confession of his own failings over
the past few years. With this act of reconciliation fellowship between them was at last fully restored. Among the fellow-workers he

was now welcomed back into a novel setting. Some kind of hier-archy had been established among the top echelon which gave to them an order of seniority, expressed by a row of chairs, in which the Number One seat was unanimously reserved for him. This, too, one may see as in part perhaps a gesture of confidence in him, but the slogan 'Bow to authority' was in fact to become a new and, to many, very disturbing feature of the work from now on. To us today it seems so entirely out of character with his past teachings and way of working that one wonders if it could possibly have originated (as a few have thought) in a change of mind in Nee him-self, or whether, at a time when he was spiritually vulnerable, he was caught off balance by the enthusiasms of others.

All present were now ready to rededicate themselves for co-operation with God in the much-talked-of migratory invasion of inland China. Watchman outlined to them what was in his mind. 'When God scattered the people abroad through persecution there were some thousands of believers in Jerusalem, and there was a constant movement outward.

'Yet when Paul returned to Jerusalem there were the same large numbers of believers. We must not remain stationary, but must move out and make room for others, for as many will be added as move out. Today China has about 450 million inhabitants and only one million Christians. Give all Christians the same training, then send them forth, and we shall see the Church proclaiming the gospel everywhere. They need not wait for persecution. Whether by perse-cution or not, go forth they must. For many of us half our time has gone. The remaining half must be spent in taking a straight course. If we are not faithful the Lord will choose others to go this way, but that would take at least another twenty years. We must save those twenty years for God.' As a first priority he laid special emphasis on the unevangelized north-west. 'I believe,' he concluded, 'that within a short time the whole of China can be won with the gospel. Let us give our all for this.'

Thereafter he addressed the packed church congregation, so many of whom had waited long to hear him, and one of his first messages to them was from the words of Jesus, 'Render to God the things that are God's.'[8] The effect was explosive, first of all in the turning to the Saviour of a large number of hitherto uncommitted men and women. Within the month as many as two hundred new believers were baptized and brought into the church. The meeting place which could only hold four hundred was strained to accommodate over 1,500 believers, with people sitting on the stairways and in the parlours behind the building or standing in the Lane. Urgent plans were made to purchase land for a new and larger meeting hall.

It was already known that Watchman had handed over the entire
C.B.C. business to the church. In the prevailing euphoria and the
rush to consecrate themselves to God, many now began to bring
gifts of cash, small and great, and pour them into the church offerings for the extension of the Work. Others arrived with substantial
gifts in kind. Already there was growing disillusion with the high
taxes, unchecked inflation and economic chaos promoted by the
corrupt Nationalist government, and this had produced in many a
revulsion from the world and its ways. There were those therefore
who turned over whole businesses, printing works, ink factories and
the like, as outright gifts for the church's use. Such giving up of
wealth by Christians had not been seen hitherto in China. It was
Acts chapter 4 over again with all its strengths, and, too, with room
left for its possible abuses, as when for example families were not of
one mind in an action taken. The slogan 'Render to God' was passed
nevertheless from one coastal city to another with revivalist fervour, and much spiritual blessing accompanied the fresh consecration
of lives to the Lord Jesus.

The trouble was however that from now on the churches attained
an unexampled material prosperity. They began to command extensive funds and to operate businesses (for even the C.B.C. itself,
instead of being quickly disposed of, had been retained for the
church) just at a time when 'capitalist' was to become a term of
opprobrium and when, in a régime without any concept of a Chari-
ties Commission, the mere possession of wealth was going to arouse
immediate suspicion. The case for ideological reformation of the
movement seems almost, by this ill-conceived development, to have
been presented to the Communist Party ready-made on a tray.

Now the Foochow training programme was resumed. By the
middle of June 1948 over a hundred young fellow-workers from
various cities were gathered for this in the green seclusion of Kuliang mountain. Simon Meek and Lucas Wu from Manila, and Faithful Luke from Singapore, were among those invited from overseas,
and a woman missionary of twenty years' experience, Joy Betteridge, was also present. A welcome to join them had even been
extended via Samuel Chang in the Chengtu meeting to two young
pioneers, Geoffrey Bull and George Patterson, who were however by
now headed for the Tibetan border.[9] In April Watchman had written to a friend in the West: 'Yes, I think China has a need for
missionaries. But for them to be useful as divine blessings they
should learn to be subject and to be one with the local assemblies.
As the brethren here are learning to see the authority of Christ as
Head in the Body and to cease from independent ways, it will be my
hope that brothers from abroad will be likewise. We are almost

"spoiled" by blessings everywhere, so send everyone you can spare.'

The wooded valley of Kuliang, high above the Buddhist monastery of Boiling Spring, commanded an extensive view of the Min Estuary from Pagoda Anchorage to the ocean and was an ideal setting for spiritual preparation. Here the group settled down to long, disciplined study. Watchman and Charity had a tiny cottage of their own, bright with flowers, where he waited upon God and set in order the thoughts he had amassed in the years of his withdrawal and comparative silence. His output in the months that followed was immense, and covered such varied themes as the qualifications of a Christian worker, the ministry of God's Word, the principles of spiritual authority, the problem of sickness, the promised fifty-two lessons for new believers, the local church's business affairs, the new principles of extension of the work of the gospel, and how to study the Bible.[10] At first on each Sunday Faithful Luke would do the long journey to Nantai and back to break bread with the local church, walking sorrowfully down the endless stone steps with their vista of green rice-fields, reddish-brown villages, and the ancient black city walls of Foochow. At length he approached Watchman who was still evidently unsure of where he stood with all the gathered workers. Earnestly he assured him that all was indeed well and obtained his agreement that they might meet for the Lord's Table in a little prayer hall in the hill-top hamlet of Kuliang amid its terraced fields.

When Watchman addressed the workers it was as if flood-gates long under pressure had opened. He would walk up and down with his hands behind his back, just speaking from his heart. After his talks he would invite questions, and his answers were valuable, never evasive but always frank and to the point. Every morning there would be one session given over to individual testimonies in which a worker would speak for half an hour, after which others were invited to give their criticisms, and finally Watchman would sum up for the benefit of the one concerned. The whole training programme was conducted under a strong sense of urgency. The political future in the nation was quite unknown. In his first editorial in May to a new Shanghai magazine, *The Ministry*, Watchman had written: 'These days are critical beyond anything we have thought.'

In the north the capture of Yenan by the Nationalists the previous year had proved an empty victory. It was the harsh brutalities they inflicted on innocent villagers whom they had 'released from land-reform' that were their undoing. Such acts exposed their brief gains to erosion by Communist guerillas who worked skilfully behind their lines to win peasant affections. In late June 1947 Mao Tse-tung had been able to launch units of his People's Liberation Army on a counter-drive through Honan that by September had penetrated to the Yangtze valley. Other units were redeployed to the east and north. Early in 1948 Manchuria was severed from China and by the same autumn many cities of Honan and Shantung had fallen without a struggle. Disciplined and well-led, the troops of the P.L.A. had unbounded faith in their cause. Chiang's forces by contrast were disheartened through self-loathing, ignorance of their trade and tyranny from above, and were swiftly losing what stomach they had had for civil strife. Soon whole regiments and even divisions were deserting or surrendering without a fight as discipline and loyalty to their Generalissimo ebbed away.

It was against this background of uncertainty that the Kuliang training programme soldiered on. In the winter months there was a break for review and for a conference of workers at Hardoon Road. Watchman and his colleagues found Shanghai troubled by hunger and economic distress, skyrocketing inflation, robbery, and mob-violence. Harsh police controls and repressions were making life hazardous and many of its citizens now longed for peace at almost any price.

At Wen Teh Li Watchman shared in the ministry of the Word under conditions of great solemnity and found people waiting on his every utterance. Much time was spent by the church in prayer, pleading that God would so control events that doors would stay open for the gospel. He himself went into close conclave with his workers and elders, making known to them his inner conviction, reached after much prayer, that in the event of a turn-over of government to the C.C.P. he himself should remain in Shanghai. He had read Marx and Engels and was sure that the Communists would behave very differently from the alien Japanese, and that conditions for Christian witness under Marxism would be intensely difficult. The Church might no longer be free to serve the Lord, even in suffering, and might face entire elimination. But his personal calling was to serve Him in China and to bring Christ to the Chinese people. Chiang and his ministers might retreat, but not the church of God. To the few workers present he said : 'When the older ones fall, you younger ones must continue to go forward.' He added his further recommendation that, if circumstances forced a movement of population overseas, Witness Lee should be prepared to go with his family and work for the spread of the gospel among the Chinese dispersion. Lee agreed to hold this plan before the Lord. Then the party of trainees returned to Foochow to resume their studies in Kuliang mountain.

16

CONSISTENT CHOICE

ON 31 JANUARY 1949 the Communist Eighth Route Army entered an undefended Peking. By April the armies of liberation were grouped on the muddy north bank of the two-mile-wide Yangtze. Nearly half a million Kuomintang troops were deployed along the southern bank facing them, supported by a powerful navy and air force. Yet when on 20 April Mao Tse-tung and Chu Teh gave the order to cross the river and liberate the south, the flotillas of junks, rafts, and sampans went over almost unopposed. Nanking, the Southern Capital of the past three decades, had yielded to the realities of the situation.

Watchman had already telegraphed from Foochow instructing Witness Lee to move with his family from Shanghai to the new field of work in Taiwan. He had also sent Charity with a small party of ladies to Hong Kong. Luke had left for Singapore and Meek and Wu for Manila. With the People's Liberation Army driving rapidly southward, capturing an average of three cities a day, it was now decided to break up the Kuliang training course prematurely. The workers descended to Foochow, and those from the north were flown to cities where they might be swiftly over-run and thus get back to their churches. Witness Lee now arrived to report briefly on the situation in Shanghai before returning to Taipei. The new light-construction hall at 45 Nanyang Road was, he said, completed and would seat four thousand. The fifty-two *Lessons for New Believers* were now in print. There was much economic distress, but the meetings were going on in life and they were proving God's faithfulness in fresh ways.

In May it was clear that Shanghai was about to fall and Watchman knew he must return there. The liberating army that entered the city on 25 May was impressive in the extreme, disciplined, well fed, and well clothed in olive-green uniforms, thoroughly indoctrinated with Communist convictions, and led by officers who lived and dressed as simply as the rank and file. To everyone's relief there was no looting and no violence, a hint of the social clean-up that was to follow. For a short while Watchman resumed the care of the church with weekly Bible studies and instruction for the workers and helpers on a wide range of subjects and needs. In addition he set aside time for a new phase in his own education. He had long ago assimilated the outline of Marxist doctrine and well understood its anti-religious character. He was on friendly terms too with several convinced but hitherto secret Party members in the city, one of whom, Charity's sixteenth uncle, lived close to his home. He now met this man several times for talks, with the object of discovering what were the Party's future plans regarding religious groups. He foresaw collision between the authorities and the rank-and-file believers on certain issues of Christian life and walk, and the C.C.P. might well prove hostile to the church's programme of nation-wide evangelism.

But this was the honeymoon period that for two years or so followed Liberation. Party members quietly observed the Christians, watching for leaders of influence and gift, and while appearing indifferent, made their calculations for the future. Thus Charity's uncle made warm promises to help Watchman, personally guaranteeing that if he stayed on in Shanghai he would be unmolested and need have nothing to fear. It is probable that Watchman, like so many others, was deceived by those Party officials he observed into thinking them reasonable men who could be dealt with wisely.

That summer, while Shanghai suffered typhoons and floods, the heart of the Yangtze valley fell to the Communists with the capture of the Wuhan metropolis. By October the Nationalists had lost Canton, and Kweiyang and Chungking fell a month later. On 1 October 1949 the People's Republic of China was proclaimed in Peking with Mao Tse-tung as Chairman and Chou En-lai as Prime Minister.

During those weeks Watchman had seized the opportunity to visit Taiwan to encourage Witness Lee and the handful of fellow-workers who had accompanied him there. The many refugees were disheartened by severe difficulties of housing and employment, but in his few days there Watchman gathered several hundred together for meetings and the nucleus was formed of a new church in Taiwan that under Lee's guidance was to go from strength to strength.[1] Drained however of strength himself and oppressed with many cares,[2] Watchman went on now to Hong Kong to join Charity at Diamond Hill in the Changsha peninsula of Kowloon.

He returned to Shanghai in the early months of 1950 during which period, on 6 February, that city was heavily bombed by Nationalist planes based on Taiwan. The electricity plant was hit and for some time light, power, and running water were severely rationed. Back once more in Hong Kong he held in May a series of meetings for young people and now saw the beginnings of revival in this so far none too thriving local church. Placing in charge two men of opposite temperament, K. H. Weigh and James Chen, to work together for the Lord's sake, he helped them with plans to secure a site in Observatory Road, Kowloon, for a new church meeting-place.

In that month of May 1950 Witness Lee joined him there to report on developments in Taiwan and was assured that he was right to return there and carry on. Before they said their last farewell in June Lee tried earnestly to dissuade him from returning to Shanghai. 'But Brother,' Watchman protested, 'it has taken so long to build up the church there. Can I possibly desert them now? Did not the apostles remain in Jerusalem under just such conditions?'[3] With Lee's experience of what the C.C.P. had done in Shantung communes they reviewed therefore their own recent plans for gospel outreach and discussed how, perhaps, Christians living communally as a visible church might disarm suspicion and ensure continuity of the work. But again on their last evening Lee lovingly renewed his personal appeal to Watchman. 'If you go back,' he said, 'it could be the end.' Watchman however had received from the Shanghai elders a telegram telling of their many problems and pleading for his early return. Peace Wang, who was present, added her support to their plea. 'The Lord sat as king at the Flood,' she reminded them. 'He sits as king for ever!'[4] Nevertheless Lee took him aside yet once more to appeal earnestly to him alone. At last Watchman exclaimed, 'I do not care for my life. If the house is crashing down, I have children inside and must support it, if need be with my head.'

To test his loyalties yet further, news now came from his birthplace in Swatow of the call to glory of his mother, Lin Huo-ping. Even so his resolution did not weaken and he instructed his eldest sister, Mrs. Chan, to attend to the funeral arrangements while he himself left for the northern provinces. He went partly to stem a movement of evacuation of believers to Hong Kong that earlier he had encouraged and partly to carry through what the brothers controlling the pharmaceutical company, chaired by Witness Lee, had finally agreed upon, namely, its disposal to a concern operating from Manchuria.

On his arrival back in Shanghai he called Charity to join him there, and soon after, spoke to the workers on 'buying up the opportunity because the days are evil'.[5] He confessed to the opportunities wasted in the past, and went on, 'No servant of God should be satisfied with present attainment. Anyone who is content with what is, is a loser of opportunities. I believe those God is now giving us are far beyond anything we can conceive. Every day God is giving us opportunities, and the aggregate who can assess? Today is July 7th 1950. To redeem the time is to seize *today* the opportunities God has appointed for us today. When the church buries a talent there is serious loss. We think that because the meeting-place at Nanyang Road has just been completed we can settle down for the rest of life. We have our preaching and ten or twenty souls are saved, and we think we have done well. But if the Lord's intention was that we win a thousand souls in one day, then nine hundred souls have been lost! When God moves let us move. As soon as the door opens slightly, enter in, for the trouble with opportunities is that they do not wait for us.' And he went on to suggest that there were whole groups of Christian believers in other movements, such as the Shantung-based 'Jesus Family' (Yeh-su Chia Ting) with its principles of communal living, to whom in the present crisis they might go out in fellowship.[6] 'We can learn from them,' he said, 'for they are ahead of us in the way they have all things in common; but as regards the truth of the Church, no doubt we can be of help to them. If this be truly God's opportunity, may we not miss it.'

It seems clear that Nee believed some degree of cooperation with the new Government on the lines of Romans Chapter 12 to be both possible and necessary, depending of course on how the clause in the constitution was applied that guaranteed freedom of religion. The Assembly Hall churches were circularized urging believers not to emigrate but to stay in China for the Lord's sake. They should be prepared to give up material comforts and, as good Christians and good Chinese, to cooperate sincerely with the State when called upon for such public work as road-building and irrigation works. Only, they must not act in conflict with the Bible nor deny their Lord.

This worked well at first, but a knowledge of Marxism-Leninism should have warned them that first impressions are illusory. Communist policy is relative, conditioned by three things, time, place, and circumstance, and when any of these changes the policy may change. Attitudes therefore may alter in a night, and there is no such thing as the Party keeping a promise.

In Shanghai it was realized that the sheer size of the Nanyang Road meetings, with three or four thousand gathering for worship on Sunday mornings, might lay them open to criticism and this again emphasized the need for dispersion for the gospel's sake. Several groups of volunteers had therefore disposed of their possessions and pulled up their roots, moving out to depopulated areas of Kiangsi. Here they had established agricultural settlements to bring the land back under cultivation. They built their own simple mud-walled houses and from the first lived a rigorous communal life governed by a strict routine which left ample time for personal devotions and nightly group edification in spiritual things.

There had been much enthusiasm about this move, especially when they won a few communists to the Lord. 'Our day has come,' they thought. But in June the government's well-tested agrarian policy of Land Reform became law. For the next year or so, whereas the cities enjoyed some respite, the villages were upheaved by mass meetings, popular trials (and in some cases executions) of landowners and rich peasants, and the redistribution of land among the poor peasants and labourers. All other work came to a standstill and all country churches were closed for the duration. The migrant Christians were not exempted from the re-education and struggle meetings and from a deliberate perversion of their motives. In due course they were to find, as did the Jesus Family, that they were no less suspect with the Communists for doing the right thing for the wrong reason than for not doing it at all.

Missionaries in Hunan at about this time describe how, when their congregation had scattered and they themselves were on the point of leaving, they were courageously befriended by a brother of a 'Little Flock' group that had lately migrated into the area. In spite of dangers he was conducting meetings by the light of a broken pressure-lamp (which they were able to replace for him with a better one). Police came and told him, 'You cannot carry on your services any more,' to which he replied: 'We have to, you know! Our Bible says we must not stop assembling together.'[7] 'Then if you must, may we attend?' 'Certainly you may!'

And a missionary in Chekiang wrote, soon after leaving, of conditions in that Province: 'The influence of the "Little Flock" permeates the country. It has begun to lay a new and strong emphasis on evangelism. It has never had any affiliation with foreign missions, and this is a great asset in the New China. May it not be that this movement is God's specially prepared instrument for the present time? It is close-knit, yet unobtrusive and adaptable in organization; it is wholly indigenous, deeply spiritual, and with a kindling missionary fervour.' A letter received a year or so later spoke of the possible union of the different groups of Christians in the town, and she comments: 'This would mean a union under the leadership of the "Little Flock", and it is perhaps the best provision against the present difficulties.'[8]

During 1949 most missionaries with evangelical vision had tried to remain in their outposts in hope of continuing their witness under the new régime. But in May 1950 there took place a series of meetings held, in the Communist manner, late at night in Peking between the Premier Chou En-lai and three liberal Protestant leaders, led by Y. T. Wu of the Shanghai Y.M.C.A. who for ten years past had secretly been a Party member. The purpose was to work out a

Christian Manifesto for the Protestant Churches, of which Chou treated the three as representative leaders and founder members of a new Christian movement whose principles he now, with every show of cordiality, dictated to them.[9] The 'Direction of Endeavour for Chinese Christianity in the Construction of New China' which emerged required the Church in all its activities to accept the leadership of the People's Government. Cooperation in the State's Common Programme of reform was to be the price of religious freedom. Chou virtually commanded the dismissal of foreign personnel and the refusal of foreign funds. Had not Leighton Stuart, the missionary head of Yenching University, served as U.S. ambassador to Chiang Kai-shek,[10] and were not all missionaries imperialists?

The men called to this conference formed the Preparatory Committee of what came to be known as the 'Oppose-America, Aid-Korea, Three Self Reform Movement of the Church of Christ in China'.[11] Its object was to make the Church self-governing, self-supporting, and self-propagating, where 'self' was the antithesis of 'imperialist'. It was made answerable to the Bureau of Religious Affairs set up under the atheist Committee of Culture and Education in Peking. Its slogan was 'Love your country; Love your Church' with a studious avoidance of the offending name of God. Its periodical *Tien Feng*, (*Heavenly Wind*) rapidly became the official, and eventually the only, published organ of Christian communication.[12]

In the months that followed there was a nationwide drive to obtain signatures to the Christian Manifesto approved by Chou En-lai, and with its publication in the secular press on 23 September it quickly became clear that the work of missionaries would in future be seriously restricted, if not rendered impossible. Indeed their presence in the field was becoming an embarrassment to the Chinese churches on whom every pressure was being brought to join the Three Self Movement. Within the year 1951 there took place the nearly total evacuation of all those who had returned after the Japanese War with such high hopes. The century-long association of Chinese and foreign Christians was thus cruelly and abruptly broken.

Not a few missionaries passing out through Shanghai or held in the city awaiting exit permits attended the Nanyang Road meetings and came away enriched, enheartened by the movement's new access of evangelistic zeal, and moved by Nee's own warmth of personality and his sustained helpfulness in Bible exposition. One such visitor observed, 'Most Christian services you feel are helpful at some point, but these are helpful right through!' At about this time Leslie T. Lyall invited Watchman Nee to meet several C.I.M. colleagues at his Shanghai flat for a discussion of the future. How should they occupy themselves in the interval before they might be asked to return? 'Translate for us some really solid commentaries such as those by Dean Alford,' was the reply. 'We have so little in that category and we need it badly. And come back as teaching elders in the assemblies; not again as evangelists. Evangelism in future must be the task of Chinese believers.'

A Chinese pastor attending the Nanyang Road hall at about this time heard Watchman, he says, speak for a whole week on Romans 1. 1. 'Each evening he delivered a different sermon of outstanding quality; but when you put them all together you got a single long and well-composed thesis. It was simply marvellous.'

On 1 January 1951 he gave to the church a New Year message on the significance of God's blessing in the miracle of the loaves.[13] One of the last we have from him, its essence is worth recording here. 'All service is dependent upon the blessing of God. We may be very conscientious and very diligent, we may believe in His power and may pray to Him to put it forth, but if the blessing of God is lacking, then all our conscientiousness, all our diligence, all our faith, and all our prayer is in vain. On the other hand, even though we make mistakes, and even though the situation we face be a hopeless one, provided we have the blessing of God there will be a fruitful issue.

'Consider the miracle of the loaves and fishes. The point was not the quantity of material in hand but the blessing that rested upon it. Sooner or later we must recognize that what counts is not the state of our treasury or the number of our gifts. It is from the blessing of the Lord alone that man derives his sustenance. One day our own resources, our power, our toil, our faithfulness, will all proclaim to us their vanity. The tremendous disappointment of future days will lay bare to us our own utter inadequacy.

'This lesson is not easily learned. The hopes of so many are still centred, not on the blessing of the Lord but on the few loaves in their hands. It is so pitifully little we have in hand, and yet we keep reckoning with it; and the more we reckon the harder the work becomes. My brothers and sisters, miracles issue from the blessing of the Lord. Only let that be upon the loaves and they will be multiplied. Where the blessing rests the thousands are fed: where the blessing is absent, much more than "two hundred pennyworth" is insufficient to feed them. Recognize that, and we would cease to ask "How many loaves have we?" There would be no need to manipulate and no need to dodge; there would be no need for human wisdom and no need for flattering speeches. We should be able to trust the blessing of God and wait for it. And we should often find that, even where we had bungled things, somehow all was well. A little bit of blessing can carry us over a great deal of trouble.

'What is "blessing"? It is the working of God where there is nothing to account for His working. For instance, you calculate that a penny should buy a pennyworth. But if you have not paid your penny and God has given you ten thousand pennyworth, then you have no basis for your calculations. When five loaves provide food for five thousand and leave twelve baskets of fragments, that is blessing. When the fruit of your service is out of all proportion to the gifts you possess, that is blessing. Or to be rather extreme, when, taking account of your failures, there should be no fruit at all from your labours and still there is fruit, that is blessing. Many of us only expect results commensurate with what we are in ourselves, but blessing is fruit that is out of all correspondence with what we are. It is not just the working of cause and effect, for when we reckon on the basis of what we put in we merely bar the way for God to work beyond our reckoning. If on the other hand we set our hearts upon the blessing of the Lord, we shall find things happen that are altogether out of keeping with our capacity and that surpass even our dreams.

'A life of blessing,' Watchman concluded, 'should be our normal life as Christians and a work with the blessing of God upon it should be our normal work. "Prove me now herewith, saith the Lord of hosts, if I will not open you the windows of heaven, and pour you out a blessing, that there shall not be room enough to receive it."[14] Here in Shanghai at the beginning of 1951 this is still the word of God.'

THE TRAP CLOSES

FOR two years Shanghai's city thoroughfares were bright with processions of workers and young people bearing paper flags and large red silk banners. To the throb of drums and the chant of slogans Yang-ko dancers swayed and pirouetted before massive portraits of Chairman Mao. But in the streets and lanes intensive organization was in process. Neighbourhood revolutionary committees had been organized and there was constant inspection of work-places and homes, everyone informing on everyone else. Human privacy was invaded by the zeal of cadres trained in indoctrination, while ready at hand to act on information received were the regular municipal police, with the secret police lurking in the shadows behind them. There were 'tiger hunts' to search out and destroy vicious capitalist tigers who preyed upon the people's wealth. To live as a Christian in such circumstances called for faith and courage of a high order.[1]

Letters in early 1951 spoke of enlargement of Watchman's ministry, but there were other affairs too to claim his attention. From 16 to 21 April Premier Chou En-lai called a conference of 181 Church leaders to allay the alarm caused by the sudden cutting off of overseas funds.[2] An edict in December had meanwhile required all receiving foreign subsidies to register full details of sources, amounts received, and the conditions of their use.[3] Watchman was required to attend this meeting, as an observer representing a group of 'self-governing, self-supporting, and self-propagating' churches. True, they had received contributions in the church offerings from visiting missionaries, as well as casual overseas gifts towards the gospel work, but there was no demand on them to register as the tools of imperialism. He was there by government design 'for the benefits received through the experience'.

In Shanghai the meetings could continue 'mostly as usual' and all the fellow workers were labouring urgently to redeem the time. But 27 April was Black Saturday in Shanghai with arrests of many thousands of intellectuals and others, followed by a programme of thought-reform of writers. Quite a few Christians were among those taken in and 'some co-workers have been in bondage and suffered for the Lord; but most are safe and well. Only all are under trials'.

On 2 May *Tien Feng* published a summons to the Christian Church in China to take part in accusation meetings. Strong persuasion was exerted on whole congregations to engage in self-criticism and reform. 'Propagandize well, accuse minutely' was the slogan.[4] Only this would qualify them to join the Three Self Reform Church. They must publicly denounce and purge out 'imperialist elements and their stooges' hidden within their own ranks and leadership. Some groups were shown whom among their leaders they were to accuse; others were told to find them for themselves. Y.M.C.A. Secretary L. M. Liu published an article on 'How to Hold a Successful Accusation Meeting', appealing to Matthew 23 as precedent and urging Christians to overcome their inhibitions by attending and learning from secular political meetings. 'Many Christians have the old-fashioned idea of "being above politics"; therefore we must hold accusation meetings to educate everybody ... To hold a successful big accusation meeting is one of the important tasks that every church must do well to wipe out the influence of imperialism.'[5]

To show the way, the Three Self Movement organized a huge meeting on Sunday 10 June for the public denunciation of Christian missionaries. It was held in the Shanghai dog-racing stadium. Carefully chosen 'accusers' representing leading Christian groups addressed an audience largely of church congregations. With rehearsed speeches and every show of indignation and hatred they vilified their brothers in Christ, both missionary figures of the past and former colleagues. The whole performance was designed to bring loss of face, not merely to the missionary-sending nations but, in the long term, to Christianity itself.[6] And any Christian's non-attendance at the meeting was carefully noted. Thus the movement gathered way as Christians turned against one another in this self-degrading form of persecution, and woe betide those churches who stood apart from the exercise. Urging its further intensification *Tien Feng* was able to announce on 11 August that sixty-three big accusation meetings had been held since May. The Christian churches were accommodating themselves to the niche prepared for them in the new society, in which 'Three Self' was ultimately to mean control by the State, financial dependence on the State, and propagation in line with the ideology of the State.[7] No wonder that letters in July reported, 'The assemblies are now in a very trying situation, and so especially are those who bear responsibility like brother Watchman Nee,' who was reported to be once again ill and on his back.

Meanwhile the People's Government was pressing on with its highly successful programme of moral clean-up aimed at eliminating crime and prostitution and all forms of corruption. Claiming to *be* the people and to rule in their name the Party sought to achieve country-wide what the missionaries had tried to tackle man by man and yet to do it using not legislation but popular persuasion. In November 1951 the State instituted two such ethical campaigns that were to occupy the country in the coming months, the *San-Fan* or 'Three Antis', opposing corruption, waste, and bureaucracy in the civil service; and the *Wu-Fan* or 'Five Antis', opposing bribery, tax-evasion, theft of state property, shoddy work, and stealing economic secrets for private speculation in the field of business. Posters everywhere called the public to Repent and Confess,[8] and there was a rash of accusations and false charges and an outbreak of suicides. This was a pointer to what lay ahead, and as if to underline it, Watchman had been notified that the transfer of the Sheng-Hua Drug Manufacturing Company (C.B.C.) to its prospective purchasers was suspended by government order pending inquiry into its accounts and tax payments.

Then in the 30 November issue of *Tien Feng*, the official Three Self Christian periodical, there appeared an article by a member of the Little Flock congregation in Nanking entitled 'A Revelation of the Secret Organization and Dark Doings of the Tsi-Tang Road Church.' He wrote: 'I am a believer who from the outset have belonged to the Tsi-Tang Road Church (in Nanking) and who regarded it as the purest of assemblies until I was indoctrinated regarding the Three Self Reform Movement, when I saw plainly what a vile place it is. I have long been deceived, but today I stand on the ground of love of country and love of religion, and with emotions of unqualified wrath I expose its professed "spirituality". In order to conceal the true anti-revolutionary nature of this movement, those in responsibility at Tsi-Tang Road persistently and emphatically affirm that it is a "local church". As a matter of fact we have been utterly misled. From its very inception it has been subject to the Shanghai assembly and is strictly controlled by Watchman Nee. It is an organized system of nationwide and occult character. Watchman Nee has an involved, secret system for controlling 470 churches all over the country, with Shanghai as his administrative base, and Shanghai governs these indirectly through "central churches" established in large cities such as Peking, Hankow, Tsingtao, Foochow, etc. The dark, mysterious control Watchman Nee exercises over the churches goes quite beyond the sphere of religion. To facilitate his totalitarian control he disseminates anti-revolutionary poison and dominates the thought of church members. He shamelessly terms himself "the apostle of God"!'

To a group of workers who wondered what action Watchman would take in self-defence he recounted his four-fold experience of being disciplined by God's hand of love: his excommunication at Foochow in 1924 and the revival that had followed; his grave illness attending the difficult choice between the role of popular preacher and the less attractive pursuit of Christian witness through the local church; his withdrawal from ministry during the Japanese War and the spiritual enrichment with which he had returned; and now this attack upon him, and, by implication, upon them all. No doubt in every criticism there was *some* element of truth. But why retaliate, he concluded, when each time the Lord's rebuke had proved so instructive, his chastening so spiritually fruitful?

Communist cadres were by now attending Nanyang Road and trying to stir up demands that the church stage their own accusation meeting. At length early in 1952, under extreme pressure from the Three Self headquarters, a meeting was called at which two of its representatives were allowed to address the assembly. Their speeches charging imperialism in the church's leaders brought only a bewildered silence. No one spoke in support. At length someone plucked up the courage to say: 'Is it not true that Paul counted all things but loss for Christ? Should we not therefore count even our honoured People's Government the veriest refuse that we might gain Christ?'[9] At this a cadre, planted in the meeting, burst out, 'Watchman Nee ordered women to cover their heads in prayer. This is despotism!' Designed to be inflammatory, the charge merely backfired on the accuser. Brothers demanded who was this outsider who had put the question. The Three-Self spokesman got up and announced: 'Obviously you are not ready for self-reform and need training in this. I put Mr Watchman Nee himself in charge of your re-education.'

All in the church now saw what they were up against. No doubt the fellow-travellers had suffered a set-back, but they would bide their time. Watchman, after talking things over with Charity and with his fellow-workers and elders, gave himself up to one thing, the preparation of Biblical material for believers. Ruth Lee and her assistants took down in writing everything he had to give. To one group of young people, for instance, he talked at length on the proofs of the existence of God. There were series too of a practical character, on Christ as the righteousness, the wisdom and the glory of God for the believer, and on the power of His resurrection. But that was not what had been ordered. Now therefore there were new government demands, this time, that he leave Shanghai. Financial questions outstanding in the pharmaceutical business with which the church was still saddled required his presence in Manchuria. So the pressure to buy up the opportunity intensified to the point of desperation. Together the team worked all day and long into the nights, expounding and recording the Lord's Word, until, that month of March, they were getting only two hours of sleep nightly.

At length the State's ultimatum could no longer be resisted. He gave a last word of exhortation to his beloved brothers and sisters in Christ, adding: 'Tell them in Hong Kong to dissociate all secular business enterprise from the church'. Sorrowfully he took leave of Charity. Then with deep misgivings he set out for Harbin. This was the last the believers heard of him until his indictment in January 1956.

In his fiftieth year he was arrested in Manchuria by the Department of Public Safety on 10 April 1952,[10] and at his first inquiry, either at Harbin or in Peking, he was charged as a lawless capitalist 'tiger' who had committed all the five crimes specified in the *Wu-Fan* campaign against corrupt business practices. He was warned that the Sheng Hua Company would be required to pay a fine of 17,200 million yuan in old currency (equivalent to nearly $1\frac{1}{2}$ million U.S. dollars). He neither accepted this unfair accusation, nor did he have the funds to pay such a fine. So he remained in prison, and the Company was in due course confiscated by the State.[11]

Initially in all such cases the conditions of imprisonment were harsh in the extreme, without, it is probable, actual physical violence but with threats, poor food, sleep-deprival, vermin, and a constant pitiless drain upon physical endurance. His Bible of course was confiscated at once. No communication was allowed with anyone outside.

He is said to have been offered the chance of reinstatement as a public Christian figure if he would lead his immense following into step with the People's Government within the Three Self Reform Church. The experience of others at this period makes it certain that, if he was thus in demand, fierce attempts were made to re-educate him into acquiescence in the national neurosis, a supine renunciation of all freedom of thought. We have ample documentation of the thought-reform methods then in use: the long hours of questioning by relays of interrogators, the political lectures, the vigilant scrutiny by relentless warders, the occupation of his cell by convinced and converted 'fellow students', and the strident speak-bitterness of the group struggle meetings.[12] That no change of heart took place and no confession worth using emerged speaks volumes for the keeping power of God.[13] But he will have been required to write and rewrite the chronicle of his life in endless detail, for from this, piece by piece, the criminal case against him was built up and he was confronted with 'evidence' that was compounded by a process of mind-deadening repetition.

There were precedents. Already by February 1952 a confession of precisely the kind they sought from Nee had been wrung after imprisonment from Isaac Wei, son of the founder of the indigenous True Jesus Church, bringing the adherents of that large group into step with the State. The same year the Jesus Family, envied for its communal success but vulnerable by reason of its rural situation, had been treated to the alternative, namely forcible dissolution and the disgrace of its leaders with 'convictions' of espionage, counter-revolutionary activity, and licentious living.[14] The Party would not tolerate in China a 'centre of darkness' where the right thing was done for what in their eyes was the wrong reason. If no 'imperialist' links could be proved in a truly indigenous movement its leaders must be arraigned as common criminals. And this therefore was the fate now in store for Watchman Nee.

Meanwhile, with his withdrawal from the scene the fences were temporarily lowered by the Three Self representatives. Elders of 'Little Flock' assemblies everywhere were assured of an unconditional welcome if they would join the steady flow of churches into this 'mountain stream which, the further it flows, the clearer and broader it becomes.' 'The door is still open', they were told, 'and we are extending friendly hands, hoping the day will arrive when we will unitedly dwell together.' With Watchman out of their reach they had no strong spiritual counsellor to whom to turn, and one by one they capitulated,[15] most of them very soon to regret the step.

In the city of Wuhan, to take a single instance, the 'Little Flock' congregation had joined the Three-Self Movement as early as 1951 and submitted to the prescribed 'learning' programme. But then one of their preachers, Ho Kuang-tao, led them out again. 'We withdraw from the movement,' the police charges report him to have said, 'purely for reasons of religious belief, for the believer and the non-believer cannot bear the same yoke.' Thereafter the elders declined to receive cinema tickets and other learning material from the Religious Affairs Bureau and gave a cool reception to its officials sent to report to the church on the government's religious policy. Many other local churches followed their example, and in 1954 Ho called a conference at Wuhan of preachers from meeting places all over central China, encouraging them in the faith and urging them to lead their congregations to independence of the Three Self Patriotic Movement and to pray for those churches which had not yet withdrawn.[16] In the four years following Nee's arrest many churches were to find again their spiritual feet in this way, that in Shanghai drawing out of the Movement late in 1955. They were to bring down wrath upon themselves as a consequence.

But meanwhile the work at Nanyang Road continued somehow to move forward with influence and power. Services for worship were able to continue and even, for a year or two, special evangelistic meetings at the New Year holiday. Because of the general uncertainty of life opportunities for personal witness were greater than ever before. The work of the Church Book Room continued with a flow of publications, mostly now anonymous but recognizable as Watchman's Bible expositions.[17]

In the spring of 1952, following a compulsory course of Marxist indoctrination of all students, there was a remarkable Christian awakening in two of the colleges and many were born again. This led to a series of summer and winter conferences that continued for several years using the Nanyang Road hall as a venue, and new Christian fellowships sprang into being in every Shanghai college, not excluding, it is said, the School of Political Studies. Saying grace at meals served students as one means of recognition. Prayer disguised as conversation between two or three with unbowed head in an open space might go undetected, and the three-quarter hour respite immediately after the weekly mass political indoctrination gave a chance, with cadres off their guard, for a larger hurried meeting. Here, at risk to their future careers, some prayed aloud who had never done so without a Prayer Book and there took place that true oecumenism under pressure which, one of them affirms, 'Watchman Nee had always prayed for'.[18] This pattern of student revival was being repeated all over China.

July 1955 saw the public attack in the *People's Daily* on the fundamentalist preacher Wang Ming-tao of Peking. This Daniel of a man was greatly loved by students who composed nine tenths of his congregation and an attempt upon him in the form of an accusation meeting ten months earlier had backfired with an 'Oppose the Persecution of Wang Ming-tao' movement. His magazine, *Spiritual Food Quarterly*, ever loyal to the Scriptures, was still in production and widely influential. Watchman Nee greatly respected him as a man of God but had no time for his church, which he likened to a roadside 'halfway house' (*pan-lu liang-ting*), a place of refreshment on a journey but not a destination.

Wang Ming-tao had firmly rebuffed all Three Self overtures and from the Party standpoint the trouble was that, as an independent preacher who neither served nor headed an organization, it was difficult to frame him on any 'criminal' charge, so political implications must be sought for in his Christian testimony alone. These were found in the courageous pamphlet he produced in June 1955 entitled *We shall be stedfast because of our faith*. The story of his arrest on 8 August is well known. A few of his former supporters were found ready to put themselves in the Party's good graces by accusing him of treasonable intent. With his imprisonment and subsequent forced 'confession' one more Christian rallying point was eliminated.[19] The field was now clear for the major storm to break.

18

ORDEAL

On Wednesday 18 January 1956 there began in the Church Assembly Hall at Nanyang Road a series of meetings called by the Religious Affairs Bureau at which the whole congregation was required to be present. They ran consecutively for twelve days lasting all day and believers were excused employment to attend them.

At these meetings items from the list of criminal charges to be brought against Nee and those associated with him were progressively made known to the believers, who were encouraged to express their views. Accusations of imperialist intrigue and espionage, counter-revolutionary activities hostile to government policy, financial irregularities, and gross licentiousness, had been accumulated in an indictment running to 2,296 pages. The object of this preliminary exercise was to prepare the church members with data and to arouse their indignation in readiness for a mass accusation meeting to be held at the month-end. Opportunity was given for the elders and senior sisters, already informed of what was required of them, to admit their own complicity and to lead the church in its denunciation of Watchman as an enemy of the people. Two elders made statements that were considered inadequate. Dr. C. H. Yu, Ruth Lee, and Peace Wang declined to make any accusation at all.

On Sunday 29 January Watchman's case came for summary hearing before the Shanghai Court of Public Security. The hearing was brief and in private. The charge was that from his hiding in the Christian Meeting Place in Nanyang Road he had conducted systematic counter-revolutionary intrigues against the People's Government. His crimes were listed under five heads. He and his accomplices had supported imperialism and the Nationalist régime; they had opposed popular movements; they had corrupted youth; they had sabotaged production; and Nee himself had acted licentiously. The charges were read and he was allowed to answer only Yes or No. No explanation was permitted. He denied the one really substantial charge, that of spying and sabotage. To the others he is reported to have remained silent. The hearing completed, the case was referred for judgement to the High Court with a strong recommendation for severity.

The same day Dr. Yu and the two women were taken into custody along with several others,[1] and in the next week thirty more workers and responsible brothers were arrested locally while a simultaneous sweep of the churches country-wide drew in some thousand key men and women throughout the movement. (Later estimates put this figure twice as high.) These all disappeared from sight, and their wives and children, debarred from visiting them, were left without support.

Next day, Monday 30 January, the promised accusation meeting took place at the Assembly Hall. It was convened by the heads of the Public Safety and Religious Affairs Departments and a total of 2,500 persons were present, including, probably by order, all the Protestant pastors and all the Nanyang Road church members. The chairman was Lo Chu-feng, Chairman of the Shanghai Religious Affairs Bureau. The charges were now proclaimed publicly in detail and backed by an exhibition of photographs and other documentary 'proofs'. The summary of them which follows is compiled from official reports of various stages in the month's proceedings.

As far back as 1941, it was alleged, Nee had engaged in transmitting to the American Air Force and to agents of Chiang Kai-shek information on Communist Army movements and secret plans. The real purpose of his last visit to Hong Kong in the spring of 1950 had been to report on the success of the Nationalist bombing of Shanghai's electric and water supplies on 6 February and to encourage more of the same thing. He had further informed Chiang's emissaries of the schistosomiasis (blood-fluke) epidemic among units of the Liberation Army in Kiangsu and Chekiang, and had advised the dropping of larva-infested snails into the Chekiang rivers and lakes together with the withholding of raw materials needed for making curative drugs.

Nee was further charged with being a lawless capitalist who had profiteered in the pharmaceutical trade. Under cover of his Sheng-Hua Drug Manufacturing Company he had imported raw materials from abroad to sell to other manufacturers, and by bribing tax officials had evaded the foreign exchange regulations covering such deals. In this way he had stolen from the nation some 17,200 million yuan (old currency). From July 1950 to August 1951 under cover of the same company he 'had stolen state secrets' by leaking news to private concerns that the People's Government was placing orders for military purposes, and by passing on details of secret technical procedures. Furthermore he had indirectly been guilty of sabotage. Fires and explosions in the Shanghai Dye Works during 1955 and the current month of January 1956 were attributable to his having detailed to these factories Christians trained by him for the long-term task of destroying production.

Nee was, it turned out after all, a running-dog of the imperialists. He had failed to register the Christian Meeting Places as a foreign subsidized mission on the specious ground that they were purely Chinese. All the time he was hiding his imperialist dealings. Since 1921 he had in fact received gifts and legacies towards the work from missionaries, from the Exclusive Brethren, from the Christian Fellowship Centre in London, and from individual donors overseas.[2] Moreover when the China Inland Mission withdrew from the country it 'had handed over to Nee' a number of church buildings, thus confirming that he and they 'were one in political thinking'.

Since long before Liberation Nee had 'carried on under the cloak of religion well planned and organized counter-revolutionary activities against the new society'. Assuming the role of founder of the Christian Meeting Places and aided by his clique of reactionaries hidden there[3] he had set up his 'emergency plan' for China, conducting training-sessions for all Church officers. In these, through lectures, sermons, and discussion meetings, he pursued his subversive activities. He had incited Christians to oppose the great enterprise of national liberation by instructing them to fast and pray that, just as Pharaoh's host perished in the Red Sea, God would drown the People's Liberation Army in the Yangtze River. In 1950 he had incited Christians in all the Meeting Places to sign their names openly attacking land reform. Yet before its introduction he had tried to anticipate it by carrying out a 'land reform' of his own, giving away to his own church his extensive holdings in Foochow. This was merely a cover for his criminal activities. Even now his harmful influence was being felt.

At a time when, under the able leadership of Chairman Mao, China was embarking on the bright path toward Socialist construction, Nee's associates were teaching that these were what the Bible calls 'the last days'.[4] They had demoralized the will of the people by, for example, attributing to the judgement of God the Wuhan flood disaster in the summer of 1954. They discouraged Christians from participating in big self-criticism and accusation meetings on the ground that Christianity was above politics,[5] and even taught that it was an honour to flunk the school examinations in political studies.

Much was made of the counselling of young Christians, many of whom Nee and his followers were said to have corrupted with their pernicious advice. For some young people they had helped arrange marriages, or in other cases advised against a particular match, and not all were satisfied. The prosecutor instanced one whose husband 'had turned out to be an espionage agent now imprisoned by the

Government'. Other young men and women had been lured into handing themselves over for training to serve the Lord, 'only to be given work that was hard and humiliating'. Worse still, they had been discouraged from joining the People's Voluntary Army, and Nee had thus posed a threat to the Resist-America Aid-Korea Movement. Quoting 1 John 2. 6 he had taught that young people should not love the world. (A transcription of his teaching on this theme may have been used here as evidence.[6]) In this advice, it was argued, he was plainly being dishonest, since what he really loved was the discredited world of Chiang Kai-shek's banditry.

Nee and his clique had harboured many Kuomintang agents: underground workers, army generals, escaped landlords, and had absorbed them into the Christian Meeting Places as preachers, elders, and deacons where they had been engaged for him in carefully planned subversivism. In 1950 they had been instructed to take cover in productive labour and to out-do even non-Christians in their supposed zeal for such State projects as road-works, but the sole object was in this way 'to set forward his emergency hidden plot'. Several of these 'underground workers' were named in the charges: 'Chen Lu-san, a former police-chief and counter-revolutionary bandit, Lu Shih-kuang, whose hands were dipped in the people's blood, Li Yin-hsin, and a great many others' (clearly some of them in the Nationalist state employment before they had given their lives to God) and these were now identified as Chiang Kaishek's 'under-cover agents'. Between 1949 and 1951 Nee had, it was alleged, posted such men to Christian Meeting Places in Kunming, Chungking, Suchow, and other cities 'to expand his counter-revolutionary influence under the guise of gospel migration and preaching the Word of God.' Through such means he had hurried into action his conquer-China-with-the-gospel plan whereby evangelism became an effective cloak for political propaganda. Madly he had announced his aim within fifteen years to cover China with Good News that should do better than a Communist revolution.

The most shameful step in this plan had been his 'Render unto God' campaign of April 1948 with its fraudulent appeal to Christians to follow the example of the Book of the Acts, and to hand over themselves and their possessions to God for the gospel's sake rather than to the Communists for (as he was charged with stating) death and destruction. This deception had spread like a bush-fire through the nation's nearly 500 Christian Meeting Places, netting an estimated U.S. $500,000 in cash and sale of goods. This was of course nothing but a political strategem to enlist cadres and funds for his counter-revolutionary programme.

Finally, for the benefit of simple God-fearing believers, Nee was charged with being a 'dissolute vagabond of corrupt and indulgent living' who frequented brothel neighbourhoods and had always been a shameless and indiscriminate womanizer. He had confessed, it was claimed, to seducing over a hundred women, Chinese and foreign. No evidence for this was produced.

Here in the Nanyang Road hall where Watchman had led the Church in prayer and had opened to them the Word that exalts Jesus Christ, the long, shoddy recital of the case against him dragged out to its conclusion. Then the chairman, Lo Chu-feng, called upon the Vice-Mayor of Shanghai to give the main address. Hsu Chien-kuo stood up. After alluding to the facts of the arrest in April 1952 (not hitherto made public) he went on to discuss the government's religious policy. 'The People's Government guarantees freedom of religious belief,' he assured them. 'Unfortunately some counter-revolutionaries slyly emphasize the difference between materialism and idealism in their writings and thus arouse the people's emotions and disrupt their unity. The question before us today is of counter-revolutionaries hidden within the Christian Meeting Places. The opposition of Nee and his gang to the Three Self Movement is not a matter of religious principle. It has had its own secret purpose.

'Religion is religion and faith is faith; they must not be mixed up with a person's private counter-revolutionary ideas and used as a cover behind which to spread the poison of hatred towards country and people. Every Christian should enter positively into the struggle to expose these arrested men's crimes.

'We still have serious questions about a number of others also, but for the present we let them alone to see if they will repent and show a new attitude. Through our investigations of the past few years we have a great deal of information on file, which we will use if need be. Those who do not heed this warning must take the consequences. And you who are members of the Christian Meeting Place should not be afraid of washing your dirty linen in public, but should vigorously seek out and expose all offenders.

'This struggle has just begun. We will not draw back until we have completed it victoriously and rooted out every counter-revolutionary hidden within the Little Flock.'

Following this Vice-Mayoral oration a medical student who was a member of the Nanyang Road meeting made a denunciatory speech, after which others who tried to stand up were promised another opportunity and the meeting was closed.

As an old school friend and fellow-worker of Watchman observed at the time, the charges against him were not religious but political and moral. 'It is one thing to suffer as a Christian; it is quite another to suffer as a criminal for sins not committed. Shall we not ask God the righteous Judge to intervene in the High Court trial to clear His own Name, deliver our brethren, and cause that His Word in China be not bound? And shall we not pray for their enemies, who are the Lord's enemies, held captive by Satan?'

On 1 February the Shanghai Municipal Government took the unusual step of publishing in its *Liberation Daily* an official statement of Watchman's arrest on 10 April 1952 and stated that he and two others, Chang Tzu-chieh and Ni Hong-tsu were held in the Shanghai First Place of Detention. Chang was a fellow-worker from Tsingtao. Hong-tsu was Watchman's third brother, the eighth child in the family, and did not claim to be a practising Christian. He was known to have been a senior political agent of Chiang Kai-shek, and had been enticed back from Hong Kong with the Party's promise that his personal finances in Shanghai were protected and would be restored to him. He was eventually executed as a traitor. Unquestionably the public association at this moment of the two brothers' names was designed to give credibility to the charge against Watchman of espionage.

On 2 February Bishop Robin Chen published a statement in *Liberation Daily* denouncing Nee and his accomplices and emphasizing how glad he was that this stumbling-block to faith had at length been removed. The same day at Huai En Church the bishop presided over an enlarged meeting of the Shanghai Council of the Three Self Movement. It was addressed by a dozen clergy and church leaders who engaged in 'furious reprimands' that echoed the official charges and praised Chairman Mao and the Communist Party for their 'perfectly correct and necessary action' in imprisoning Nee and his group. These fierce wolves in sheeps' clothing should be given the severest punishment. The meeting passed a resolution that spoke of 'the grave and momentous sins of these evil leaders in their traitorous rebellion against the Government' which had aroused Christians to 'an unprecedented righteous indignation'. Their teachings were incompatible with Christian doctrine and all Christians who had been deceived and poisoned by them 'must without exception be required to engage in studies designed to elevate their patriotic conscience and uncover their sins.'

One woman speaker at this meeting described Nee as an anti-revolutionary profligate and shameless adulterer. 'We women, hearing this, could not but hate him,' she said. Taking its cue from this the Shanghai *Liberation Daily* featured next day a cartoon bearing the caption *Chiao Chu Lai*, 'Render Up'. It depicted two levels or floors of a house. On the upper floor people were pressing forward to where a man sat masked on a step-ladder, urging them to pour their possessions into a great funnel labelled 'render unto God the things that are God's'. Every kind of gift was going in, right down to that of the coolie who had stripped off his shirt and the little jacket of his weeping child. On the floor below to which the receptacle extended it was differently labelled: 'For the Work of Counter-Revolution'. Here from the funnel's outlet a stream of gold and silver, watches and jewellery and money gifts came pouring out at the feet of the admiring Ni To-sheng who relaxed with a prostitute seated in his lap.

By such calculated measures was Watchman dethroned if possible from his place of affection in the Christians' hearts. Few dared openly to speak his name, but silently many Christians all over China supported him in prayer.

Pastors and evangelistic workers throughout Shanghai were now instructed to organize study in small groups from 5 February onwards to acquaint Christians everywhere with 'the crimes of Ni To-sheng'. At Nanyang Road all meetings other than Sunday worship were closed to make way for this special indoctrination. For guidance *Tien Feng* of 6 February devoted eleven pages to a review of Nee's case. Its editorial was headed, 'Drive the Cruel Wolves out of the Church', and ran, 'From the recital of their crimes, it can be seen that this gang have been destructive of our economic reconstruction, dangerous to the people's livelihood and social order, and a threat to national safety. Their presence within the Christian Church has been a dishonour to the holy name of the Lord, a blot on the Church's reputation and a corruption of gospel truth. They are very clever and devious, and like to talk about holiness. Their own actions however are far from holy, and the life of Ni To-sheng himself is too adulterous to repeat.

'Brothers and sisters of the Christian Meeting Place: We are very happy that this gang can never again disturb and harm our beloved Church, and so without hindrance we may now unite freely in mutual love. Fellow Christians, let us celebrate our common victory and consider it cause for rejoicing. It is only by exposing and expelling such wolves that we can purify the Church so that it may glorify the Lord.'

Subsequent issues of *Tien Feng* maintained the flow of invective. That of 29 February told also of another big denunciation meeting at the Nanyang Road Hall with more than three thousand 'Little Flock' members present, including representatives from Nanking, Changsha, Soochow, Wusih, and other places. Their presence was designed to give weight of authority to the election of a governing committee of fourteen who should take the place in Shanghai of the imprisoned leaders. This meeting proceeded with much more emotional pressure than the one on 30 January. Hesitations and ques-

tionings had in some degree been overcome and *Tien Feng* reported
that all were ready to join in a frenzied demand for vengeance. Its
fifteen-page report of charges and denunciations was followed by a
devotional article entitled, 'Now abideth faith, hope, and love, these
three.'[7]

A large number of delegates from the Church Assembly Halls
now attended the second national conference of the Chinese Christian Church held in Peking from 15 to 23 March 1956. Here the
Chairman of the Three Self Movement, Y. T. Wu, gave his report of
progress since the previous conference in July 1954. At that time, he
said, 'just as we were going ahead in full confidence, a little group,
on the empty pretext of its being a "question of faith", opposed the
Three Self Movement and broke up our unity.' He described how,
during the national campaign in late 1955 and early 1956, 'some
counter-revolutionaries hidden within the church were uncovered.
Under the cloak of religion these men acted as spies, spread rumours,
and disrupted the central campaign of the Chinese people. Within
the church they used the pretext of "faith" to oppose the Three Self
Patriotic Movement, trying with a religious slogan to confuse their
fellow-Christians, to corrupt youth and to destroy Christian unity.
Their exposure removed the obstacle to the unity of the Chinese
Christian Church. Today all Christians are united on a wider and
firmer basis than ever.'[8]

Soon opportunity was given for the 'Little Flock' representatives
to make their public confessions and join the ranks of the Movement. In a later speech the Anglican Dr. H. H. Tsui stated, 'Elder Yen
Chia-le of the Peking Little Flock and Miss Hsu Ma-li of the Shanghai
Little Flock have made accusations in this very conference. Who
has ever been compelled to make accusations? We simply could not
do otherwise but grasp such opportunities to reveal and accuse these
proponents of imperialism and anti-revolutionism when we fully
recognize their horribly criminal acts.' He spoke of the 'hidden
claws of the wolf under the sheepskin' of those whom the West
chose to describe as 'brave Christian leaders'.[9]

On the last day a letter from the Committee of the Three Self
Movement was sent out to all Chinese Christians, which included
the following paragraph: 'We remember that in the national conference of the Chinese Christian Church of July 1954 there were still
some believers who did not understand the meaning of coming together in the Three Self Patriotic Movement. They took a destructive
attitude and tried to prevent the union of Christians. But today the
situation is very clear: we see now that the obstacle to union at that
time was the presence of counter-revolutionaries hidden within the
church, who, wearing the cap of "faith", tried to destroy the patri-

otic movement against imperialism. Now they have finally been exposed, and the deluded brothers and sisters have come to realize the true situation; and so the grace of brethren living together in harmony has now finally descended upon us. Brothers and sisters, let us together before the Lord rejoice and give thanks.'[10] Provincial conferences followed, that for Chekiang being held at Hangchow, the place where Watchman and Charity were married. When this conference was thrown open for speeches members of the Assembly Halls were specially eager to stand up and disavow their former attitude and to join in condemnation of their imprisoned leader.[11] In Anhwei province it was officially reported in March that 'as many as possible of those who had been perverted by Ni To-sheng's widespread influence had been re-educated, and the remainder arrested'.

By mid-April reorientation of the church at Nanyang Road, Shanghai, was pronounced complete. Its formal entry into the Three Self Movement took place on 15 April at a meeting with representatives of the other member churches. The themes of the meeting were 'The Clarification of Our Faith' and 'How to Participate in the Three Self Movement'. Bowing to 'the desires of the masses' the church publicly announced its 'rebirth'. It was addressed by a representative of the Religious Affairs Bureau and several church-leaders made speeches of welcome. The whole Protestant Church in China was now, it was claimed, united under a single authority.

Afterwards however the *Tien Feng* reporter observed plaintively : 'But a small number of brothers and sisters who had been deeply affected by the anti-revolutionary poison still were uneasy and could not in conscience agree, thinking that the question was one which involved their faith.' So the authorities set to work to close the bolt-holes. All informal Bible classes, prayer meetings, and other unauthorized activities in private homes were actively proscribed. Independent evangelists and preachers were classed as outlaws. Freedom of Christian worship was loudly proclaimed but it was a conditioned freedom, reserved for those under State surveillance within the approved fold.

Throughout these proceedings Watchman Nee himself had of course remained out of sight. On 21 June 1956 he appeared before the High Court in Shanghai. As before, and as in all such cases, it was not a public trial but simply a public meeting to condemn him. It lasted five hours. During the hearing it was announced that he had been excommunicated by his own church. He was found guilty on all charges and was sentenced to fifteen years' imprisonment with reform by labour, to run from 12 April 1952.[12]

SUPPRESSIVE ACTION

WHEN the storm broke in Shanghai in January 1956 Charity had
been among those 'wanted'. She was however under strict medical
care in hospital. Hypertension with associated retinopathy was
threatening her eyesight, and she was too ill to attend the accusation
meetings or to produce the confession demanded of her. But by
June, at the time of Watchman's High Court trial and sentence, she
was herself in prison. At the year's end her confession was still not
completed.

It was some time in 1957 that Charity was released to begin her
long home vigil. She lived now in a room off the Siccawei Road not
far from the First Medical School. Few dared visit her, and to do so
openly took great courage, for she was related to a criminal reactionary and so was herself without civil rights. Association with her
could be dangerous. Her neighbours rarely talked with her; but now
and again a Christian student or one of the believers would seek her
out, usually after dark to escape detection. Avoiding mention of her
husband they would speak together about the Lord Jesus and then
unite in prayer. Always the visitor went away uplifted, amazed at
her fortitude and inward rest of spirit, for she was a woman with
considerable inner resources.[1]

A prisoner serving sentence might appoint one relative as visitor,
so now, after an interval of five years, Charity was permitted to see
Watchman. She crossed the city to Amoy Street in the old International Settlement where the vast and forbidding First Municipal
Prison backed upon the Suchow Creek. Their interview, which was
supervised, took place in a hall with an open-mesh barrier between
them and lasted half an hour. The permission was renewable
monthly. Watchman could also send and receive one strictly censored letter a month.

The prison had been built by the British in 1913 in traditional
style with walls grey and hideous. Turret stairways led to each of
the five floors of its eleven blocks. Watchman's single cell measured
9 ft. × 4½ ft. As furniture it had only a wooden platform on the floor
to sleep on. The padlocks on most of the doors had been made in
London. Outside the door was a gallery 200 ft. long upon which the

cells opened like cupboards, with windows in its facing wall. Because of the 'livestock' sleep was difficult.

The day was divided into eight hours of labour, eight of education
and eight of rest. He rose at 5.00 a.m. to mingle with the throng of
lost and sullen men at work in the prison factory or at exercise in
oppressive quadrangles that were devoid of open greenness. There
was no prison uniform and the prisoners' own clothes were worn
and tattered, or, if the wearers were diligent, a mass of patches.
They made a drab and depressing sight. Meals, prepared by the
women prisoners, were three a day, two of them solid (for labour)
or light (for non-labour) and the third of gruel. Though they included fresh vegetables and occasional meat, the heat of summer
brought to light the prisoners' cage-like ribs and prominent veins.
Clearly they lived barely above subsistence. They were allowed an
occasional hot bath and a fortnightly hair-cut. In winter with no
heating the extreme cold called for many layers of clothing merely
to keep alive.

As a criminal against the civil code Watchman received the same
educational reform as a political prisoner. Lectures were given in
politics, current events, and production techniques. In each section
there was a library of approved books and newspapers, and there
were discussions, drama groups, and films. Much of the day there
was a blare of political propaganda over the loudspeakers.

As in due course Watchman's circumstances became known outside, small quantities of food, clothing, soap (which was severely
rationed), and money, were sent to Charity from Hong Kong and she
was able to take in a little for his use. It was learned that his mind
was clear and was being kept occupied. He was allowed writing
materials, and a part of his reform through labour meant employment in translating from English to Chinese such scientific textbooks
and journal articles as were of use to the authorities. He could buy
approved books for this purpose, and at a later date two volumes of
a Medical Dictionary were purchased in Hong Kong and sent in for
his use. It is practically certain however that he was never allowed a
Bible. For that source of spiritual comfort he depended therefore
upon his prodigious memory.

The summer of 1956 had seen the beginning of the 'Hundred
Flowers' period of relaxation of thought, but a year later, at the
time of Charity's release, there followed the phase of 'Blooming and
Contending' with its harsh Rectification Campaign against liberal
thinkers. Nevertheless a student visitor to Nanyang Road in 1957
found a congregation of courageous people proclaiming: 'The Lord
is my strength and song; and he is become my salvation.' There was
a morning service, holy communion in the afternoon, and a meeting

for young people in the evening. It was, she says, most refreshing. There was also a five-day student conference in the meeting hall that July.[2] Indeed there was a widespread Christian awakening that summer among students throughout China, fed, it would seem, by the stimulus of carefully preserved writings of Wang Ming-tao and Watchman Nee. Many students too were taking very seriously the question of committing large sections of the Chinese Bible to memory against a day of trial.

In November of the same year the first of Watchman's popular writings, *The Normal Christian Life*, appeared in print in Bombay, India. It is unlikely that he was ever aware of their wide spiritual fruitfulness outside China.

With January 1958 came Mao Tse-tung's Great Leap Forward, aimed to make the nation's production 'faster, better, and more economical'. Guided by his infallible thoughts as interpreted by the cadres, the Chinese people threw themselves into overtime effort in everything from close-planting of rice-seedlings to the backyard smelting of pig-iron. Exhaustion from this cause led inevitably to the dwindling of church attendances, but the year had begun too with an intensive campaign of socialist education of Christian pastors, designed to identify them as members of the exploiting classes, 'parasites on society', and to draft them into productive labour. *Tien Feng* was full of reports of the wicked things discovered, such as faith healing and the casting out of demons. 'Imperialism' was said to have raised its head again, and there were the usual baseless charges of immorality. Lists were supplied of pastors sent to prison or to work in the mines. Many Christian leaders who had mistaken the Party's temporary strategies for its ultimate aims and had joined in the early denunciations now found themselves in their turn denounced. 'One did not know,' says a close-up observer, 'whether to mourn most over those accused or those who made the accusations.'[3]

The corollary to this was the unification of worship for which a campaign was now set on foot. Everywhere congregations were fused and church buildings made available for secular use. By September the churches in Peking were reduced in number from 64 to 4, in Shanghai from 150 to 20. The Nanyang Road hall became a factory. Compulsory reform of the 'Little Flock' included the abolition of its women's meetings and of its weekly breaking of bread with the personal interviewing of members before it. Hymns were to be unified and approved by a committee. In all churches preaching on the theme of the last days and the Lord's return was banned, as also was preaching about the vanity of this world. Teaching should favour church union and socialism. All books used in the interpretation of the Bible were to be examined and judged, and those containing poisonous thoughts rejected. Buildings and church property as well as church accounts were to be handed over to the Standing Committee of the Three Self Patriotic Movement.

Inside the First Place of Detention, where pressure to step up productivity was no less strong, a quietly defiant song of praise was rising to God. A foreign prisoner in another block tells us how he himself contrived a year or so later to sing, each morning before the loud speakers came on, four or five songs that he had composed from Scriptures he had memorized. This gives credibility to the report of more than one prisoner released in the summer of 1958 that the singing of hymns was frequently to be heard from Watchman's cell. Those who remember his pleasant baritone voice, or who are familiar with the many lovely hymns he composed or translated into Chinese, will feel this story is wholly in character and will even have some idea of what he sang. They will be reminded by it too of a first century occasion when 'the prisoners were listening'.⁴

The trial and denunciation of Ruth Lee and Peace Wang took place that summer of 1958. They had steadfastly refused to accuse Watchman Nee, and were each given fifteen years imprisonment to run from January 1956. In due course it was known that they were employed under harsh conditions of labour making cloth shoes. Dr. C. H. Yu had also resisted every inducement to denounce Watchman, even when his wife and son were sent in to persuade him to accept release by doing so. He was by now suffering from cancer and was too ill, when the time came, to stand trial. A little later, when out on parole, he died in one of the former upstairs offices at Hardoon Road, firm in his faith to the last.

The New Year of 1959 saw no firecrackers, no gay new clothes, and of course no evangelistic meetings. *Tien Feng*, now a bi-weekly and the last surviving Christian magazine, limited itself to propaganda articles. People everywhere had been exhorted to 'hand their hearts over to the Party', and all were now fully occupied with being productive. But by the time that three Chinese mountaineers, spurred on by Mao's strategic thinking, had placed a small plaster bust of the Chairman at the summit of Chomolungma (Everest) in May 1960, China was already plunging into economic crisis. A combination of gross mismanagement and natural disasters had compelled food rationing and brought near-famine conditions in many areas, and Mao's Great Leap Forward policy was having to be reversed. Naturally enough the famine penetrated into the Places of Detention. In 1962 when two frail and aged 'Little Flock' elders were released after serving ten-year sentences it was said that Watchman weighed less than one hundred pounds. Eighteen months later he was ill in the prison hospital with coronary ischaemia and was relieved from manual work for a while. Drugs advised were allowed to be purchased in Hong Kong and sent in to him.

In June 1966 the Great Proletarian Cultural Revolution exploded on the nation, taking by surprise even the shrewdest of observers close to the heart of affairs.[5] It appears that the personal ambitions of the present generation of privileged administrators were thought to be threatening the collective interest. On 18 August at a mass parade in Peking student Red Guards received the blessing of Mao Tse-tung, 'our great teacher, leader, supreme commander and helmsman', upon their crusade for ideological enthusiasm and purity. Armed with his 'thoughts' they attacked the nation's leaders, from President Liu Shao-chi down, as bourgeois Soviet revisionists. In Shanghai within months the administration was in upheaval and the Municipal Committee had fallen. Factories closed, vituperative posters covered every blank wall, clashing crowds filled the streets, and no one knew a moment's privacy. On one occasion Red Guards appeared at the gate of the municipal gaol and, charging Fu Wei-jen the governor with revisionism, burst into and took over the building for a while. Storming through its cells and lecture-rooms they violently molested some of the inmates. There is evidence that in this episode Watchman was knocked down and suffered a fractured arm.[6] Certainly from now on the New Thought took precedence over all other studies in the reform of the prisoners, and the selection of approved books in the prison library was made to conform with it.

In April 1967 Watchman's fifteen years were completed. Frequently throughout this period the loudspeakers in the First Municipal Prison had warned prisoners: 'If you have a five-year or a seven-year sentence, and if when your term is up we are not satisfied that you have changed, you will be given a further five or seven years.' So though many round the world were praying for his release, and though Charity who was now in poor health was confidently expecting it, perhaps few others were so hopeful. Postcards were exchanged between his two elder sisters in Hong Kong and Shanghai. 'Is elder brother at home?' 'Elder brother is not at home.'

The year 1967 saw the distribution of 86 million of the four-volume *Selected Works* of Mao Tse-tung, 350 million *Quotations* ('The Little Red Book') and a further 100 million of the *Selected Readings* and the *Poems*.[7] Now it became dangerous to possess a Bible. Thirteen times in as many months the Red Guards sacked Charity's little home, rooting through her personal possessions, ridiculing and destroying everything Christian. At the end, like so many others, she was left in an acute anxiety state that verged on total collapse. Though the believers did what they could to support her, only God upheld her then.

From this year on, church services were discontinued throughout the country and the few remaining clergy were ordered to return to their native villages. All religious buildings of all faiths were 'secularized', and anti-religious propaganda was put up on their walls. *Tien Feng* suspended publication and has not so far reappeared.

But in September word was received by the elders at the Church Assembly Hall in Hong Kong, apparently from high authority in the People's Republic, to the effect that Watchman and Charity might be ransomed out of China if a considerable sum in U.S. dollars were deposited in the Hong Kong branch of the Bank of China. There was some precedent for this. A political prisoner with his family, reported in Peking as having 'defected to the West', was widely believed to have been bought out for a very large sum by just such a mutual arrangement. So great was the love felt for Watchman by Chinese believers in South-East Asia and beyond that very quickly the ransom was collected and placed on account as specified. Then, early in 1968, word came from the same official source that the deal was off. The money was released intact for return to the donors. We may ask ourselves what lay behind this reversal of plan.

Assuming that the offer was real and that it reached Watchman, he was certainly fit to form a decision on it one way or the other, since a September letter in his handwriting which found its way to Hong Kong with a refugee affirmed that he was in very good spirits and reasonable health. It is therefore held by the young fellow-workers who had been closest to him that, like those earlier men of faith who 'disdained release',[8] he himself turned down the proposal. This is inherently probable. By staying firm to his principle of co-operation with the State in things neutral—study, labour, translation work—he would do least harm to the image of Christians as loyal Chinese, 'subject to the governing authorities'.[9] His model behaviour might even help to ease the lot of others, whereas for him to 'defect to the West' would certainly involve them all in an appearance of compromise.

But there was another thing. He was not, after all, in the hands of unscrupulous men, but of God. The men doubtless knew in their hearts that he had been framed and that his 'crimes' were fictitious, but that was their concern. What mattered was that God was handling him in His own way, and that God could say, 'Blessed are you.'[10]

At some point early in his life Watchman had learned the lesson of 'brokenness' whereby the Christian, being once touched by God as to his own strength and permanently crippled there (as was Jacob at Jabbok) discovers in that experience the ever new strength of God. When he is weak, then, *in God*, he is strong.[11] 'I cannot hold Thee, but I can plead with Thee. I have no faith and can scarcely even pray, yet I believe!' And when that is so, God, *because He is being leaned upon*, must act. Watchman never sought to graduate from that school. 'We shall always be learners,' he had said at Wen Teh Li, 'but at some point we shall each learn that fundamental lesson, after which nothing can be the same again. There is now no way of *not* being a cripple. From that point begins a knowledge of God beyond anything we have ever dreamed.' Once, to the present writer, he made the point most tellingly by taking a biscuit from the plate between us at supper and snapping it in half, then fitting the two halves together again carefully. 'It looks all right,' he said with a smile, 'but it's never quite the same again, is it? You are like that. You will yield ever after to the slightest touch from God.'

Watchman's inward peace derived thus from a sense of destiny, which in this life is perhaps God's greatest gift to a man. In 1949 he had elected to return from Hong Kong in the conviction that God had a task for him in the new China. It would be wholly consistent for him to feel now that, whatever the appearances, this was still where God could use him and therefore wanted him to be. 'Nothing hurts so much,' he used to say, 'as dissatisfaction with our circumstances. We all start from rest, but there is another rest which we discover when we learn from Jesus how to say, 'I thank Thee Father, for *it seemed good to Thee*.'[12] God knows what He is doing and there is nothing accidental in the life of the believer. Nothing but good can come to those who are wholly His.

'To what are we consecrated? Not to Christian work, but to the will of God, to be and to do whatever He pleases. The path of every Christian has been already marked out by God. If at the close of a life we can say with Paul, "I have finished my course", then we are blessed indeed. The Old Testament saints served their own generation and passed on. Men go, but the Lord remains. God Himself takes away His workers, but He gives others. Our work suffers, but never His. He is still God.'

20

UNHINDERED

THROUGH the spread of his devotional writings in the West the name of Watchman Nee became, during the 'sixties, a rallying point for prayer on behalf of Christians in China generally. Yet this interest in him was quite new, and it is disconcerting to compare it with the suspicion he had earlier aroused in those mission circles where his work encroached upon established interests. Inevitably today his readers feel they have more in common with such indigenous Chinese witness as his than with the professional foreign missionary enterprise that had so sadly failed to read the signs. One heart-searching admission of this failure was to come from an Anglican missionary after the forced departure from Fukien. He describes Nee's work as 'both a real and an expanding fellowship' and admits that such movements 'began as protests against our errors'. What he calls the tragic opposition between the catholic order and the freedom of the Spirit 'would not have happened if we had not exported to China our own torn and mutilated Western post-mediaeval Christian traditions'.[1] But a Chinese observer in the West could hopefully see in the suspension of the foreign missionary endeavour a prelude to a richer evangelical future. 'It is reasonable to expect,' he wrote, 'that a new type of missionary movement will be started in China.'[2] Can it be said, we may ask, that to such a future Watchman Nee made any positive contribution?

He had been born into an age of revolution. Once won to Jesus Christ he saw the need to work out afresh for himself the Christian programme of life and witness free of irrelevancies in a Chinese context, and he settled for the Bible as a sufficient source-book. Reading it constantly through and through he hoped thereby to escape the danger of selectivity, and he expected problems arising from action upon it to find their solution in fresh encounters with the living Christ who is its theme. Thus, to quote a missionary's comment, 'The movement of which he was the leader had tremendous appeal as an embodiment of the gospel not only radically Biblical but also radically Chinese.'[3]

When it came to ecclesiology his chief weakness (but one in which down the ages he has had plenty of company) lay in treating as mandatory the principles he had derived merely from New Testament example. His insistence upon the geographical 'locality' of the churches (one secular city : one local church administration) may have opened the door too readily to State control just because it is so static. By contrast his rediscovery a decade later of the first century concept of migration evangelism seems truly inspired. By it, ideas of Christian flexibility and opportunism were planted in the minds of many whose destiny was very soon to be a forced dispersion. As the Party began to play general post with the population, seeking by this means to liquidate the church, these more fluid and pragmatic concepts of Christian life and witness were destined to come into their own. You have then what may be termed the 'extempore' church, contriving not just to survive but to do battle while itself under fire.

But Watchman's most valuable contribution to the survival of faith and of lively Biblical thinking in China may lie elsewhere. His unforgettable teaching on the Christian's walk with his God contains seed with life in itself. The grain of wheat may die, but will not remain alone. The word uttered will not return empty, but will accomplish the thing for which it was sent. 'Erudite and profound, comprehensive and thorough, he is one of the best preachers I have ever met,' says a Chinese pastor of the Alliance Mission.[4] And in the words of a Western missionary : 'There is no doubt that Mr. Nee was a man raised up by the Lord to inject the truths of the gospel into the very blood-stream of the Chinese people. His words stuck like burrs. His books and tracts ran everywhere. If one was asked to draw up a short list of the most influential Chinese Christians there have ever been, it would be hard to leave him out.'[5]

But what did Watchman Nee achieve by electing—if indeed he had any choice—to stay in China, shut up, as was Paul 'like a common criminal'?[6] What message have his final years to bring to us?

First there is his situation itself. It can be argued that this is what Christianity is all about. 'You will be dragged before governors and kings for my sake, to bear testimony before them and the Gentiles' —thus Jesus warned the Twelve. 'What you are to say will be given you in that hour; for it is not you that speak, but the Spirit of your Father speaking through you.'[7] This was borne out in their experiences in the Book of Acts, and as F. F. Bruce points out, it establishes also Paul's true motive in appealing to Caesar. 'If Caesar in person heard Paul's defence, what might not the outcome be? It would be precarious to set limits to Paul's high hopes, however impracticable they might appear in retrospect to us who know more about Nero than Paul knew in A.D. 59.'[8] To Paul, imprisonment was not punishment for preaching the gospel but a platform for its preaching,[9] and others throughout the Christian era have made this their experience. Mme Guyon, the story of whose life had so influenced Watchman in his early years, wrote of her official interrogation under threat of the scaffold in 1688, 'Our Lord did me the favour which He promised to His disciples to make me answer much better than if I had studied.' This aggressive outspokenness for the kingdom calls forth always that response from God that lies behind the final word of the Book of the Acts—'unhindered'.

In May 1968 a Chinese visitor to a Western capital asked for asylum. The story he told to the authorities there was that he had at one time been a prison guard in the Shanghai First Place of Detention and that through Watchman's witness to him he had found Jesus Christ as Saviour. If this offers a glimpse of what Chinese Christians are today achieving through 'the word of their testimony'[10]—and it may indeed do so—it must prompt also a further consideration.

In His discourse on the last days Jesus uses, *to us* by implication, the identical words about witnessing before the authorities that he used earlier to the Twelve. There is however a significant addition, for sandwiched between the two sentences above quoted is the familiar statement, commonly thought of in the more usual context of world mission, that 'the good news must first be preached to all nations'.[11] In other words, the classic setting for proclaiming the gospel of Christ today is still the criminal court and the interrogation room. For by the very nature of his task the interrogator himself is wide open to the witness of his victim. His role is to ask questions and to search for motives and causes. He may believe himself to be the aggressor holding all the cards in his hands, but before God he is a lost and dying man. The prisoner, aware of the man's need, is the one ideally placed to confront him with the news which 'is the power of God'.[12]

This does not mean that, even if falsely charged, the prisoner gets off. Our Lord Jesus Himself was held on fabricated criminal charges, and it took a trial and an execution to call forth from His judges, from a fellow prisoner, from his executioner, and from the common people the admission that he was a faultless man. We are not faultless. 'We are afflicted, perplexed, persecuted, struck down, always carrying in the body the death of Jesus, so that the life also of Jesus may be manifested in our bodies.'[13]

This privilege of fellowship with Christ as 'overcomer' through participation in His triumph over death had long been Watchman's ambition for his fellow Christians. Back in the forties he found himself intrigued by John's stormy symbolism in the Book of Revelation of a woman confronted by a hungry red dragon when she is about

to give birth to an infant boy.[14] This child, to the dragon's discomfiture, escapes being devoured by finding his place at the throne of
God. Evidently his escape is a figure of resurrection, since 'they (who
are represented by the child) love not their lives even unto death'.
Some may feel that the attenuated and serpentine dragon of China
has little in common with John's Grecian symbolism;[15] yet to Chinese believers today the concept of a disappointed dragon—and a
Red one—must surely possess a certain innocent charm!

In his night-long meeting with the founders of the Chinese Christian Three Self Patriotic Movement Prime Minister Chou En-lai
made clear the Party's position on freedom of Christian witness.
'We are going to let you go on trying to convert people, provided
you also continue your social services. After all, we both believe
that truth will prevail. We think your beliefs untrue and false;
therefore if we are right, the people will reject them and your
church will decay. If you are right, then the people will believe you;
but as we are sure that you are wrong, we are prepared for that
risk.'[16] It was a gracious presentation of a quite ruthless intent, and
it already has its answer in the assurance of Jesus to His church that
against her even the bars of death will prove ineffective.[17] When
Jesus said this He was Himself about to put those bars to the test. It
is certain therefore that we shall see in our day the reawakening in
China of a vital Christian faith. 'The old superstitions are reviving,'
complain the discouraged Party watchdogs—and they should know.

Open collision is inevitable. For God's children there, as here, the
Christian life is not generally lived out of sight or under ground, for
'quite openly' is the other adverb with which the Book of the Acts
concludes. 'Christianity is not a religion of recluses and mountain
retreats; it is social and bound up with the community; therefore it
must be a challenge to Communism.'[18] It would be unwise however
to hint further at the many evidences that the Spirit of truth is still
at work where once Watchman Nee and Wang Ming-tao and so
many others preached so faithfully, and is even now bringing conviction to a world whose unseen ruler is already judged.

In January 1970, at the age of 66 and after eighteen years in the
Shanghai goal, Watchman was moved to an open prison or work
camp in the country. There however either exposure to the climate
or the light labour he was given proved too much for him. His
ischaemic heart-condition flared up once more causing him great
discomfort, and as a result he is thought to have been returned to
Shanghai for a time. That year passed and he was well into the next;
the twenty-year term was in sight and Charity's hopes began to
rise. Then one evening in late September 1971 she was fixing something in her little home to which, perhaps now within a matter of

months, she hoped to welcome Watchman back. She was standing
on a stool when, all at once, she lost her footing. Possibly she had a
slight stroke; anyway she fell heavily fracturing several ribs. Friends
sent word to her own sister in Peking whom she had not seen since
before Watchman's trial, and who now arrived in time to be with
her briefly in hospital before she passed away. God had in kindness
taken His child.

Having completed the funeral arrangements this sister visited
Watchman in the labour camp some distance from the city. He had
already received the news and was feeling the loss deeply. They had
so looked forward to their reunion in April. She reported, nevertheless, that he was in good heart.

What precisely happened next in the summer of 1972 we do not
know. On 12 April he completed twenty years in detention, five
years over his published sentence. Ten days later he wrote to his
sister-in-law a letter in his clear, firm hand. In it, addressing her as
'Elder Sister', he first thanked her for some gift parcels. 'I have received your letter of 7 April, and learn from it that you have not
had my acknowledgement of the things you sent me. Everything
you name has in fact reached me and I am most grateful to you.'
Then he goes on to reassure her about himself. 'You know the
chronic condition I have is always with me. The attacks of course
are distressing, but in the intervals it is not so difficult. The only
variation is in its degree of activity, for there is no question of
recovery.' His next sentence indicates perhaps that he is in a country place. 'The summer sunshine,' he says, 'can give a little colour to
the skin, but it cannot affect the illness.' And then he concludes:
'But I maintain my own joy, so please do not worry. And I hope
you also take care of yourself, and that joy fills your heart. Wishing
you well, Shu-tsu.' He has signed with his childhood name, the one
they used as playmates together long ago in Foochow.

Six weeks later he was, we are told, in Anhwei Province. Was the
long journey there too much for him? Or were there fresh priva-
tions? As an unreformed intellectual without civil rights, was the
treatment he received less than generous? Or did his illness strike
suddenly again? We have no details. We do not know whether he
had any Christian companionship at the end. All we know is that on
1 June 1972 in his sixty-ninth year he passed into the welcoming
presence of his Lord.

It is from a perusal of his last letter that something more emerges.
He accepts his situation and speaks of the sunshine which can enter
from without and do something to modify it a little. And then of
course he concludes on a welcome note of joy, and those who knew
him will feel this is wholly in character. There is no self-pity, for his

concern is for the letter's recipient, that the inward joy he is experiencing may be her experience also. Let us remind ourselves that he cannot name the name of God. The letter will be censored and may well be destroyed.

So he does something else. In expressing his wish for her that her 'heart within be filled with joy' he uses four characters: *hsi-loh*, 'joy', and '*man-tsu*', full. Can we perhaps detect here a twinkle in his eyes? For they are the four characters used in translating the words of Jesus to His disciples: 'Ask, and you shall receive, that your *joy* may be *full*.'[19]

This, then, is his coded message to us all: 'Ask!' Since God is always there in the Unseen, there is no situation on this earth in which you and I are powerless to do anything. Whether shackled by foes or hampered by circumstances, whether totally paralysed or walled up in solitary darkness, we can pray, we can appeal to Him, we can *ask*. We shall surely receive. God will act again. If we will but go on asking, our sorrow will be turned to surpassing joy. 'And your joy no one will take from you.'

NOTES ON THE TEXT

Chapter 1

THE GIFT

1. I Samuel 1. 11.
2. The similarity of sound is fortuitous. There is, we are assured, no etymological connection between *to-sheng* and the French *tocsin*.
3. I Samuel 3; Isaiah 21. 6, 11 f.; 62. 6.

Chapter 2

HONOUR YOUR ANCESTORS

Background Reading. Christopher Hibbert, *The Dragon Wakes: China and the West 1793–1911*, London 1970. F. Schurmann and O. Schell eds, *China Readings 1, Imperial China*, London 1967. J. Doolittle, *Social Life of the Chinese*, London 1868; written in Foochow and an invaluable source of the local background. Eugene Stock, *The Story of the Fuh-Kien Mission of the Church Missionary Society*, London 1882; and the 4th Edition revised T. McClelland, 1904. D. MacGillivray, *A Century of Foreign Missions in Foochow*, Shanghai 1907.

1. Quoted in E. R. Hughes, *The Invasion of China by the Western World*, London 1937, p. 65.
2. 'The four pupils were all baptized in 1857. They subsequently all became helpers in the work. Pastor Nga our first ordained native pastor was one of them. He died in 1890.' Charles Hartwell, *Reminiscences*, Foochow 1904, p. 27. See also D. MacGillivray, *op. cit.*, p. 255. It is probable too that Nga was one of the three young men whose sermons preached one evening in September 1860 are paraphrased in J. Doolittle, *op. cit.*, pp. 599 f.
3. I Samuel 1. 27 f. Her story is vividly told by herself in : Ni Lin Huo-ping, *En Ai Piao Pen (An Object of Grace and Love)*, Shanghai 1943, which provides some of the family's history during this period.

Chapter 3

REVOLUTION

Background Reading. F. Schurmann and O. Schell, eds, *China Readings 2, Republican China*, London 1967. E. R. Hughes, *The Invasion of China by the Western World*, London 1937.

1. Stephen Chen and Robert Payne, *Sun Yat-sen, A Portrait*, New York 1946, p. 130.
2. They included the virtual surrender of harbour works at Foochow.

3. W. S. Packenham-Walsh, the founder of Trinity College, records its beginnings in *Twenty Years in China*, Cambridge 1935. Watchman's English teacher at Trinity was Betty M. Williams, wife of the College Principal, David Williams. I am indebted to her for some account of this period.
4. Wing-tsit Chan, *Religious Trends in Modern China*, New York 1953, pp. 228 f.
5. See Chow Tse-tsung, *The May Fourth Movement; Intellectual Revolution in Modern China*, Cambridge, Mass. 1960, pp. 92 ff.
6. Genesis 3. 3.
7. Stuart Schram, *Mao Tse-tung*, London 1966, pp. 56 f.

Chapter 4

DEDICATION

1. Luke 5. 11.
2. H. A. Franck, *Roving Through South China*, London 1925, p. 181.
3. Romans 6. 13.
4. C.M.S. Report for the Year.
5. Genesis 18. 16 ff.
6. Psalm 91. 7.
7. Mark 1. 11.
8. Romans 6. 3; 1 Peter 3. 21 f.; John 16. 11; Acts 3. 15. See W. Nee, *The Normal Christian Life*, pp. 61 ff.; *Love Not the World*, pp. 26 ff.

Chapter 5

ACROSS THE GRAIN

1. Is it mere coincidence that in this year of 1922 the Chinese Communist Party was created in Shanghai?
2. See Christiana Tsai, *Queen of the Dark Chamber*, Chicago 1953, Chapter 9.
3. This spiritual awakening in Foochow is remembered as the Chien Shan Revival.
4. See W. Nee, 'Two Principles of Conduct', in *Twelve Baskets Full*, Vol. 2, Hong Kong 1966, pp. 36 ff.
5. Matthew 17. 26 f.
6. Jessie Penn-Lewis, *The Cross of Calvary and its Message*, Bournemouth 1903, and *The Logos of the Cross*, 1920, reprinted as *The Centrality of the Cross*.

Chapter 6

THE PROOF OF FAITH

1. John 15. 5. Compare Roland Allen's observation that groups that have learned the gospel from relatively ignorant and untrained Chinese are often found to have learned it both truly and deeply and to be anxious for more. *The Spontaneous Expansion of the Church*, London 1927, p. 65.
2. See W. Nee, *Spiritual Knowledge*. New York 1973, pp. 40 ff.; *Concerning Our Missions*, London 1939, pp. 212 f.
3. Luke 6. 38; 3 John 7. And see *Concerning Our Missions*, Chapter 8.
4. The novelist Pearl Buck echoes this opinion, writing in *My Several Worlds* of 'the beautiful sweet oranges from Fukien, where such oranges grow as I have never seen elsewhere', even, she adds, in California.
5. John 5. 19; 2 Corinthians 12. 9.

6. Joshua 6. 12 ff.; 1 Samuel 5.
7. Numbers 17.
8. Years later a missionary sympathizer would say of him, 'He was liable to make a telling point by pressing on beyond what was written.'
9. Hollington Tong, *Christianity in Taiwan*, 1961, pp. 116 f., simplifies the difference into one of moderation or extremism in the matter of a breach with the mission churches, but he is possibly reading back later history into the situation.
10. 2 Kings 2. 14.
11. On the 'Great King' of Animist villagers in Fukien see J. Doolittle, *op. cit.*, pp. 85, 124, 382.
12. See W. Nee, *Sit, Walk, Stand*, Bombay 1957, and London 1962, Chapter 3.

Chapter 7

FOREIGN FIELDS

1. There are six more stanzas. This was to become No. 128 in his collection *Hsiao Chun Shih-ko* (*Little Flock Hymns*).
2. Luke 4. 43.
3. See W. Nee, *Sit, Walk, Stand*, p. 26, and compare *Twelve Baskets Full*, Vol. 2, Hong Kong 1966, pp. 43 f. His two somewhat different accounts suggest that there may have been more than one such episode.

Chapter 8

THE OLD WINESKINS

1. David M. Paton, *Christian Missions and the Judgment of God*, London 1953, pp. 48 f.
2. John 13. 35.
3. 1 Peter 5. 6.
4. Romans 6. 1 ff.; 1 Corinthians 1. 30; Galatians 2. 20. See W. Nee, *Changed into His Likeness*, London 1967, pp. 78 ff.; *The Normal Christian Life*, p. 46.

Chapter 9

FRAGILE CLAY

1. Zechariah 4. 10.
2. W. Nee, *The Spiritual Man*, English translation in 3 Volumes, New York 1968. The two prefaces are dated Shanghai 4 June 1927 and 25 June 1928. (At pp. 179 ff. of Volume 3 the 1968 editors have added also the transcription of a 1948 address by Nee on the subject of sickness.)
3. This appears to have been Nee's fixed view during the forties, reaffirmed several times to his co-workers. The 1968 publisher may be right in believing that he would by then have changed his mind, but 'doubtless' is too strong an adverb in the circumstances.
4. 1 Corinthians 10. 16 ff.; 11. 23 ff.; 14. 26, 29 ff.; Acts 20. 7 ff.
5. 1 Corinthians 11. 5 ff.; 14. 34 f.; 1 Timothy 2. 11 ff.
6. Some account of the periodicals edited by Watchman Nee, including extracts from his 1928 editorials, is supplied by his eldest sister's son, Stephen C. T. Chan, in his excellent memoir, *O-tih Chiu Fu Ni To-sheng* (*My Uncle, Watchman Nee*), Hong Kong 1970, Chapters 8, 10, and 14 and appendixes. Chan states that 'his open letters in *Revival* for 1928 reveal the agonies of mind through which his long illness put him'.
7. 2 Corinthians 1. 8; 2. 4; 4. 8; 6. 10.

8. 2 Corinthians 4. 7.
9. Margaret E. Barber, *Verses of a Pilgrim*, Foochow, October 1931, published by her colleague Margaret L. Ballord.

Chapter 10

DISENCHANTMENT

1. For details see Stephen C. T. Chan, *op. cit.*, Chapter 22.
2. W. Nee, *The Latent Power of the Soul*, New York 1972, p. 69. He was musical and could be pained by the dissonance.
3. Officially just *Hymns*, or more fully, *A Few Hymns and some Spiritual Songs, selected 1856, for the Little Flock*, revised by J. N. Darby, London 1881. The allusion in the title is to the words in Luke 12. 32, 'Fear not, little flock, for it is your Father's good pleasure to give to you the kingdom.'
4. W. Nee, *The Latent Power of the Soul*. See especially pp. 51, 54 f., 71 ff. This book was first published in 1933 as a postscript to *The Spiritual Man* and owed something to Jessie Penn-Lewis's *Soul and Spirit*.
5. L. T. Lyall, *John Sung*, London 1954, p. 88.
6. They were: from Britain Mr. C. R. Barlow and Mr. and Mrs. A. Mayo, from San Francisco Dr. Powell, and from Australia Mr. and Mrs. Joyce, Mr. Phillips and Mr. W. J. House.
7. Miss Ling had married and was to become the mother of nine children, all of them brilliant.
8. They are popularly known, along with some smaller groups, as 'Exclusive Brethren' (with reference to their principles of Christian fellowship) in distinction from the very much larger and more missionary-minded 'Open Brethren'. Both stem from the same beginnings, and the term 'the Brethren' is commonly of wider application therefore than in the present chapter.
9. See the quotations from life in W. Nee, *The Orthodoxy of the Church*, p. 90.
10. For an account of an exorcism see W. Nee, *What Shall This Man Do?* p. 152.
11. Taylor wrote from New York at the time, 'The person through whom he was converted, a woman, taught him something on prophecy, according to what is generally accepted by the saints—which makes his erroneous views seem more serious. He has given up truth for error.'
12. For an account of this whole episode from the standpoint of the London Group see 'Events Relating to China' in A. J. Gardiner, *The Recovery and Maintenance of the Truth*, Second Edition, Kingston-upon-Thames 1963, pp. 272 ff. This edition contains some relevant letters of James Taylor.
13. It is necessary in fairness to add here that this exclusive view of Christian fellowship is not representative of the Brethren movement as a whole.
14. This, one of the most satisfying of Watchman Nee's presentations of Christian truth, is dealt with several times in his recorded preaching; see: *Sit, Walk, Stand*, p. 30; *The Normal Christian Life*, pp. 127 f.; *Changed into His Likeness*, pp. 79 ff.; *Twelve Baskets Full*, Vol. 1, pp. 32 ff.

Chapter 11

NEW HORIZONS

1. They were published as W. Nee, *The Meeting Life* (in Chinese), Shanghai 1934.
2. W. Nee, *The Song of Songs*, Fort Washington 1966.
3. See also his account of the early Brethren writings in *The Orthodoxy of*

the Church, Los Angeles 1970, pp. 69 ff. Darby, Bellett, Muller, Mackintosh, Kelly, Anderson, Miller are among those he was familiar with, and he constantly used J. N. Darby's *New Translation* of the English Bible.

4. Hollington Tong, *Christianity in Taiwan*, 1961, p. 117.
5. F. P. Jones, *China Bulletin* Vol. 4, 21 February 1955.
6. The story is told in L. T. Lyall, *John Sung*, London 1954.
7. Elisha Wu, magazine article (source not traced).
8. Frank Rawlinson, ed., *The China Christian Year Book*, Shanghai 1935, pp. 104 f.
9. Isaiah 54. 17.
10. See W. Nee, *What Shall This Man Do?* p. 108.
11. A. J. Gardiner, *op. cit.*, p. 287.
12. The English version of their letter was supplied for them by Miss Elizabeth Fischbacher.
13. Witness Lee, *The Baptism of the Holy Spirit*, Los Angeles 1969, p. 12.
14. Compare 1 Corinthians 12. 30.

Chapter 12

RETHINKING

1. As in Foochow where, in the one town, the assembly was already split into two competing groups.
2. There seems no evidence that Nee ever met Roland Allen or even that he read his well-known writings. *Missionary Methods: St Paul's or Ours*, 1912, and *The Spontaneous Expansion of the Church and the Causes which Hinder It*, 1927, but it must be remembered that, whatever he may have read, he rarely if ever quoted Christian writers who did not share his own conservative evangelical position.
3. Charles E. Notson, 'Individualism Gone Astray: II, The "Little Flock" of Watchman Ngnee', in the *Alliance Weekly*, 12 November 1952, pp. 729 f.
4. *Ibid.*, p. 729.
5. George A. Young, *The Living Christ in Modern China*, London 1947, p. 91.
6. Shanghai 1938. The book has a Chinese and an English preface.
7. *The Keswick Convention 1938*, London 1938, p. 245.
8. 2 Corinthians 4. 7 ff.; Galatians 2. 20.
9. Matthew 7. 1 ff.
10. Genesis 23. 4; Psalm 39. 12.
11. W. Nee, *The Normal Christian Life*, Bombay 1957, London and Fort Washington 1961, edited by conflation of several series of his addresses on the same and related themes.
12. 1 John 5. 4; Revelation 2. 4; 12. 11; 21. 7.
13. W. Nee, *Concerning Our Missions*, London and Shanghai 1939. Abridged and reissued as *The Normal Christian Church Life*, Washington D.C. 1962, echoing the title of the above book. But in *The Normal Christian Life* 'normal' is Nee's own calculated understatement for 'victorious' and is a challenge to the subnormal, whereas here 'normal' can only mean 'correct' with the implication that every other pattern of church life or mission is therefore abnormal! Furthermore, *Concerning Our Missions* is not even a book about the 'Church' but about the Work. And of it he says explicitly: '*The title of the book explains its nature.* It is not a treatise on missionary methods but a *review* of our past work in the light of God's will as we have discovered it in His Word' (p. 11, his italics).
14. G. H. Lang on pp. 92, 94, in a privately communicated review. (Jerusalem's population, too, was of course occasionally swelled by pilgrims.) Lang also points out that in Acts 9. 31 Nee strengthens his case by following (p. 95) the plural reading 'churches' where the weight of manuscript authorities is for the singular.
15. Nee saw this problem, (*ibid.*, pp. 90 f.), but his suggested solution of equating London boroughs or postal districts with New Testament cities

subjects the church's 'locality' to sudden change by secular whim. Did he intend this?

Chapter 13

HEYDAY

1. W. Nee, *Changed into His Likeness*, London 1968.
2. W. Nee, *The Glorious Church*, Los Angeles 1968.
3. The C.I.M. Editorial Secretary, Norman Baker, had kindly shown Nee the current edition of the Mission's *Principles and Practice*, and Nee had had to point out that under the heading of 'church government' the document gave little or no room for Chinese opinion as to the pattern of worship to be followed in any given case.
4. Especially was this so now in Chekiang Province. As had been noted already in the *China Christian Year Book* of 1935 (pp. 104 f.), in this, 'the field of the Little Flock', the movement's opposition to a paid ministry was commanding respect in the prevailing economic climate, while its emphasis on the return of Christ aroused a response in the hearts of many discouraged by the worsening political conditions.
5. Ephesians 4. 11; 2 Timothy 4. 5. See W. Nee, *What Shall This Man Do?* Chapter 3, 'Catching Men'; and also his instructions in *The Good Confession*, New York 1973, pp. 75 ff.
6. With an explicit reference to Acts 20. 30.
7. H. T. Ku, pamphlet entitled *Hsiao Chun*, Shanghai 1940. It is probable that this, with others like it, was seized upon twelve years later as source material for the charges of 'imperialist' associations.
8. 2 Timothy 3. 12.
9. Luke 6. 36 ff.; Galatians 6. 7.
10. Genesis 45. 5; 1 Samuel 1. 23; Isaiah 49. 5; Galatians 1. 15; Jeremiah 1. 5; Romans 9. 11, 16.

Chapter 14

WITHDRAWAL

1. Luke 9. 62. See W. Nee, *What Shall This Man Do?* pp. 64 f.
2. Luke 16. 9. W. Nee, *Love Not the World*, Chapter 11.
3. Titus 3. 8, 14.
4. Acts 18. 3; 20. 34. Compare W. Nee, *Concerning Our Missions*, p. 200.
5. John of the Ladder, *Scala Paradisi*. Accidie is from the Greek *akedia* of Psalm 61. 2, LXX: 'is overwhelmed'.
6. Geoffrey Chaucer, *Canterbury Tales*, 'The Parson's Tale: Remedium Accidiae'. See Francis Paget, *The Spirit of Discipline*, London 1891; Introductory Essay.
7. These talks on Revelation Chapters 2 and 3 were published in Chungking in 1945. See W. Nee, *The Orthodoxy of the Church*, Los Angeles 1970. They are built on the theory of progressive recovery of original truth with the author's own choice of final revelation at the apex, a theory used by many exponents to give authority to as many different doctrinal emphases.
8. Stephen C. T. Chan *op. cit.*, Chapter 24.
9. *chia*, 'family', perhaps originally with the concept of a household church as in Romans 16. 5, but soon developing, with increasing numbers, into congregations in large meeting halls (as later in Taiwan) yet still under a single city church eldership.
10. Hebrews 13. 17.
11. *pai*, a military term for a row or squad.
12. Published as W. Nee, *Basic Lessons on Practical Christian Living* (6

Volumes) New York from 1972. The titles are: 1, *A Living Sacrifice*; 2, *The Good Confession*; 3, *Assembling Together*; 4, *Not I, but Christ*; 5. *Do All to the Glory of God*; 6, *Love One Another*.

13. This system readily played later into the hands of a totalitarian State police.
14. 'Report of a Fellowship Gathering' by Witness Lee in the first issue of a new magazine, *The Ministry* (ed. W. Nee), June 1948.

Chapter 15

RETURN

Background Reading: F. Schurmann and O. Schell, *China Readings 3; Communist China*, London 1967. C. P. Fitzgerald, *The Birth of Communist China*, London (Pelican) 1964, a quite excellent account.

1. John 12. 24. W. Nee, *The Release of the Spirit*, Mt. Vernon, Mo. 1965.
2. Acts 8. 1, 4; 11. 19 f.
3. Report in *Believers' News*, (Ed. C. H. Yu) Shanghai, October 1944.
4. This view was elaborated in subsequent instructions, e.g. in an address to workers at Kuliang in August 1948. See W. Nee, *Further Talks on the Church Life*, Los Angeles 1969, Chapter 6.
5. Witness Lee, 'The Merciful Leading of the Lord', in the first issue of *The Ministry*, (Ed. W. Nee) Shanghai, May 1948.
6. See W. Nee, *Concerning Our Missions*, p. 104.
7. The reconciliation in Foochow was not, however, complete. Since 1928 there had been two assemblies in Nantai with two sets of elders, violating the 'one city, one church' principle that the movement held so dear. Chang Chi-chen, successor of John Wang, was the senior elder of the group that met 'near the football ground', and though present in these discussions he stood out against the new ideas and, rightly or wrongly, would not at this time bring his fellow elders to break bread with the workers and representatives of the other group. This caused great sorrow to those who placed their hopes in a completely new beginning at Foochow, and though Watchman Nee himself made generous overtures the situation remained unresolved. See Stephen Chan, *op. cit.*, pp. 51 ff.
8. Mark 12. 17
9. George N. Patterson, *God's Fool*, London 1956, p. 151.
10. All but the last of these are in English translation: *The Normal Christian Worker*, Hong Kong 1965; *The Ministry of God's Word*, New York 1971; *Spiritual Authority*, New York 1972; an appended chapter in *The Spiritual Man*, New York 1968, Vol. 3, pp. 179 ff.; The 'Basic Lessons' Series, New York 1972–4 (6 volumes); and Chapters 5 and 6 of *Further Talks on the Church Life*, Los Angeles 1966.

Chapter 16

CONSISTENT CHOICE

Background Reading: Leslie Lyall, *Come Wind, Come Weather*, London 1961. Edward Hunter, *The Story of Mary Liu*, London 1956. George N. Patterson, *Christianity in Communist China*, Waco, Texas 1969. W. C. Merwin and F. P. Jones, *Documents of the Three Self Movement*, New York 1963. Katherine Hockin, *Servants of God in People's China*, New York 1962.
1. Allen J. Swanson, *Taiwan: Mainline versus Independent Church Growth. A Study in Contrasts*, Pasadena 1970, p. 62.
2. With the Shanghai local church's move to new premises in Nanyang Road a Chinese Christian in another group had circulated a booklet *Seven Open Letters to Watchman Nee* attacking Watchman for his

'spiritual arrogance' which compared unfavourably with his self-effacing preaching.

3. Acts 8. 1.
4. Psalm 29. 10.
5. Ephesians 5. 16.
6. The Jesus Family, founded at Ma-Chuang in 1921 by Ching Tien-yin, applied the principles of early communal Christianity to the Chinese family system, quietly practising on a small scale what the Communists alleged was their own objective. Though somewhat erratic in doctrine and practice, the movement was Bible-loving and warmly evangelical. See D. Vaughan Rees, *The Jesus Family in Communist China*, London 1954. Writing of this development, L. T. Lyall observed: 'Instead of the lonely pioneer who, by painfully slow and sometimes discouraging processes, sought to establish a witness for Christ among the heathen, a zealous Christian community and a live active church are transplanted into the same heathen area. No imagination is needed to see the possibility of such migrations if they can be undertaken on a wider scale and to even needier unevangelised fields of China,' *China's Millions*, London, January 1951.
7. Hebrews 10. 25.
8. Mary Weller in *China's Millions*, November 1951, p. 103. With this compare the observation of a reviewer writing two years later: 'It is interesting to note the emergence of the Little Flock, or Christian Meeting House as they prefer to be called, as a major Christian denomination in China.' Francis P. Jones, *China Bulletin*, iii, 22, 7 December 1953.
9. Ostensibly they were offered for discussion and subsequent review, but it was soon found that they had already been accepted as final by the Premier. His kindly official reception of the delegates had veiled other motives and sinister designs.
10. Unlike John R. Mott, who, a generation earlier, had earned Chinese student admiration by declining the same post.
11. Because the idea of doctrinal reform proved offensive to many, the term Patriotic was substituted in the title. Support of the new régime was equated with patriotism.
12. Merwin and Jones, *Documents*, pp. 19 f., 34 ff.; Edward Hunter, *op cit.*, pp. 138 ff.; Leslie Lyall, *op. cit.*, pp. 21 ff.
13. Mark 6. 35 ff.; John 6. 1 ff.
14. Malachi 3. 10.

Chapter 17

THE TRAP CLOSES

1. An excellent account of the ten years in Shanghai from 1949 to 1959 is given by Helen Willis of the Christian Book Room in *Through Encouragement of the Scriptures*, Hong Kong 1961.
2. Merwin and Jones *op. cit.*, pp. 27 f.
3. *ibid.*, pp. 22 ff.
4. *The Story of the Year 1951*, China Inland Mission, London.
5. New China News Agency, 15 May 1951, quoted in Merwin and Jones, *op. cit.*, pp. 49 ff. No New Testament preacher or writer in fact takes Matthew 23 as a precedent. The chapter is unique.
6. Edward Hunter, *op. cit.*, pp. 190 ff.
7. Wing-tsit Chan, *Religious Trends in Modern China*, New York 1953, p. 262.
8. Many have detected a Christian origin in the very puritan tone of this phase as well as in some of the techniques used. See e.g. C. P. Fitzgerald, *op. cit.*, p. 134. Need one add that ethics is not the whole of Christianity?
9. Philippians 3. 7.
10. *Liberation Daily*, Shanghai 1 February 1956.

11. *Kung Shang Er Pao*, Hong Kong Daily, 18 February 1956.
12. Robert Ford, *Captured in Tibet*, London 1957, ch. 16 ff. Geoffrey T. Bull, *When Iron Gates Yield*, London 1955, ch. 17 f. Robert Jay Lifton, *Thought Reform and the Psychology of Totalism*, 1961; Edward Hunter, *Brain-Washing in Red China*, New York 1951; Suzanne Labin, *The Anthill*, London 1960.
13. So far as is known the confession obtained amounted to an admission that he had used paid employees to set the Foochow properties in order without participating himself in the physical labour involved.
14. Merwin and Jones, *op. cit.*, pp. 60 ff., 89 ff.
15. Some 'Little Flock' representatives were present as observers at the National Christian Conference of the Three Self Movement in May 1954, one of them participating on the twelve-member Standing Executive Committee.
16 *Tien Feng*, Shanghai 1956, Nos. 4, 7 and 8.
17. A number of editions are extant, produced under Ruth Lee's supervision, with the Shanghai imprint dated as late as 1953 and 1954.
18. See also Mary Wang, *The Chinese Church that Will Not Die*, London 1971, p. 75.
19. *China Bulletin* v, 12 and 17–20; Leslie T. Lyall *op. cit.*, Chapter 6. Merwin and Jones, *op. cit.*, pp. 99 ff. Released a year later in a state of nervous breakdown, he recovered sufficiently to withdraw his confession publicly, whereupon he was reimprisoned for an indefinite term.

Chapter 18

ORDEAL

The events and accusations summarized in this chapter were reported in Shanghai in *Liberation Daily* for February 1956; in *Tien Feng* ('Heavenly Wind'), Shanghai, the official periodical of the Chinese Three Self Patriotic Movement, Nos. 3 to 8 for 1956; and in *Hsueh Hsi Tung Hsun* ('Studies Reporter'), for February 1956, a Shanghai news-sheet of the same movement. Extract translations have appeared in F. P. Jones, *The China Bulletin* of the Far Eastern Joint Office of the Division of Foreign Missions, National Christian Council, New York, Vol. VI, 1956, and in Clayton H. Chu, *Religion in Communist China*, U.S. Joint Publications Research Service, New York 1958, pp. 30 ff. I am also indebted to Thomas I. Lee, *China News Release No. 11*, Minneapolis, 17 July 1956.

1. Others arrested in Shanghai at this time included Lan Chih-i, Chu Chen, and Tu Chung-chen.
2. In those instances where documentation can be checked, the gross misconstruction or exaggeration of the facts suggests that 'evidence' was multiplied by the mindless repetition of question and answer.
3. They are named as 'Ruth Lee, Peace Wang, Cheng Yu-chih, Lan Chih-i and others'.
4. 1 Timothy 4. 1.
5. 'For the past hundred years the dexterously planned strategy against Chinese Christians of applying poisonous ideas of "religion above politics" has been the malicious scheme of the missionaries of imperialism.' Dr. H. H. Tsui, Address to the National Conference of the Chinese Christian Church, Peking, March 1956. (Merwin and Jones, *Documents*, p. 141.)
6. See W. Nee, *Love Not the World*, London 1968, of which the substance dates from about 1941.
7. 1 Corinthians 13. 13.
8. Merwin and Jones, *Documents*, pp. 122 f.
9. *ibid.*, p. 141.
10. *ibid.*, p. 134.
11. According to incomplete reports, the 'Little Flock' had at this time 362

places of worship and 39,000 members in the one province of Chekiang. These figures were interpreted as indicating that members of the 'Little Flock' made up 15–20 per cent of the whole Protestant Church in China, and that they may have been the largest single denomination (*Ecumenical Press Service*, Geneva, 22 November 1957). It is certain, however, that many of these were congregations founded by the China Inland Mission and absorbed, with other independent groups, into its ranks (*The Millions*, London, July 1958).

12. Fifteen years was the period officially announced and widely accepted at the time. For some reason, however, in 1963 Merwin and Jones, in *Documents of the Three Self Movement*, p. xii, give 'twenty years' as the sentence, and in fact this was the time he served.

Chapter 19

SUPPRESSIVE ACTION

A useful general survey of this period is supplied by Leslie T. Lyall, *Red Sky at Night*, London 1969. For information on the conditions in the Shanghai First Municipal Prison I am indebted to Leslie Haylen's description in *Chinese Journey*, Sydney 1959, pp. 73 ff., and to the experiences of two Jehovah's Witnesses confined there, Harold G. King, *The Watchtower*, 15 July 1963, pp. 437 ff., and Stanley E. Jones, taped report.

1. Mary Wang, *op. cit.*, pp. 90 f.
2. *ibid.*, pp. 89, 92.
3. Helen Willis, *op cit.*, pp. 58 ff. Merwin and Jones, *Documents*, pp. 180 ff.
4. Acts 16. 25.
5. A close-up view of the period is provided by two Australian residents in Peking and Shanghai, Colin Mackerras and Neale Hunter in *China Observed 1964–67*, London 1967, Chapters 12–14.
6. Possibly both arms. This episode may lie behind the stories of his physical mutilation circulating in the West, where it has been affirmed that 'because he would not stop testifying to Christ, the Communists gouged out his eyes, cut off his tongue, and also cut off his hands'. So, R. Wurmbrand (quoting Harold Martinson) in publicity material for May 1970, and again for December 1972, of 'Jesus to the Communist World Inc.,' Glendale, Calif. To this the handwriting of Watchman's last letter, which we are told is recognizably his own, seems a sufficient answer.
7. *China Reconstructs*, Peking, April 1968, p. 2.
8. Hebrews 11. 35.
9. Romans 13. 1.
10. Matthew 5. 11.
11. Genesis 32. 24 ff.; 2 Corinthians 12. 10.
12. Matthew 11. 25 ff.

Chapter 20

UNHINDERED

1. David M. Paton, *Christian Missions and the Judgment of God*, London 1953, p. 49. See also Victor E. W. Hayward, *'Ears to Hear': Lessons from the China Mission*, London 1955.
2. Wing-tsit Chan, *Religious Trends in Modern China*, New York 1953, pp. x f.
3. This must be seen, however, in the context of contemporary China as one of God's original movements in history. As a technique transferred to another setting it is likely only to disappoint.
4. Elisha Wu, Saskatchewan.
5. David Bentley-Taylor, letter to *The Life of Faith*. December 1963.

6. 2 Timothy 2. 9.
7. Matthew 10. 17 ff.
8. F. F. Bruce, *New Testament History*, London 1969, p. 341.
9. Ephesians 6. 18 ff.; Philippians 1. 16; Colossians 4.3; 2 Timothy 4. 16 f.
10. Revelation 12. 11.
11. Mark 13. 9 ff.
12. Romans 1. 16.
13. 2 Corinthians 4. 7 ff.
14. Revelation 12. 1 ff. See W. Nee, *The Glorious Church*, Los Angeles 1968, Chapter 4. The 'child' could be Christ alone, but more probably it figures those who are victorious with Him.
15. Though a Chinese with the character for 'dragon' in his name will prefer to change it at baptism.
16. Quoted by C. P. Fitzgerald, *The Birth of Communist China*, London 1964, p. 138.
17. Matthew 16. 18.
18. Fitzgerald, *op. cit.*, p. 141.
19. John 16. 24. Jesus equates Christian fruitfulness with the receipt of answers to prayer in John 15. 16.